国际商务硕士研究生课程配套原创教学案例

国际经济与贸易专业实务类课程配套原创教学案例

国际物流专业实务类课程配套原创教学案例

U0674752

Teaching Cases:
Marine Cargo Claims

海上货物
索赔教学案例 （第二版）

李勤昌　编著

东北财经大学出版社
Dongbei University of Finance & Economics Press

大连

图书在版编目（CIP）数据

海上货物索赔教学案例 / 李勤昌编著. —2 版. —大连：东北
财经大学出版社，2025.9. —ISBN 978-7-5654-5633-6

Ⅰ. D912.280.5

中国国家版本馆 CIP 数据核字第 2025AD0023 号

海上货物索赔教学案例
HAISHANG HUOWU SUOPEI JIAOXUE ANLI

东北财经大学出版社出版

（大连市黑石礁尖山街 217 号　邮政编码　116025）

网　　　址：http://www.dufep.cn

读者信箱：dufep@dufe.edu.cn

大连金华光彩色印刷有限公司印刷　　东北财经大学出版社发行

幅面尺寸：170mm×240mm　　　字数：257 千字　　　印张：15.5

2025 年 9 月第 2 版　　　　　　　2025 年 9 月第 1 次印刷

责任编辑：李　彬　王芃南　　　　　责任校对：那　欣

封面设计：原　皓　　　　　　　　版式设计：原　皓

书号：ISBN 978-7-5654-5633-6　　　定价：68.00 元

前言

本教材自 2016 年出版至今已有 9 个年头。为反映作者最新案例开发成果，更好服务国际商务专业学位硕士研究生相关课程教学和国际经济与贸易、国际物流、国际商务等专业本科生的实务类课程教学需要，特做本次修订。

1. 主要内容

本次修订仍围绕海上货物索赔这一主题编辑综合性案例，涉及承运人保证船舶适航义务、管理货物义务、及时交付货物义务、承运人责任区间、倒签提单、共同海损分摊、国际商务仲裁和滞期费等国际货物贸易领域的核心问题。

各案例均分为案例正文和案例使用说明两个部分。在案例正文中，除案例背景外，各二级标题下的案情描述中均隐含着一个法律规则或实践技能问题，读者可根据随后给出的讨论思考题到案情描述中寻找这些问题，然后到教材或其他文献中学习相关理论知识，并围绕思考问题提出解决方案。案例使用说明为教师提供了案例使用指导，包括教学目的、分析思路、理论分析和教学技术指导等内容，一些案例还附有参考判例或程序性的规则，供学习和使用时参考。

为方便案例讨论，各个案例还附有参考资料，特别是不易检索到的与案例主题密切相关的国内外法院判例、国际仲裁机构的相关规则、国外著名保险公司保函、专业性国际展会介绍等。

2. 应用场景

编辑的案例可以应用于国际贸易实务、国际货物运输、国际物流、国际货运代理、国际商务等案例教学场景，为这类课程的案例教学和学生综合能力培养提供素材。需要提及的是，尽管编辑的案例仅涉及海上货物索赔范畴，但其中贯穿的国际商务索赔一般性知识和解决问题思路同样适用于其他商务合同索赔问题。因此，其他专业商务合同索赔的案例教学同样可以借鉴使用，本教材也可作为相关领域业务人员的工作参考书。

3. 特色优势

一是专业性突出。作者具有30多年本科和研究生的国际贸易实务类课程教学和研究经验，主编该领域教材16部，又有10余年的国际贸易和国际货物运输商务管理经验，主持过在中国香港以及新加坡、菲律宾、德国、荷兰、美国、委内瑞拉、海地等地的商务诉讼，保证了该教材的科学性、专业性和可用性。

二是典型性突出。本教材聚焦"海上货物索赔"主题，紧紧围绕国际贸易海上运输过程中事故率高、涉案金额大的八个方面编写案例，便于重要知识点教学选用。

三是综合性突出。教材中编辑的案例均为中型和偏大型案例，案例正文描述的案件错综复杂，涉及不同国家的国际货物贸易法律规则及差异、货物运输法律规则及差异、诉讼程序规则及差异、文化差异、索赔技巧等众多问题，具有高阶性和挑战度，适合相关课程落实综合能力培养目标使用。因此建议，本科生教学层次，每学期规划4次左右的此类案例教学；硕士研究生教学层次，可实施全案例教学。

四是真实性突出。本教材全部案例素材均来自作者在国际贸易和远洋运输公司工作期间主持国际商务诉讼时或在外贸公司做顾问工作中处理跨国纠纷时积累的第一手资料。目前呈现给大家的案例，更像作者当年工作的回忆录，有时间，有地点，有人物，有跌宕起伏甚至是惊心动魄的事件发展过程，只不过出于教学目的，将当年这些错综复杂的事件做了合理取舍和逻辑编排而已。因此，沉下心来阅读案例，从专业角度仔细品味每一个情节，既能加深对专业知识的理解，又能产生和积累学习案例的兴趣，这对教师推动案例教学是大有裨益的。

五是国际性突出。为培养学生的国际视野，大部分案例正文编入了当事双方的英文原文往来信函，鉴于国际仲裁案例当年基本是以英文沟通，索性整个案例正文以英文编辑。这样做，既容易把读者带入案例故事情境中，增加学习兴趣，又有利于培养学生国际视野和提高学生英文阅读和使用能力。

致　谢

本教材中的全部案例素材均来自相关企业的国际业务活动，特别感谢他们无私提供详尽的真实材料以及在案例加工过程中给予的帮助与指导。

感谢东北财经大学出版社对教学案例出版给予的大力支持和编审人员精益求精的工作态度和辛苦努力。

感谢读者对本教材的厚爱和修改建议。

感谢广东省普通高校人文社会科学重点研究基地项目"广东服务贸易双循环研究中心"（项目编号：2021WZJD002）、2024年度广东省普通高校创新团队项目"数字贸易与智能商务研究创新团队"（项目编号：2024WCXTD019）、广州工商学院"国际商务重点学科"资助出版。

本教材由李勤昌教授原创性编著，佛山大学硕士研究生刘浩天参与了部分编辑工作。作者拥有著作权中的署名权、修改权、改编权、翻译权。未经允许，本案例的任何部分都不能以任何方式复制或传播。案例的理论依据与分析部分为编者个人观点，不妥之处欢迎读者提出宝贵修改意见。

李勤昌

2025年3月于广州工商学院

目　录

绪 论

　　国际经济与贸易、国际商务和国际物流等专业中的各类国际商务合同课程教学目的主要有两个：一是培养学生在相关法律和国际惯例规则基础上，掌握制定和履行各类商务合同的基本技能；二是培养学生运用知识解决合同履行过程中发生的各类纠纷的实践能力。实现上述目的一个很好方法就是案例教学。

　　何谓案例教学？概括地说，案例教学就是在教师的引领下让学生通过对来自真实世界的带有特定问题的案例进行讨论，培养学生主动学习和运用理论知识分析和解决实际问题的能力，同时培养学生逻辑思维、准确表达、团队合作和跨专业知识运用能力的教学过程。

　　与传统的讲授式教学法相比，案例教学法是颠覆性的。在这种教学方式下，课堂的主体是学生，通过对问题的讨论，锻炼学生前述各项能力，教师只是课堂的组织者和学习促进者。为解决来自现实世界的特定问题，学生必须在课堂讨论之前主动地收集和学习相关理论知识，运用自己的智慧分析特定问题并提出解决问题的方案，由此提高学生学习的主动性和自觉性，培养学生的知识运用能力和决策能力。正因为如此，自哈佛商学院在1921年正式采用案例教学法后，这一方法在全球商学院迅速传播开来，我国的相关专业也在大力推行这一教学方法。

　　实施案例教学的一个先决条件是要有好的教学案例。这里所说的教学案例不是传统教学中使用的简短的说明性案例，而是一个需要学生运用所学知识和综合能力来解决特定问题的真实事件描述，具有很强的复杂度和挑战度。一个标准的教学案例应当包括案例正文和案例使用说明两个部分。案例正文是对某个企业发生的需要解决的问题的客观情景描述，有时间、地点、人物、事件发生过程和所遇困惑的交代，结构通常包括背景、情景描述、思考问题和参考资料等，其编写目的是让学生能够识别案例设置的问题，然后通过主动学习相关理论知识，提出解决这些问题的方案。案例使用说明是为了教师组织和引导学生课堂讨论提供指导，通常包括教学目的、分析思路、理论指导、教学组织等内容。

案例教学的实施过程也是颠覆性的。在经典的案例教学课程中，教师应当指定课前阅读材料，包括案例正文、思考问题、相关教材和理论文献等。学生必须课前阅读所有材料，识别和认真分析案例中设置的特定问题，提出问题的解决方案。在进入正式课堂讨论前，学生还应当进行小组讨论，通过相互学习，完善自己的决策方案。在课堂讨论中，教师是学习的组织者和促进者，而不是简单的知识灌输者。教师应当努力将教室营造成一个合作性的讨论场所，围绕特定问题，组织和动员每个学生有序地参与各具体问题的讨论，通过讨论让学生去发现知识、运用知识，使课堂成为自主学习和锻炼合作决策的场所。

就各类国际商务合同的履行而言，根据本人在国际贸易和国际海上货物运输领域的10余年从业经验，但凡合同制定得比较妥当，双方当事人能够诚实守信和务实，一般性的纠纷凭借通常的智慧和专业知识都可以通过友好协商得以解决。但如果遇到涉及重大利益的纠纷，就远不是情感上的宽宏大量和通常的智慧与知识所能够顺利解决的。因为事件伤筋动骨，双方往往会据理力争，互不相让，于是便诉诸仲裁或诉讼，导致仲裁庭或法庭案件积压，排期很久，耗费了当事人大量的法律成本。

人们有个错觉，认为案件只要提交到仲裁庭或法庭就一定会得到公正解决，其实不然。要知道，仲裁庭和法庭判案是一个查清案件事实和运用法律的过程。他们掌握法律规则的水平通常很高，但查清事实则主要依靠当事人提供证据，有时一个看上去微不足道的事实证据可能完全改变判案结果。因此，当事人能够既懂得法律规则，又懂得"打官司"技巧十分重要。遗憾的是，实际工作中这种"能人"并不多，以至于遇到复杂的纠纷就去找律师，耗费了大笔的律师费。其实，凭我个人的经验，应付复杂"官司"的技能，也是可以通过专业课堂教学培养出来的，关键在于我们的教学目标定位要准，教学方法要得当。

正是基于上述认识，作者长期以来在积极尝试推行国际贸易和国际商务专业的案例教学和案例编写工作，现在呈现给大家的案例集就是其中的部分成果。

第一章

船舶适航

海运公司应对不适航索赔的9年商战

摘要：本案例正文描述的这场持续9年的船舶不适航索赔商战发生在20世纪末，主战场在荷兰的鹿特丹。索赔方是荷兰和德国的多家收货人，被索赔方是大连的H海运公司，索赔还波及当事船舶的英国保赔保险人W。商战因H海运公司所属的G轮不适航导致严重货损引发。案例首先介绍了案件发生的背景，细致地展示了收货人发现的承运船舶不适航和货物损坏的证据，客观地描述了收货人采取的主要索赔方式和战术，以及承运人的应战战略和战术。案例使用说明部分对案例正文描述的各场较量进行了理论分析和评价。

关键词：船舶适航　货物索赔　船舶扣押　残损检验

1.本案例描述的对H海运公司船舶不适航索赔的9年商战是一个真实的事件，案例编者是当年的主要参与者。尽管事件发生在20世纪末，但鉴于事发至今的相关法律规则没有发生实质性变化，因此案例对船舶适航问题的教学仍具有使用价值。为了锻炼学生的实战能力，案例正文部分资料保持了当年的英文原文。由于企业保密的要求，在本案例中对有关当事方做了必要的掩饰性处理。

2.本案例只供教学之用，并无意明示地或暗示地褒奖或贬低案例中涉及的公司的相关行为。

案例正文

本案例描述和分析的是因船舶不适航导致的货物索赔商战。这场商战发生在20世纪末的荷兰，持续了9年之久。索赔人是荷兰和德国的多家收货人，被索赔方是大连的H海运公司，案件还波及当事船舶的英国保赔保险人W。索赔人因H海运公司所属的G轮不适航导致其货物严重损坏，扣押了当事船舶，向被索赔方索要33万美元的赔偿，后者也展开了激烈的反击。

1.背景

1998年春季对于中国烟台市的出口是一个春暖花开的季节，数家贸易公司利用当地丰富的花岗岩资源，将其初步加工成不同规格的花岗岩产品后，以很好的价格分别销售给了意大利和荷兰的数家公司，共计14 300多吨，其中荷兰的买家又将大部分货物转卖到德国的不来梅和汉堡。

根据买卖合同约定的交货期，该批货物的最大买家BSK公司与在中国大连注册的H海运公司（以下简称H）签订了该批货物的运输合同，其他买家的货物均委托BSK公司运输。运输合同约定，承运船舶为H所属的G轮，货物为不同规格的花岗岩产品，部分散装，部分捆装，其中3 300多吨运往意大利的Marina di Carrara，11 000多吨运往荷兰的鹿特丹，装货港口为中国烟台，装卸条件为FIO。G轮为载重吨16 100吨的钢质杂货船，共5个货舱，设有二层舱，1977年由德国船厂建造，有欧洲的远洋运输经历，船舶的各项法定证书显示该轮处于适航状态。

1998年5月14日，G轮按照运输合同约定抵达烟台港并开始装货，5月24日装船完毕并开航。该航次G轮收取了不同发货人的清洁提单保函共签发了12份清洁提单。6月26日，G轮抵达Marina di Carrara卸货，之后开往鹿特丹并于7月9日抵达鹿特丹港。前往欧洲的船舶都知道，欧洲所有港口对到港船舶的卫生检疫要求特别严格，有多艘国内船舶抵达欧洲时因检验不合格而被扣留。该轮在烟台港装货前在此方面做了大量的准备工作，船舶抵达上述两个港口时顺利地通过了卫生检疫，船长高兴地通过卫星电话将这一消息告知了当时在新加坡出差的船东主管，大家都处在兴奋之中。但是，谁也没有意识到，一场灾难正在悄悄地降临。

2.收货人发现货损

G轮在鹿特丹港靠泊后，除值班船员外，其余船员在取得了船舶代理帮助办理的登陆证后，纷纷下船，开始了这个国际名城的参观之旅。鹿特丹是个好客的城市，考虑到船员们的长途航程辛苦，当地的海运劳工协会还免费向船员提供了足球衫和足球鞋，请他们到绿茵场上踢了一场足球比赛，大家玩得不亦乐乎。当班船员也在琢磨，这个城市是否像人们传说中的那样美好？第二天下船一定好好参观一下。

然而，意想不到的货损事故发生了。当该轮的5个货舱打开后，人们发现，上层货物表面大面积被锈水污染，捆装货物倒垛、位移，部分货物散捆、折断。进一步检查发现，底层货舱积水达20多厘米，底层货物浸泡在锈水之中，受到严重污染。此外，船上有部分货物是转卖到德国的，这部分货物被安排直接卸到驳船上运往德国的汉堡和不来梅。面对如此严重的事态，不同的收货人（或他们的保险人）立即委托公正检验机构分别在鹿特丹和德国港口对货物进行残损检验。鹿特丹港口的独立检验人V的检验报告主要内容如下：

In compliance with instructions received, we attended on board of the m. v. "G" and subsequently on the quay, in order to survey, without prejudice as to our principals' liability, a number of consignments of granite products, loaded at Yantai into the vessel's cargo holds, destined for discharge at Rotterdam.

Receivers of the various consignments of granite products at Rotterdam claimed that part of their cargo showed rust stains, while after completion of discharge, also some oil stains were claimed.

It was moreover claimed that in some of the vessel's cargo compartments, the stow of bundles of granite products had collapsed, due to which bundles had fallen apart and sometimes the granite products became broken.

As per the relevant cargo documentation the following consignments were involved:

B/L no.	Marks & Numbers	Number	Packing	Cargo description	Weight	Consignees
01	B W – E		Bundles	Granite kerbstones		BSK
	B6 15×15–17 CM	52				
	A2 15×18–25 CM	51				
	A5 12×15–30 CM	72				
	B6 14×25–26 CM	228				
	B6 12×13–16 CM	64				
	B6 14×13–16 CM	81				
	8×20–22 CM	15				
	Total	563			743 000.0	
02A	NM	1 366	Bundles	Granite kerbstones	1 707.5	Rheintrans
02B	NM	408	Bundles	Granite kerbstones	510.0	Rheintrans
04	B W – E		Bundles	Granite kerbstones		BSK
	B1 15×18–20 CM	10				
	B6 10×25–26 CM	168				
	B12 15×17.5–12 CM	1				
	B6 12×25–26 CM	282				
	G3 10×17–18 CM	190				
	Total	651			805 000.0	
05	B N – X	388	Pallets	Granite kerbs	501 000.0	BSK
06	B W – X	108	Pallets	Granite kerbs	151 000.0	BSK
07	B W – X	835	Pallets	Granite kerbs	1 185 000.0	BSK
08	B W – I	218	Pallets	Granite kerbs	154 700.0	BSK
09	B N – I	1 039	Pallets	Granite kerbs	1 379 310.0	BSK
110A	3 8 6 K	360	Big bags	Stone products	333 000.0	BSK
110B	3 8 0 K	52	Bundles	Stone products	75 000.0	BSK
111	M K B		Bundles	Granite kerbstones		BSK

B/L no.	Marks & Numbers	Number	Packing	Cargo description	Weight	Consignees
	A1 =	210				
	A3 =	100				
	A4 =	167				
	A5 =	417				
	B6 =	56				
	B6 =	375				
	B6 =	142				
	Total	1 467			1 837 000.0	
12	M K B		Crates	Granite kerbstones		BSK
	10 × 30 CM	15				
	10 × 45 CM	20				
	Total	35			36 000.0	

The abbreviation "BSK" stands for Messrs. BSK Brüll Spedition of Bremen, which company took delivery of their consignments partly overboard onto barges and partly onto the quay.

Messrs. Rheintrans of Rotterdam, acted as forwarding agents for Messrs. Raiss, in Germany, receivers of the consignments carried against Bills of Lading nos. 2A and 2B. These receivers took delivery of their consignments directly overboard into barges "NECKARFRACHT 15" and "TRIO".

The consignments carried against Bills of Lading nos. 2A and 2B were discharged as last consignments after the vessel had shifted to the premises of Messrs. Klapwijk, pier 1, Waalhaven, Rotterdam, whereas the balance of the cargo was discharged at the premises of Messrs. Steinweg.

In view of the stowage position on board, some 300 bundles of granite products belonging to Bills of Lading nos. 2A and 2B, were however, discharged by Messrs. Steinweg into receivers' barges.

Findings upon survey

When we attended on board, in the afternoon of the 9th January, 1998, we found discharge with the aid of shore cranes, partly overboard into barges and partly onto the quay in progress.

The consignments mainly consisted of bundles of granite blocks, which were bundles as follows:

On top of two wooden bulks, 6×8 cms., 2 layers of granite blocks, 7 blocks per layer were stowed. These blocks measured 14×25 cms.. The whole was bound with two steel wires, which were twisted.

We observed that a large number of these steel wires were somewhat slack. The surfaces of the granite blocks were uneven.

We inspected the various cargo holds and observed the following:

No.1 lower hold

We found a stow of bundles of blocks of granite to be present in the aft part of the hold. A restricted quantity of wooden planks etc. had been used to fill up the open spaces between the bundles and between the stow and the sloping sides of the hold.

The bundles were stowed 5 high and 10 up to 14 wide. We observed that bundles which held different lengths of blocks of granite were stowed mixed in the hold.

We noted at starboard side on top of the stow, rust stains to be present on top of the granite blocks. These stains gave a positive chloride reaction when submitted to a silver nitrate test. It was estimated that 12 bundles in the top layer showed visible rust stains.

In the wings, we found wooden constructions made of 1 cm. thick dry brittle wood, which were obviously meant to chock off the stow onto the sloping shell plating. At starboard side this very weak construction had partly collapsed and the stow of bundles of granite blocks had fallen towards the starboard side.

A large number of bundles had partly fallen apart and we noted that several granite blocks were broken.

On the tank top we found some free water to be present. This water gave a positive chloride reaction when submitted to a silver nitrate test.

The free water had a rusty colour and caused rust water stains when in contact with the bottom layer of bundles of granite stones.

No.2 hold

We found in the lower hold aft part, a stow of bundles of granite blocks.The stow of bundles of granite blocks was locally leaning over.Rust stripes were visible in the hatch coaming of the hold.On top of the cargo rust stains were visible.These rust stains revealed a positive chloride reaction when submitted to a silver nitrate test.

No.3 hold

We found in the middle part of the lower hold, over the full width, a stow of bundles of granite blocks.These bundles were stowed 5 or 6 tiers high.The stow was leaning over and some unites had collapsed.On top of the stow we found rust water stains to be present on the blocks of granite.

No.4 hold

We found in the forepart of the no.4 lower hold, a stow of bundles of blocks of granite to be present.These bundles were stowed up to 6 tiers high.Liquid marks on the base of this stow indicated that in the hold some 20cms.of free water had been present.The granite blocks which had been in contact with the rust water showed rust stains.

No.5 hold

In this lower hold, a stow of bundles of granite blocks was present in the forepart, while at port and starboard side, cobble stones, in bulk, were stowed.

Again we observed that free water was present on the tank top plating.This free water was rust coloured and marks indicated that the cargo had been in contact with the rust water up to a heigh of about 30cms.above the tank top level.

Further steps taken

We suggested to receivers to keep the allegedly damaged items separate during the discharge operations. Such was however, as we understood, in view of the adverse effect of such a separation on the discharge rate, not carried out.

We checked the discharge operations regularly.We observed that the majority of the cargo was directly loaded onto barges for on-transport to final receivers.

Counter surveyors invited us for a close inspection of the consignments carried against Bills of Lading nos.10A and 10B.These consignments were discharged onto the quay.

We inspected these consignments jointly, on the 3rd August, 1998, and noted the following:

Bill of Lading no.10A: 360 big bags of stone products - 333m.tons

In used polypropylene woven big bags, granite cobble stones were present. We found a total of 18 big bags, which outwardly showed rust water stains. Opening of these big bags revealed that the cobble stones present adjacent to the stained fabric also showed rust stains.

Bill of Lading no.10B: 52 bundles of stone products - 75 m.tons

We found this consignment to consist of unpacked bundles of granite blocks, 30×12 cms.and 12 blocks per bundle. We found 9 bundles, which showed rust water stains to varying extents.

Outturn remarks

We learned that the following remarks were inserted by stevedores/receivers on the relevant outturn report:

Bill of Lading no.	Remarks
1	54 stones broken 21 bundles loose 47 bundles covered with rusty water Covered with hold dust 8 bundles without skids
2	Several stones broken About 150 pallets covered with rusty water, loose or without skids
4	27 stones broken 13 bundles loose 51 bundles covered with rusty water Covered with hold dust
5	12 stones broken 11 pallets loose 5 pallets without skids 18 pallets covered with rusty water

Bill of Lading no.	Remarks
6	3 stones broken 4 pallets without skids
7	53 stones broken 21 bundles loose 18 bundles covered with rusty water
8	11 stones broken 1 bundle loose 23 bundles covered with rusty water
9	41 stones broken 8 bundles loose 48 bundles covered with rusty water 1 bundle covered with oil
10A	Covered with hold dust Weak packing Covered with rusty water
10B	3 stones broken 3 bundles without skids 12 bundles covered with rusty water
11	45 stones broken 34 bundles loose 18 bundles green stained 45 bundles covered with oil 108 bundles covered with rusty water Covered with hold dust
12	Weak packing-2 crates loose 1 crate repackd in 2 big bags

These remarks were in line with our findings upon survey.

<u>Further developments</u>

We requested the relevant final receivers to keep us informed about this final claim.After some time had elapsed, we learned however, that the vessel's P&I Club had instructed local surveyors to inspect the various consignments at final receivers' premises on their behalf.

Therefore we restrict ourselves to the above mentioned statement of facts.

With regard to the cause of the damage, we discussed the matter with the vessel's Master, and from information obtained, perusal of the relevant documentation and from our own observation, we learned and/or noted the following particulars:

The vessel loaded at Yantai, between the 14th and the 24th May, 1998, ex quay, with the aid of shore cranes, a cargo of granite products, destined for discharge at Marina di Carrara and Rotterdam, into her cargo holds.

The cargo had been secured in the vessel's holds by means of wooden chocks and steel wires.

These were applied by stevedores to the satisfaction of the vessel's staff.

As per stowage plan, the vessel loaded the following cargo:

Marina di Carrara: 2 663 packages =   3 328 750 kgs.

Rotterdam: 7 490 packages =   11 201 197 kgs.

The following remarks relating to the cargo destined for Rotterdam, were inserted on the relevant Mate's receipts upon loading:

Bill of Lading no.	Remark on the relevant Mate's receipt
SGR 01	5 bundles hoops slack
SGR 04	5 bundles hoops slack
SGR 05	25 bundles hoops broken, 5 stones broken
SGR 06	2 bundles hoops broken
SGR 07	12 bundles hoops broken
SGR 10	21 bags chafed, contents visible
SGR 11	All crates insufficiently packed, not responsible for contents loss 10 bundles hoops slack

The subject remarks were handwritten on the subject Mate's receipts.

The vessel left Yantai on the 14th May, 1998 and proceeded via Marina di Carrara (discharge) to Rotterdam, where she arrived on the 8th July, 1998.

During this voyage the vessel encountered heavy weather on the following dates:

Date	Wind direction/force		Course
11-06-1998	SW	6	296°
12-06-1998	SW	7	299°
13-06-1998	SW	8	285°
14-06-1998	SW	8	272°
15-06-1998	SW	7	348°

During these periods of heavy weather, the vessel had been rolling, sometimes up to 30 degrees to either side in a period of 12 seconds, and pitching, labouring at times, shipping water over deck and weather deck hatches.

The vessel's speed had been reduced and her course altered, as circumstances required, in order to ease her.

According to the vessel's staff, the adverse weather conditions prevented a daily sounding of the hold bilges, but the bilge pump was used every day on these bilges in order to keep same dry.

In view of the stowage position, some 30 bundles had been shifted at Marina di Carrera from the forward to the aft part of the no.4 tween deck.It was said that upon arrival at Rotterdam, it was observed that in the no.4 tween deck, some 10 bundles of granite blocks had toppled over.

When we attended on board, the cargo carried in the no.4 tween deck had already been discharged.

The vessel's Master made a "sea protest" at Rotterdam.

When we inspected the cargo in the vessel's holds we found in the no.3 tween deck some 6 bundles of granite blocks, which were visually contaminated with oil.

As far as could be ascertained no oil pipes were running through the hold at this location.We take it that the subject bundles became contaminated with oil prior to loading or during discharge operations at the vessel's previous discharge port.

We inspected the stowage of the bundles of granite blocks and observed that these bundles were bound together with two twisted steel wires.

Occasionally these wires were rather slack, due to which the integrity of the bundles was affected.

The bundles were stowed up to 5 high in the various cargo compartments.The inevitable open spaces between the bundles and between the stow and the vessel's sides were filled with constructions made of thin wooden planks.

Apparently these constructions were too weak when the vessel was rolling and same partly collapsed, as a result of which the stows sometimes collapsed.

When such a stow had collapsed, we found broken pieces of granite and broken bundles.

We found in the various lower holds, indications that free rusty coloured water had been present.

Attached below is part of pictures we take during our survey:

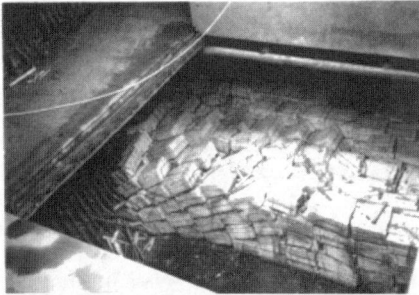

3.收货人扣押 G 轮

鉴于货物严重受损，收货人申请法院扣押了 G 轮，要求船东 H 提供相当于 33 万美元的赔偿担保。这一消息如雷击顶，H 公司上下顿时陷入一片吃惊和茫然之中。他们本以为，G 轮这次欧洲航程运送的花岗岩制品是他们运送过的货物中最简单的货物之一，船员稍微照顾就不可能发生货损事故。只要船舶能够顺利通过严苛的卫生检疫，就应当是一个顺利的航次。怎么可能发生如此严重的货损事故呢？当下最要命的是，船舶被扣押了，为了释放船舶，收货人索要 33 万美元的担保，对于这样小规模的海运公司而言，上哪去筹集这笔巨额的资金呀？

无奈，H 向 G 轮的英国保赔保险公司 W 求救。遗憾的是，W 在向荷兰的代理了解情况后告知 H，本航次的货损主要是由船舶不适航导致的，而船舶不适航导致的货损不在保赔保险承保的范围之列，因此无法代替 H 出具担保，除非 H 能够向 W 提供等额的反担保。

这一答复对 H 来说无疑又是当头一棒。眼看 G 轮卸货即将完毕，如果无法提供担保，该轮将被扣留在鹿特丹无法动弹。

H 在万般无奈的情况下又转向 G 轮的财产保险人 P 求救，请求帮助船东向 W 出具 33 万美元的反担保。P 在研究了本案案情后回复称，G 轮的货损事故系船东责任所致，而本公司承保的是 G 轮的财产险，非船东责任险，因此无法向 W 出具反担保，除非船东能够向本公司提供等额的反担保。

H 又当头挨了一棒，几乎被彻底打晕了。H 走到了绝境，因为，当时公司账户中只有几十万元人民币的流动资金，还不到索要担保额的四分之一，公司的船舶都设有银行贷款抵押，再也没有任何资产可以抵押了。绝境中的 H 开始绞尽脑汁地寻找解决办法。

他们首先与 W 协商，声称全部货损中有部分货物损坏是由于恶劣海况引起货物位移导致的，这是保赔保险承保的范围，因此请求 W 出具 10 万美元无反担保的担保。W 再次了解了全部货损情况，尽管细节当时仍然不明，但还是同意了 H 的请求，这稍微减轻了 H 的压力。

H 又向兄弟公司借入 40 万元人民币，加上自有的流动资金共筹集了 100 万元人民币，并承诺将其所属的其他船舶的下一航次运费收入交给 P（这类似于空头支票），以此作为反担保，请求 P 考虑多年的合作关系，向 W 出具 23 万美元的反担保，P 最终同意了 H 的请求。于是，P 向 W 出具了 23 万美元的反担保，W 向收货人提供了 33 万美元的担保。至此，G 轮获得了释放，H 总算暂时松了口气。

4.收货人提供了 G 轮的不适航证据

为了支持自己的索赔，收货人指定了独立检验人 V 对当事船舶 G 进行了船况检验。V 后来出具的检验报告主要内容如下：

REPORT OF SURVEY

Place of survey：the premises of C.Sterinweg Handelsveem B.V.，Rotterdam.

Date of survey：14th July 1998

In compliance with the instructions received, we attended on board the aforementioned vessel in order to carry out an inspection of the weather deck hatches.

The subject inspection was carried out on the 14th and 15th July 1998 and during the entire inspection, the vessel's Chief Officer was presented.

Major deficiencies were moreover reported and shown to the vessel's Master.

We reported our findings per telefax message to our Principals on the 14th and 15th July 1998; below we set out these findings.

The vessel is equipped with steel McGregor single pull hatches and the vessels cranes are used to open/close same.

The following deficiencies were found：

No.1 hatch

Hatch closed with 5 steel pontoons, opening to aft.

Hatch inspected in open position as the crane, which is used to operate the hatch, was out of order

−Coaming port and starboard aft drain pope missing.

−Starboard side 2 quick acting cleats bent.

−Compression bar heavily corroded and uneven.

−No.4 pontoon from forward cross seam packing channel wavy and bent over 1 metre.

−Rubber packing in general in worn condition with deep permanent imprints.

−Stripes in coaming indicate hatch leaking.

No.2 hatch

Closed with 5 pontoons opening to forward.

−Aft pontoon forward transverse vertical plating 3 corrosion holes, each about 30×30cm and plating signs of heavy wastage.

−Aft pontoon starboard aft corner packing channel deformed.

−2nd pontoon from aft packing channel (transverse) wavy.

−3rd pontoon from aft top plating signs of wastage with small corrosion holes.

−4th pontoon vertical transverse forward plating corrosion hole 32×2 cm.

−4th pontoon transverse packing channel heavily bent and torn over 2 metres and channel at port bent over 30 cm.

−19 out of 32 wedges missing at top.

−Coaming drain pipes port and starboard forward corroded away.

−Compression bar heavily rusted and uneven.

−Port aft quick acting cleat clamp out of order.

No.3 hold

Hatch closed with 5 pontoons opening to forward.

Forward pontoon:

−Aft vertical transverse plating corrosion holes 80×30 and 120×20 cm.

−Port forward connection pint quick acting cleat out of order.

No.2 pontoon:

−Transverse packing channel heavily bent over 1 metre.

−Starboard side packing channel heavily deformed over 30 cm.

No.3 pontoon:

−Transverse packing channel locally corroded away over about 30 cm.

No.4 pontoon:

−Transverse packing channel wavy.

−Top plating signs of heavy wastage.

No.5 pontoon:

−Packing channel deformed in way of middle.

−Coaming aft port drain pope broken off.

−Compression bar rusty and uneven.

<u>No.4 hatch</u>

Hatch closed with 7 steel pontoons, opening to forward.

−Starboard forward drainpipe of coaming table corroded away.

−Compression bar on coaming table heavily corroded and uneven.

−Starboard side one quick acting cleat connection broken.

−No. 3 pontoon (counted from aft) corrosion hole on top plating in way of middle.

−No.4 pontoon forward transverse vertical plating corrosion hole of about 80×40 cm.

−Wedges on cross seams, 8 wedges per seam, total 42 out of 48 wedges missing.

−Rubber packing locally deep permanent imprints.

<u>No.5 hatch</u>

−Compression bar on coaming table signs of heavy corrosion and uneven.

−Starboard aft drainpipe of coaming table partly corroded away.

Hatch closed with 5 steel pontoons, pontoons counted from aft:

−No. 2 pontoon forward vertical transverse plating corroded through in 3 locations, viz.

80×15 cm

40×15 cm

20×15 cm

−Starboard packing channel deformed.

−No.1 pontoon forward vertical transverse plating corrosion hole of about 80×20 cm.

−Cross seams provided with wedges, total 28 out of 32 wedges missing.

<u>General remarks</u>

• We observed that the steel pontoons were for the major part rather recently painted. The adjoining clamps for the quick acting cleats on the pontoon did sometimes not show paint damages, giving the impression that only part of the quick acting cleats was actually used.

• We observed that the wheels of the hatch pontoons were sometimes seized and not in line with the tracks.

The chains used to interconnect the hatch pontoons occasionally showed considerable wastage and were sometimes too long.

• The areas around the hatches, such as coaming stanchions, hatch pontoon tracks, etc.showed signs of considerable wastage.

• The No.1 hole forward access door lower flange was partly corroded away.

• No hose test was performed in view of the obvious leakages of the weather deck hatches.

In witness, whereof this report is issued, to serve and avail, when and where required.

Enclosure: pictures we take during the survey.

At Rotterdam, 20th July, 1998.

5. View on compression bar

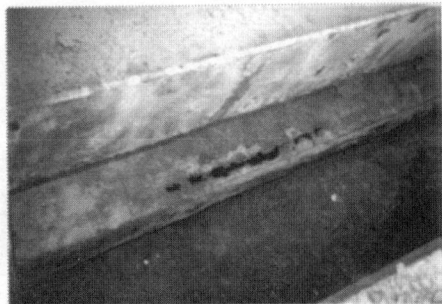

1. Corrosion holes in hatch pontoons.

16. Quick acting clamp out of order.

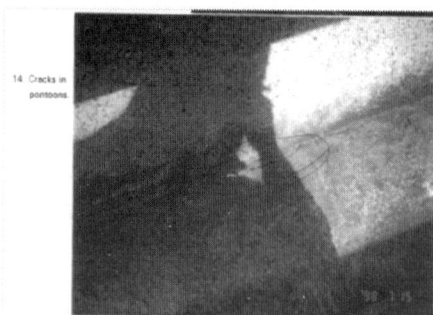

14. Cracks in pontoons.

13. Serious corrosion holes hatch pontoons.

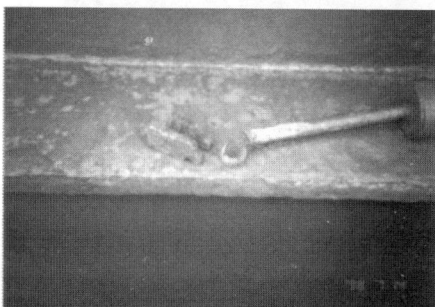

11. Broken quick acting cleat.

5.收货人索赔及船东 H 的应战

    凭借独立检验人 V 对受损货物和船况的检验报告，以及不同的收货人在德国港口对驳船驳运的到港货物的检验报告，不同的收货人分别指定律师于1998 年 9 月通过 G 轮的保赔保险人 W 向承运人 H 提出具体的索赔。各收货人在索赔函中除了提出索赔金额外，还附上了相关的提单、烟台各出口公司开具的商业发票、货损检验报告、其他费用开支单据等。从此双方长达 9 年的漫漫索赔谈判及法院诉讼的大幕正式拉开。

面对收货人的33万美元巨额索赔，H与W的律师一道对收货人的索赔逐一展开了应战。

H与W明白，无论是从索赔人提供的检验报告看，还是从他们自己委托的检验人出具的检验报告看，船舶不适航和货物损坏有客观证据在，白纸黑字是赖不掉的。因此，他们首先承认船舶不适航和货损的事实，然后从货损检验的地点、货物损坏范围及程度的认定、货损金额和航行期间遭遇恶劣海况等方面入手，对索赔人提出的赔偿金额展开了反击。

在切入正题之前，H首先虚晃一枪指出，本航次的运输合同系H与BSK公司签署的，只有后者才有权依据该合同向本承运人索赔，而其他收货人凭借提单向本承运人索赔是没有法律依据的，因为该航次运输合同约定适用《海牙-维斯比规则》，该规则中没有提单持有人可以凭借提单向承运人索赔的规定。相关国内法也规定，提单只是运输合同的证明，而非运输合同本身。

关于货物的检验地点问题，H认为，收货人的货物检验地点违反了法律规定，因此检验报告应当认定为无效证据。本案例中各项索赔所依据的提单背面条款规定，本提单适用《海牙-维斯比规则》。根据该规则的规定，承运人的责任期间为从货物装到船上时起到货物卸下船舶时止。因此，本承运人对货物的责任应当在鹿特丹港货物卸离G轮时终止。据此，收货人应当在鹿特丹港进行货损检验，并邀请承运人的代表参加。遗憾的是，收货人除在鹿特丹港安排了检验外，还在货物最终目的地德国的不同港口邀请了不同的检验人对货物进行检验，并且，这些检验报告对货损的认定与鹿特丹港的检验报告存在矛盾。而索赔人却依据这些无效的、相互矛盾的检验报告向承运人索赔。因此，本承运人不接受当前的索赔金额。

关于货物损坏范围及损坏程度的认定问题，承运人认为，在鹿特丹港卸货时，收货人没有尽到法律规定的减少损失义务，好坏货物混淆，加大了损失程度；按照合同规定，本航次的卸货责任和费用由收货人承担。但是，收货人雇用的码头工人在卸货过程中野蛮操作，造成部分货物损坏；在直接卸往驳船过程中也造成部分货物损坏。这些事实在索赔人委托的检验人的检验报告中都有记载。这些损失不是承运人履行合同义务所致，不应当由承运人承担，但是索赔人却将这些损失一并向承运人索赔，明显违背了公平公正原则。

此外，本航次的所谓货损，一部分为货物表面被锈水污染，其中绝大多数石条只是一个侧面被污染，无论将其用于马路边石，还是用于其他建筑，都不影响其使用价值，但索赔人却认定其全部丧失使用价值，这明显夸大了损失程度。

关于索赔金额的计算问题，H认为，根据《海牙-维斯比规则》，货物损坏的赔偿额，应当按照货物受损前后实际价值的差额计算。然而在本案例中，索赔人没有邀请承运人对受损货物的价值进行认定，也没有请公证机构进行这项认定，而是自己进行认定，然后计算差价向承运人索赔，这也明显违反了相关法律规定和公平公正原则。因此，当前的索赔金额承运人是不能接受的。

关于部分散捆货物折断受损问题，H认为，这部分货物的损坏完全是不可抗力原因导致的，根据提单的法律规定，应当免除承运人责任。G轮本航次的航海日志和索赔人指定的检验人出具的检验报告均显示，该轮在经过印度洋的航行途中，适逢西南季风季节。在从6月11日至15日的5天时间里，船舶遇到恶劣海况，西南风在7~8级，船舶露天甲板大量上浪，并且以12秒的短周期横摇达30度。为了航行安全，船舶需要不断改变航向。这些不利因素才是导致货舱内货物位移、散捆和折断的根本原因。而当前收货人将这类损失一并向承运人索赔，这也是违反法律规定和公平公正原则的。

综上，承运人明确告诉索赔人，不接受当前的索赔金额，请索赔人根据上述情况重新计算索赔额。

收货人收到承运人上述陈词后，对各项索赔金额进行了重新计算，将索赔金额降到20万美元。对此，承运人仍表示难以接受，双方的谈判陷入僵局。但为了谈判能够进行下去，双方将诉讼时效多次延展。

时间到了2002年9月，双方的谈判虽然有了一定的进展，但收货人的索赔金额与承运人的愿意赔付额仍相去甚远。双方进行博弈，索赔人多次以提起法律诉讼相威胁，而H则采取拖延战术，意在消磨索赔人的斗志，反正一天不答应他们的诉求，他们就一天拿不到钱。到2002年的9月17日，在经历了整整4年的反复较量后，第1号和第4至9号共7份提单下的收货人与承运人达成了赔偿协议，接受H的3万德国马克赔付提议，2号提单收货人放弃了索赔，至此，本次索赔中的主要战斗宣告结束。

然而，第10、11和12号提单下的索赔谈判仍无法达成一致，收货人终于将案件提交到法庭，法庭的程序是复杂的。在法庭上，双方的辩护律师提出了各自的主张并提交了大量的文件，利用法律的程序性规定各自施展博弈技巧，一直将案件拖到了 2007 年 6 月。大概是承运人的战术有效了，最终，双方以 H 赔付 3 个提单持有人总计 2.5 万欧元结束了这场战斗。

至此，在经历了 9 年漫长的谈判和庭审过程之后，H 遭遇的这场 33 万美元船舶不适航索赔案以 H 总共赔付不到 6 万美元而彻底宣告结束。看上去 H 是个胜利者，但这场本不该有的索赔案也让他们尝到了船舶管理不善的苦头。如果当年在船舶技术状况的管理上能够稍微认真一些，如果这 9 年的精力不是用在与欧洲人的博弈上，而是用在市场开发上，结果会是怎样呢？

6.讨论思考题

(1) 什么是船舶不适航？船舶不适航具体包括哪些内容？

(2) 法律对承运人保证船舶适航义务是如何规定的？

(3) 哪些人有权向承运人发起船舶不适航索赔？

(4) 索赔人应如何申请诉前扣押船舶？

(5) 索赔人应如何进行货物索赔？

(6) 涉案双方应当从本案例中吸取什么教训？

7.参考文献

[1] 海牙-维斯比规则 [EB/OL]. [2025-04-10]. https：//wenku.so.com/d/2f3095c038eb703c4fa525b2a94a24cf？src=ob_zz_juhe360wenku.

[2] 英国 1992 年海上货物运输法 [EB/OL]. [2025-01-10]. http：//wenku.baidu.com/view/e0443f18964bcf84b9d57b0f.html.

[3] 中华人民共和国海商法 [EB/OL]. [2025-01-10]. 中华人民共和国海商法_相关规定_中国政府网.

[4] 1999 年国际扣船公约 [EB/OL]. [2015-08-10]. http：//www.un.org/chinese/documents/decl-con/docs/12-8.htm.

[5] 中华人民共和国海事诉讼特别程序法 [EB/OL]. [2025-01-10]. 中华人民共和国主席令（第二十八号） 中华人民共和国海事诉讼特别程序法__2000 年第 2 号国务院公报_中国政府网.

[6] 司玉琢. 海商法 [M]. 5 版. 北京：法律出版社，2023.

［7］杨良宜，杨大明，杨大志. 证据法：国际规管与诉讼中的证据攻防［M］. 北京：法律出版社，2020.

［8］杨良宜. 合约的解释：规则与应用［M］. 北京：法律出版社，2015.

［9］李勤昌. 论海运提单的运输合同属性［J］. 世界海运，2002（5）.

8.案例英文信息

The Nine-year Defence for Unseaworthiness Claim by H Shipping Company

Abstract： The nine-year fight describes in this case happened at the end of last century in Netherland. The claimants are several Dutch and German cargo receivers and the respondent is H Shipping Company in Dalian City in China. W Shipowners' Mutual Protection and Indemnity Association is also involved. The battle is incurred by the unseaworthiness of MV G owned by H Shipping Company. With the introduction of the background of the fight at the beginning, this case exhibits in details the evidences of unseaworthiness of the carrying vessel MV G and the specific damage of the cargo discharged presented by the claimants. It also describes objectively the tactics and measures taken in the claim by the claimants, so does the strategy and tactics used by the owner of the carrying vessel in their fight for the claim. The second part of this case is the theoretical analysis and comments from the writer.

Key words： seaworthiness, cargo claim, arresting ship, damage survey

案例使用说明

一、教学目的与用途

本案例适用于"国际贸易实务"、"国际货物运输"和"国际物流"等课程中关于船舶不适航索赔知识点的教学。案例的编写目的是通过讨论案例中描述的各争议焦点，引导学生领会船舶不适航索赔的相关法律规定并掌握索赔技能，培养学生处理船舶不适航索赔实际问题的实践能力。通过阅读、分析和讨论本案例资料，帮助学生思考和掌握下列五个具体问题：一是提单持有人索赔权的确定；二是诉前扣押船舶的法律规定；三是索赔的程序；四是索赔金额计算的法律规定；五是商务索赔技巧。

本案例的概念难度、分析难度和陈述难度均适中，适用对象包括国际贸易专业、国际物流专业和国际商务专业的本科生、研究生和国际商务专业学位研究生。对于缺乏专业基础理论知识的本科生，可以根据教学大纲，有选择地引导阅读案例相关材料，重点熟悉船舶不适航的概念和具体内容，掌握船舶不适航索赔的基本法律依据和基本程序；对于缺乏实践经验的研究生，可以引导其将所掌握的理论知识运用于本案例中每一个具体问题的分析，对案例中争论的几个焦点问题，作出自己的是非判断，锻炼其处理实际问题的能力。

本案例规划的理论教学知识点包括：

（1）索赔人对船舶不适航导致货损的索赔权的法律依据；

（2）诉前扣押船舶的法律依据；

（3）索赔金额确定的法律依据。

本案例规划的能力训练教学内容包括：

（1）对船舶不适航导致货损的检验的正确组织能力；

（2）对船舶不适航证据和货物损失证据的搜集能力；

（3）诉前扣押船舶的实施能力；

（4）索赔金额的计算能力；

（5）整体索赔的筹划与组织能力。

二、分析思路

本案例的核心问题是船舶不适航情形下对承运人的索赔权问题，这也是本案例教学的核心知识点。围绕这一核心知识点，建议案例的课堂讨论按照下列思路和顺序展开：

首先，讨论索赔的性质问题。围绕这一核心问题引导学生具体讨论下列问题：（1）发生货损的原因是什么？（2）船舶不适航包括哪些主要内容？（3）相关法律对承运人保证船舶适航义务有哪些具体规定？（4）承运人违反保证船舶适航义务须承担哪些后果？

其次，讨论提单持有人的诉权问题。围绕这一问题，引导学生讨论下列问题：（1）提单持有人作为托运人时具有诉权吗？（2）提单持有人非托运人时具有诉权吗？（3）提单持有人持有未背书指示提单具有诉权吗？（4）提单持有人持有记名提单时，需要背书才具有诉权吗？（5）上述提单持有人同时又是租船合同的承租人时，索赔依据是什么？

再次，讨论索赔金额认定问题。围绕这一问题，引导学生讨论下列问题：（1）相关法律有何规定？（2）市场差价如何认定？（3）残值应如何认定？（4）存在发货人导致的货损应如何处理？（5）转售合同额外损失应如何处理？

最后，讨论向承运人索赔的技术性问题。围绕这一问题，引导学生讨论下列问题：（1）应采取何种索赔方式？诉讼和仲裁有何区别？（2）何谓诉前保全？应如何进行？（3）获取证据的意义是什么？应如何获取？（4）应如何进行仲裁或诉讼？如何将保函出具人列为被告？

在通过上述问题讨论完成本案例知识点教学任务后，还可以引导学生深入讨论两个延伸问题：一是若是卖方租船，可否向卖方索赔？二是可否向保险人索赔？索赔时应注意什么问题？

三、理论依据及分析

1.船舶适航及其具体内容

船舶适航（seaworthiness）有狭义和广义之分。狭义的船舶适航是指船舶的船体、机器、设备在设计、结构、性能和状态等方面能够抵御航次中通常出现的或能够合理预见的风险。它不要求船舶能够抵御航次中遇到的一切风险，所以，适航要求是相对的。广义的船舶适航是指在船舶本身适航基础上，还要求配备充足适任的船员、装备船舶和配备供应品，保证货舱适货。按照英国法院的众多判例和其他国家的司法实践，船舶适航包括以下几个方面：

（a）The ship's structure must be sufficiently strong to withstand the weather and sea conditions likely to be encountered on the voyage and her hull plating and hatch covers must be sufficiently watertight to protect the cargo from the risk of seawater damage.

（b）The propulsion machinery and other machinery and equipment necessary for the safe navigation of the vessel on the voyage must be adequate in design, and in adequate state of maintenance and repair, to undertake the voyage safely.

（c）Proper manning is an essential element in the concept of seaworthiness under law. The vessel must have an adequate number of persons employed to serve on board to perform functions for which they are qualified and in fact competent and efficient. Thus， however well qualified a vessel's master or chief engineer， if they are drunkards or too ill or too institutionally lazy to perform their functions， then the vessel is unseaworthy.

（d）A vessel's equipment as well as the vessel herself must be reasonably fit to meet and undergo the perils which are likely to be encountered and to keep the cargo in sound condition. Thus， a reefer ship with a refrigerated cargo was held unseaworthy because of defects in her refrigeration machinery and a vessel with an insecure bullion room was held unseaworthy for the carriage of gold bullion.

A vessel must also be supplied with those necessary provisions required for the voyage. She must have sufficient and adequate bunkers to complete the voyage， allowing a reasonable margin for contingencies to which the vessel may be subject. When bunkers are intended to be taken at an intermediate port， she must set out for that port with enough bunkers to reach it in safety. Also those bunkers must also be suitable for use in the vessel's engines.

There must likewise be sufficient food for the crew as well as drinking water or the means of making it.

The vessel must also be supplied with all necessary charts， pilot books and other navigational aids to perform the required voyage.

（e）A vessel is not seaworthy unless she is in possession of documents necessary to her legal and efficient performance of the voyage undertaken， such as those required by the law of her flag， by her classification society and by the laws.

（f）The holds must be properly cleaned of rust， residues of previous cargoes， insects and the like， which might contaminate the contemplated cargo or render the carriage of the cargo dangerous resulted from any defects caused by improper stowage， which give rise to instability during the voyage， e.g.through the consumption of bunkers or the handling of cargo.

2.承运人保证船舶适航的法律规定

对于承运人的"适航义务"，有关国际公约和主要航运国家的法律对此都作了严格规定。《中华人民共和国海商法》（以下简称《海商法》）第47条规定："承运人在船舶开航前和开航当时，应当谨慎处理，使船舶处于适航状态，妥善配备船员、装备船舶和配备供应品，并使货舱、冷藏舱、冷气舱和其他载货处所适于并能安全收受、载运和保管货物。"

《International Convention for the Unification of Certain Rules of Law Relating to Bill of Lading》Article 3 stipulate that：

The carrier shall be bound before and at the beginning of the voyage to exercise due diligence to：

（a）Make the ship seaworthy.

（b）Properly man，equip and supply the ship.

（c）Make the holds，refrigerating and cool chambers，and all other parts of the ship in which goods are carried，fit and safe for their reception，carriage and preservation.

根据有关法律，承运人承担的适航义务是相对的，即承运人只要谨慎处理（with due diligence）使船舶适航即可。如果承运人已尽谨慎责任，船舶仍存在不能发现的潜在缺陷（latent defect），也视为承运人履行了谨慎处理使船舶适航的义务。

根据《海牙规则》，承运人履行保证船舶适航义务的责任期间是在"船舶开航前和开航当时"（before and at the beginning of the voyage）。关于该英文词语的解释，应当指从预备航次开始之时（可能在运输合同生效之前）到船舶在装货港离泊之时，但从实际意义出发，更多的是指在装货阶段。根据上述规定，船舶装货驶离泊位后，承运人的保证适航义务便终止了。承运人对航行途中船舶发生的事故是否采取措施恢复船舶的适航性，包括船舶正常航行的途中在加油港口加燃油，都属于承运人管理船舶义务范畴，与适航义务无关。

本案例中，索赔人出具的船况检验报告显示，G轮的5个货舱舱盖和舱口围及其附属构件多处锈损严重，有的弯曲变形，有的构件锈掉了、遗失了，更有甚者，几处舱盖侧板锈出了大小不等的洞孔。所有这些明显构成G轮不适航的充分证据。这明显违反了相关法律强制规定的承运人恪尽职守保证船舶适航的义务，从货损的原因看，大量的证据显示，货物锈损是G轮货舱舱盖不水密导致的，因此必须对由此导致的货物损坏承担全部赔偿责任。

3.提单持有人的货物索赔权利

本案例中争议的其中一个问题就是提单持有人是否具有货物索赔权。这是一个法律问题，回答这一问题需要回到相关法律规定上。

英国《1992年海上货物运输法》对提单持有人作出详细规定。该法第5条第2款规定：本法所称的提单持有人是指以下各种人：（a）在提单上载明因而成为提单项下货物收货人的占有提单的人；（b）通过提单的交付而完成了提单的背书转让或在空白提单下通过其他方式完成了提单转让，因而占有提单的人；（c）因任何商事交易而占有提单的人，但该商事交易进行时，占有提单已不再赋予占有人对承运人主张提单下货物的权利，若非如此，该商事交易的进行将使提单占有人成为前述（a）、（b）两项所指的持有人。同时，该法第1条第2款（a）项将提单限定为"不包括不能通过背书即可转让，或不能像空白提单那样无须背书，通过交付即可转让的单证，但包括收妥待运提单"。

收货人和提单持有人两个概念主要与提单合同相联系，在实际使用中常常混用。我国《海商法》第78条第1款规定："承运人同收货人、提单持有人之间的权利、义务关系，依据提单的规定确定。"英国提单法也强制性规定收货人或提单持有人取得提单时，同时获得了提单的权利和义务，这里所说的权利包括提单项下的货物索赔权。因此，不论何种提单，只要合法持有，持有人就应当拥有提单下对承运人的货物请求权，或在承运人存在过失导致货物灭失、损坏情况下向其主张赔偿。

因此，本案例中，即使索赔人不是本航次租船合同的缔约人，但他们是提单持有人，享有提单合同下的货物索赔权，他们的索赔是有法律依据的，H的主张也就是虚晃一枪罢了，是没有法律依据的。

4.索赔人的诉前保全

海上索赔权利保全也称为海事请求保全，是指对海事请求具有管辖权的法院根据海事请求人的申请，为使其海事请求民事权利得以保障，对被申请人的财产或行为所采取的民事强制措施。这些强制措施通常包括：强迫被申请人提供可信赖的担保、扣押义务人的船舶、要求义务人实施某种作为或不作为等。

海事诉前保全的目的是保证海事请求人民事权利的顺利实现。例如，在卸货港发生重大货物损失，金额巨大，此时如果不对卸货船舶采取海事请求保全，该轮一旦离去，收货人索赔可能就非常困难。所以，海事请求保全是海事请求人实现其索赔权利的重要且行之有效的措施，货物索赔人应当懂得运用这一措施保全自己的权利，顺利实现索赔。

海上索赔权利保全可采取担保书和扣押船舶两种形式。

货物赔偿担保书（letter of undertaking，LOU），或赔偿担保函（letter of indemnity，LOI）是指承运人就其承运货物的灭失或损坏或延迟交付导致经济损失，向收货人提供的保证将按照仲裁机构的裁决或法院的判决作出赔偿的书面保证。为提高担保书的可信赖性和可执行性，担保书应由信誉卓著的机构作出，例如银行、船东互保协会、船舶保险人、具有足够经济实力的大公司等。

扣押船舶是海事请求保全中最主要、最典型的形式。船舶不同于一般财产，作为海上运输工具，船舶具有名称、国籍等拟人化特征，因此，扣押船舶是民事诉讼中的特殊海事诉讼制度。《统一扣押海运船舶若干规定的国际公约》（以下简称《1952年扣船公约》）《1999年国际扣船公约》以及《中华人民共和国海事诉讼特别程序法》（以下简称《海诉法》）都对扣船的有关问题作出特别规定。

诉讼前的扣船属诉前保全措施，它是指在实体争议开始解决之前通过法律程序对船舶实施强制留置措施，其目的是迫使被申请人提供足够担保，保证将来海事请求权利的实现。为了使仲裁裁决得以实现，也可以在仲裁开始之前，由申请人向海事法院申请扣押船舶。

本案例中，收货人很好地运用了法律给予的扣押当事船舶的法律武器，其依法扣押G轮的行为既符合相关国际公约的规定，又符合相关国内法的规定。通过扣押G轮成功地获取了W的33万美元担保，为后来的谈判和赔偿金的获取奠定了非常好的基础。

5.收货人的货物索赔操作

货物损失索赔应按照一定的程序进行，主要包括：

（1）及时发出事故通知

根据有关国际公约、国内法规或合同的规定，在发生海上货物损失时，收货人或其他货物索赔人应在规定的时间内向承运人发出货物损失通知书，声明保留货物损失索赔权。《海商法》第81条规定："承运人向收货人交付货物时，收货人未将货物灭失或者损坏的情况书面通知承运人的，此项交付视为承运人已经按照运输单证的记载交付以及货物状况良好的初步证据。"按照此项规定，如货物索赔人未向承运人发出货物损失通知，事故的举证责任就由承运人转到收货人。如果收货人不能举证承运人存在过失，则可能在索赔中败诉。

货物索赔人发出货物损失通知是有时间限制的。《海商法》第81条规定："货物灭失或者损坏的情况非显而易见的，在货物交付的次日起连续七日内，集装箱货物交付的次日起连续十五日内，收货人未提交书面通知的，适用前款规定。货物交付时，收货人已经会同承运人对货物进行联合检查或者检验的，无需就所查明的灭失或者损坏的情况提交书面通知。"

（2）准备索赔文件

在收货人作出货物损失通知的情况下，因为货物灭失或损坏的举证责任在承运人一方，所以，收货人在提出索赔时，出具的索赔文件比较简单。通常，收货人在提出索赔时应出具以下文件：

一是索赔函。索赔函是货物索赔人向承运人提出货物索赔的正式文件，该文件无固定格式，但应包括以下主要内容：索赔人的名称和地址、船名、装卸港口名称、船舶抵达卸货港的日期、提单号码及提单中的货物描述、货物灭失或损坏的情况、索赔日期、索赔金额及索赔理由等。

应当注意的是，索赔人按照法律规定向承运人提出的货物损失通知并不表示已经向承运人提出索赔，只有索赔人向承运人提出索赔函时，才表明索赔正式开始。索赔人提出索赔请求后，应当抓紧催赔。如果在诉讼时效临近时承运人仍未赔付，或仍未就赔偿事宜作出正式承诺，索赔人应当在诉讼时效到期前依法提起诉讼，防止承运人故意拖延，错过诉讼时效，丧失索赔权利。

二是提单。提单是海上货物索赔的重要依据。提单作为货物收据，表明承运人收到货物的数量和外表状况；提单作为运输合同，表明承运人应当承担的责任，是处理索赔的重要法律依据。索赔人提出索赔就是因为承运人交付的货物与提单记载不符，要么货物灭失，要么货物损坏，要么货物短少，要么延迟抵达导致经济损失，根据提单合同及相关法律规定，承运人必须对上述损失承担赔偿责任，除非承运人能够举证，根据提单合同及有关法律，它可以免除赔偿责任。

三是卸货报告、理货报告、货物溢卸（短卸）报告、货物残损单等卸货单证。上述各种单证是对船舶卸下货物的原始记录，由船方和理货人或装卸公司共同作出并会签。如果卸下的货物与提单或出口载货清单（export cargo manifest）不符，会在此类报告中作出记录。此类单证是货物灭失或损坏的原始记录，所以是货物索赔时的重要依据。

四是货物残损公正检验报告、重理单。当收货人和船方对货物的损坏程度、数量、损坏原因无法作出正确判断或存在争议时，往往需要双方共同指定公正检验机构对残损货物进行检验，确定损坏程度、数量、价值，以及导致货物残损的原因等，并出具货物残损检验证书（inspection certificate for damage and shortage）。当船货双方对卸货数量发生争议时，可以对所卸货物重新理货，并出具重理报告。这两种报告同上述三中的报告性质一样，是货物索赔最直接的原始依据。

五是商业发票、装箱单、重量单等。商业发票是由贸易合同中的卖方开给买方的商业票据。它记载了货物的单价和货物总值，是索赔时计算索赔金额的直接原始依据。如果发票中记载的是货物的CIF价值，索赔金额应当按此价值计算；如果发票是以FOB、CFR开具的，计算时还应加上运费或保险费，但索赔人应提供运费或保险费收据，以兹证明。装箱单或重量单通常是商业发票的随附单证，用以证明提单项下货物品种和数量的详细情况，因此是提单中货物记载的辅助性证明。

（3）正确计算索赔金额

索赔金额应当按照法律规定计算。《海牙-维斯比规则》第2条（a）款规定："全部赔偿应参照该项货物，根据合同从船上卸载或应卸载的当时当地的价值计算。货物价值应按照商品交换价格确定，或如无此价格时，则按现时市场价格，或如无商品交换价格或现时市场价格时，则按该相似种类和质量货物的正常价值确定。"

《中华人民共和国民法典》（以下简称《民法典》）第584条规定："当事人一方不履行合同义务或者履行合同义务不符合约定，造成对方损失的，损失赔偿额应当相当于因违约所造成的损失，包括合同履行后可以获得的利益；但是，不得超过违约一方订立合同时预见到或者应当预见到的因违约可能造成的损失。"因此，索赔金额除了货物本身的损失外，还可以包括因货物灭失或损害所丧失的合理合同利益。提供索赔证据时，应当包括与合同利益损失的有关证据。

《海商法》第55条规定："货物灭失的赔偿额，按照货物的实际价值计算；货物损坏的赔偿额，按照货物受损前后实际价值的差额或者货物的修复费用计算。货物的实际价值，按照货物装船时的价值加保险费加运费计算。前款规定的货物实际价值，赔偿时应当减去因货物灭失或者损坏而少付或者免付的有关费用。"

本案例中，在索赔程序上，收货人首先对受损货物进行了检验，取得了货物受损的详细情况，对船舶状况的检验提供了G轮货舱不适货的充分证据。然后他们通过扣押G轮，向承运人H通告了货损情况。这些做法基本符合货物索赔的一般性程序，但对检验地点的选择和对受损货物的处理问题上，仍有不当之处，即应当只在鹿特丹港口进行检验，残损货物处理应当公正。他们对索赔范围和索赔金额的认定是违反前述法律规定和公平公正原则的，夸大的索赔金额，为承运人提供担保制造了麻烦，承运人就此事可以索赔。好在后来在无充分证据反驳承运人赔偿主张的情况下，他们实事求是地降低了索赔额，使案件最终得以解决。

6.涉案双方从本案例中应当吸取的教训

先从索赔人说起，根据相关法律规定和前文关于索赔程序的分析，索赔人应当在卸货港邀请承运人一道对货物的损失范围、损失程度作出检验。在对受损货物的处理上，要么邀请承运人一道处理，要么请求公证人参与对受损货物的处理，从而体现公平公正精神。如果索赔人能够按照上述程序操作，就不会出现承运人抓住的那些把柄，获赔金额应当能够高于最后的实际获赔金额。在战术上，索赔人如果能够不犹豫，及早果断地采取法律诉讼手段解决问题，就会给承运人很大的压力，后者可能会被迫接受较高的赔偿金额。

再说承运人，从案件的处理过程和最终结果看，承运人是这场战役的胜利者。他们充分运用了各项证据的漏洞和索赔人的处理不当，再结合持久战的战术，将原本33万美元的索赔降低到不到6万美元。然而，本案给承运人的教训也是深刻的。本案货损主要源于承运船舶的不适航，这是索赔人抓住的要害。案件反映了承运人对船舶技术状况管理的疏忽。如果承运人能够对当事船舶的货舱舱盖进行认真的检查，是能够发现这一明显缺陷的。如果这些缺陷被消除，就不会发生货舱漏水，从而就不大可能发生这场索赔之战了，至少不会如此复杂和如此旷日持久。

四、关键要点

阅读本案例并正确回答讨论思考题，需要学生把握以下要点：

（1）船舶适航涉及很多具体内容，货方从使用船舶和货物索赔角度看应当掌握这些内容。

（2）法律严格规定了承运人的保证船舶适航义务及其违反该项义务的法律后果，货方应当准确把握，以便在发生因船舶不适航导致货损时依法索赔。

（3）货方遇到因船舶不适航导致严重货损时，应首先考虑实施诉前保全措施。

（4）在进行货物索赔时，应当准备充足的书面证据，并及时地向承运人提出索赔。

（5）索赔人应注意诉讼时效的适时延展。

五、课堂教学计划建议

本案例可以作为专门的案例讨论课来进行。以下是按照时间进度提供的课堂计划建议，仅供参考。

对于本案例教学，建议在给出本案例前，教师用50分钟的课堂时间预先讲授相关知识，并在相关知识讲授完毕后，立即给出本案例素材和讨论思考题，然后根据思考题的数量将全班学生分成若干组，每一组分配一个问题，要求各组在课后阅读案例材料，根据所学知识对分配的问题作出分析性答案，并将主要分析依据和结论做成PPT。准备100分钟全班同学听取汇报和教师评论。课中计划：

简要的课堂前言，明确主题：2～5分钟

小组发言：每组10～15分钟，控制在80分钟内

引导全班进一步讨论并进行归纳总结：15～20分钟

第二章

管货责任

D轮疏于管货引发收货人索赔

摘要：在国际货物贸易中，有相当一部分货物损坏是因承运人在运输途中疏于管理货物造成的。本案例的正文部分以Z进出口公司提单项下管货责任索赔为主要线索，描述了该公司与H海运公司之间，以及与当事船舶的保赔保险公司和货物保险公司之间的索赔商战的全过程。案例在介绍了索赔发生的背景之后，细致地描述了相关当事人在长达3年多的时间里围绕货物损坏索赔所进行的船舶扣押、一审法院起诉和应诉、二审法院上诉和抗辩、最高法院的申诉等多场激烈的交锋，揭示了提单项下货物索赔的复杂性和艰巨性。案例的使用说明部分对案例正文描述的各场较量进行了理论分析和评价，同时提供了案例使用指导。

关键词：货物索赔　管货义务　船舶扣押　残损检验

1. 本案例描述和分析的Z贸易公司提单下货物索赔商战是一个真实的故事，案例编者是当年的主要参与者。尽管描述的事件发生在20世纪末，但鉴于事发至今的相关法律规则没有发生实质性变化，因此案例对提单下货物索赔的教学仍具有使用价值。由于企业保密的要求，在本案例中对有关当事方做了必要的掩饰性处理。
2. 本案例只供教学之用，并无意明示地或暗示地褒奖或贬低案例中涉及公司的相关行为。

案例正文

本案例描述和分析的是一场提单项下因承运人未尽妥善谨慎管理货物义务导致的货物损失索赔商战。20世纪末，Z进出口公司因D轮承运的印度豆粕到达南通港后发现严重货损，扣押了该轮，并向H海运公司、当事船舶的保赔保险公司和货物保险公司发起了长达3年之久的索赔商战，战斗在一审法院、二审法院和最高法院进行得异常激烈。

1.背景

1997年，中国豆粕市场供货出现紧张，豆粕价格一路上扬。饲料加工企业感到了压力，担心价格继续上涨，便开始大量订购豆粕，结果加剧了市场价格的上扬，短短几个月内，国内市场价格比国际市场价格高出了30%还多，国内有能力的农产品贸易公司便开始到国外大量抢购豆粕。

Z进出口公司（以下简称Z）是当年一家国有大型农产品进出口公司，总部设在北京，常年经营饲料出口业务，拥有一批精明强干的业务人员，在国内外积淀了广泛的交易渠道。豆粕市场的这种悄然变化Z当然不会没有觉察。他们通过各种渠道从印度市场陆续订购了数万吨豆粕，其中就包括Z从C国际贸易公司（以下简称C）订购的1.1万吨印度豆粕。Z初步估计，按照当时的差价计算，这数万吨豆粕全部售出后可净赚数千万元人民币。

C的母公司是一家专门从事农产品进出口的大型跨国贸易公司，是世界上四大农产品跨国贸易公司之一，业务范围几乎囊括全球的各类农产品贸易，在世界农产品主要贸易国设有许多子公司。1997年11月6日，C与Z签订了一份合同号为S0187的销售合同。合同主要条款如下：11 000吨（增减10%）散装印度片状黄豆粕，蛋白质含量45%，最大含水量12.5%，砂石含量不超过2.5%。价格为CFR每公吨278.5美元，结算方式为不可撤销的即期信用证，装货港为印度的维沙卡帕特南，卸货港为中国的南通，交货期为1998年1月15日至2月15日。其他条款以谷物与饲料贸易协会（GAFTA）100格式合同为准，仲裁规则以GAFTA 125规则为准。事实上，C销售的豆粕是从其母公司旗下的印度子公司P（以下简称P）购买的，后者是这笔交易的真正发货人。12月8日，Z按照合同约定通过国内某银行向C开出了金额为3 063 500美元的即期付款信用证。

C 与 Z 签订了 1.1 万吨豆粕销售合同之后，于 1998 年 1 月与 H 海运公司（以下简称 H）签订了其所属 D 轮的该批货物运输合同，受载期为当年的 1 月 15 日至 2 月 10 日。2 月 9 日，D 轮按照运输合同约定抵达印度的维沙卡帕特南港并靠泊装货，至 16 日 16 时，全部货物装船完毕。其后，发货人 P 向 D 轮大副出具了倒签提单和清洁提单保函，D 轮大副签发了装运日期为 2 月 15 日的清洁大副收据，并委托船舶代理人依据大副收据签发提单。D 轮的这一行为引发了后来 Z 与 H 的倒签提单之战（请参看本人编写的"D 轮倒签提单引发的商业大战"案例）。

商人的头脑虽然精明，但也有糊涂的时候。几个月过后，由于多家贸易公司在国外抢购的豆粕陆续运抵国内港口，国内豆粕价格开始下滑。至 D 轮 3 月 5 日抵达南通港时，不但 Z 的预期利润跌没了，据后来他们向船东 H 索赔的数据，还倒赔进去 520 多万元人民币。Z 于是以倒签提单为由申请海事法院扣押了 D 轮，向 H 索赔市场差价损失。由于 D 轮有银行抵押，Z 索赔不成，又依据买卖合同向 C 提起仲裁索赔。又由于 Z 错过了仲裁时效，与 C 就此问题在伦敦仲裁庭舌战了很久前景也不明朗，于是，Z 决定转向再战 H，但理由改为货物损坏索赔。Z 到底是大公司，业务技能高超，出招凶狠。专业人士一看就明白，Z 的此役与上次的倒签提单之战大不相同，因为告货损就会将 D 轮英国的 W 保赔保险公司（以下简称 W）和货物保险公司拖进来，如果案子胜诉，就不怕没人赔得起了。再者，与 C 交战会伤害自己长期贸易伙伴的感情，最重要的是，C 是豆粕专家，向他索赔货损不那么容易。而告 H 就不同了，后者不懂豆粕，战斗会顺利得多。后来的战局演进证明，Z 的总体判断是对的，但 H 也不甘示弱，双方在连续 3 年的时间里你来我往地交战了多个回合，打得难解难分……

2.D 轮在南通港卸货出现货损

D 轮于 3 月 6 日在中国南通港靠泊开始卸货。Z 的代表在卸货过程中发现，大比例的豆粕呈现褐色而非提单中描述的黄色，有部分货物结块变黑，呈现碳化，可能已经丧失了使用价值。Z 马上邀请中华人民共和国江苏南通进出口商品检验局派员对 D 轮所载豆粕进行检验。据该局 1998 年 9 月 28 日出具的编号为32061C9850031号的货物残损检验证书，D轮卸货时发现的货物受损情况如下：1舱2层舱和底舱后部货物出现严重碳化现象，所载720吨货物有389吨碳化、变黑，有64.5吨变色并与炭化货物相混，有266.5吨变色；2舱所载2 145吨货物全部变色；3舱所载2 799吨货物全部变色；4舱所载2 226吨货物全部变色；5舱所载2 589吨货物全部变色。检验人员分析认为，上述货物受损系卸货前就已存在，不排除承运人管理货物不当的原因，受损货物已不能正常使用和销售。检验局收取了49 445元人民币检验费用。

3.Z申请扣押D轮

4月24日，Z迫不急待地以货损为由向海事法院申请扣押D轮。Z在诉前扣押申请中写道：

"申请人Z是01号正本提单的持有人，提单项下的承运人为H，承运船舶为D轮，提单显示已装船印度黄豆粕10 479吨，品质良好。但D轮在南通港卸货过程中发现，部分货物严重碳化，已完全丧失使用价值；部分货物变色，发生贬值。经估计，申请人的损失约为人民币830万元。申请人认为，承运人H未能尽到妥善管理货物的义务，致使货物在其掌控期间发生损失，应当承担全部赔偿责任。为保证本案判决能够顺利执行，申请人根据《中华人民共和国民事诉讼法》规定，特提出诉前保全申请，请贵院裁定许可并立即执行。"

海事法院在收到Z的扣船申请的当日进行了快速审理。法院审查后认为，申请人的申请符合法律规定。依照《中华人民共和国民事诉讼法》第93条、第251条第2款的规定，裁定准许申请人的诉前财产保全请求，从即日起扣押H所属的D轮，判令D轮船东H向法院提供人民币830万元的担保。同时，海事法院下达了扣船令，并于当日送达D轮，在南通港正式对该轮予以扣押。多难的D轮再次失去了自由。

4.Z正式发起对H的货损索赔之战

D轮被扣押给H带来了巨大的经济损失和精神压力，每天的船期损失在5 000美元以上，还要支付海事法院指定的看船人不菲的看船费用。为应对这一不利局面，在与Z协商将担保额降低到人民币647.4万元后（按当年8.3的汇率约折合78万美元），H向W提出申请，请求他们根据保赔保险合同，向海事法院提供该项担保金。后者了解案情后随即委托中国某保险公司上海分公司于5月4日向海事法院提供了78万美元的担保，法院在收到该笔担保金后，于当日裁定释放D轮，多难的D轮暂时获得了自由。

6月21日，Z在海事法院正式以货损为由对H提起诉讼。起诉书称：1997年11月，我司向C购买印度产片状黄豆粕10 479吨，交由被告H所属D轮从维沙卡帕特南港运往南通港。该轮签发的提单表明货物品质良好，但该轮在南通港卸货过程中，发现部分货物严重碳化、变色，经初步检验发现货损金额达人民币647.4万元。我司认为，该次货损的发生是由于承运人H管货过失所致，如雨天装货、货物在航行过程中未按指示通风等，因此H应当承担管货过错责任。请求法院判令H赔偿我司人民币647.4万元。令人不解的是，Z在后来的庭审中，变更诉讼请求，请求法院判令H赔偿损失共计人民币12 808 922.34元。

关于D轮雨天装货的证据问题，Z向法庭提交了D轮的航海日志相关记载：2月9日，D轮在维沙卡帕特南装货，18时10分，5舱作业；19时20分，3舱作业；21时，工人休息；21时40分，下雨关1、2、4舱；22时关3、5舱；23时30分开3、5舱继续装货。据此，原告向法庭推断，D轮在雨中装货，是导致后来货物碳化变质的重要原因之一。

关于货物品质的证据问题，原告向法院提供的2月16日装货港检验人出具的品质证书，表明装载于D轮的豆粕没有杂乱谷壳，没有结块。向法院提供的同年9月28日江苏南通进出口商品检验局出具的残损证书表明，1舱有部分货物碳化变黑，其他货舱货物变色，已不能正常使用和销售。向法院出具的D轮航海日志表明，D轮在航行途中没有对货舱适当通风和测温。

关于转卖合同损失的证据问题，Z向法院提供了与国内Y公司（以下简称Y）签订的该批豆粕转卖合同。该合同内容显示，转卖数量为12 000吨，单价为人民币2 630元，Y在合同签订后向Z支付人民币300万元定金，如Z违约，需向Y双倍返还定金和支付合同金额10%的违约金。3月6日，Y致信Z称，合同规定3月5日交付货物，但时至今日贵公司仍未能交付货物，我们宣布因贵公司违约而解除该项合同，要求贵公司在5个银行工作日内双倍返还300万元定金并支付违约金915.6万元人民币。

关于受损货物贬值销售的损失证据问题，Z向法院提供了以下出售记录：

在4月、5月、6月期间，Z以每吨人民币1 800元销售该批豆粕130吨，以每吨1 260元销售30吨，以每吨1 240元销售2 000吨，以每吨1 700元销售70吨，以每吨1 300元销售650吨，以每吨1 050元销售99.57吨，以每吨1 000元销售2 659.7吨，以每吨1 160元销售4 292.375吨，以每吨500.98元销售499.015吨，共计降价销售10 430.66吨。Z申请南通市价格事务所出具的价格鉴定报告显示，委托鉴定的变色印度豆粕（不包括碳化、变黑部分）4—6月份的南通市场平均可销售价格为每吨人民币1 150元左右。

5.H对Z索赔的应战

对于Z的起诉，H及W共同指定了代理律师N处理此案。对于Z的各项诉求及诉由，N代表H和W在法庭作了如下抗辩：

N首先对Z的诉讼资格进行了抗辩：我的当事人认为，D轮本航次的豆粕运输是基于航次租船合同进行的。该租船合同表明，合同的承运人为H，承租人为C，如果存在货物损坏，也只有C有权对本公司提起诉讼。而Z并非该运输合同的当事人，H对Z没有任何合同义务，因此Z没有权利对本合同的承运人主张任何权利。Z出示的与C的买卖合同中的CFR贸易条件也证明了此点。

Z以提单为依据向H提起诉讼也是没有法律根据的。我国1992年颁布的《海商法》第71条规定，提单是指用以证明海上货物运输合同和货物已经由承运人接收或者装船，以及承运人保证据以交付货物的单证。D轮签发的本航次的提单显示，货物的托运人为C，承运人为H。《海商法》第42条第3款规定：托运人是指"本人或者委托他人以本人名义或者委托他人为本人与承运人订立海上货物运输合同的人"或者是"本人或者委托他人以本人名义或者委托他人为本人将货物交给与海上货物运输合同有关的承运人的人"。本航次使用的是"CONGENBILL"格式提单，提单内容显示，托运人为C，并非Z，因此，Z并不是提单的当事人，在提单项下没有诉权；本航次D轮签发的提单是租船合同提单，该提单合并有H与C的航次租船合同，而该租船合同内容也显示，Z并非本航次运输合同的当事人。因此，Z无论是依据提单还是依据租船合同向H起诉，都是没有诉讼资格的，请求法院驳回其起诉。

再者，D轮签发"CONGENBILL"提单背面的首要条款表明，本提单项下的任何争议的解决适用《海牙-维斯比规则》，本航次租船合同使用的是

"GENCON" 1976年版格式合同，该合同第26条追加条款规定，本合同下的任何争议应当根据英国1979年仲裁法在伦敦申请仲裁，适用英国法律。据此，中国法院应当尊重当事人的约定，根据国际司法礼让的精神，驳回Z的起诉。

关于D轮航海日志记录的在装货港口雨中装货问题，时任船长后来向法庭作证如下：本航次装运的豆粕是绝对怕湿的，因此不允许下雨后再关舱。航海日志记载的"下雨"是要下雨的意思，这一记载看上去不准确，但却是驾驶员的记载习惯。事实上，在下雨之前，D轮的所有货舱都已关闭，雨停后才打开继续装货。

关于所谓的D轮在航行途中没有进行适当货舱通风问题，我的当事人认为，货物装船时的平均水分含量达到11.8%，但表面状况良好，船长签发了清洁提单并无过错。在运输过程中，D轮根据货舱通风的一般规程对货物进行了适当的通风，只是根据本公司管理习惯，没有将通风过程记录在航海日志中，承运人在货物运输过程中已尽到妥善谨慎地管理货物义务。货物本身含水量较高，有自然吸收水分的特性，属于货物内在缺陷，这是导致货物损坏的根本原因。从Z提供的目的港残损检验报告中可以看出，货物的碳化发生在底舱，全船货物存在变色，这足以证明货物损坏与货舱通风没有任何关系。因此，根据相关法律，由货物内在缺陷导致的货损承运人无须承担责任。

关于Z对Y的所谓违约赔偿问题，我的当事人认为，Z与任何人达成的任何条件的转售合同均与本公司无关，本公司并非所谓的转售合同的当事人，对该转售合同的内容一概不知，Z也没有书面或口头告知本公司转售合同的任何内容，特别是合同的定金、高额违约金的规定。因此，我的当事人对于Z对Y的所谓双倍返还定金和支付高额的违约金无须承担任何责任。退一万步说，即使本公司被法庭判定需要赔偿，根据《民法典》第584条的规定，违约方的赔偿金额应限定在违约人在订立合同时能够预见的程度。而对于Z与Y约定的合同金额10%的高额违约金，完全超过了承运人的预见能力。再者，Z向本公司既索赔双倍返还的定金，又同时索赔违约金的行为明显是违法的，是一种投机取巧。《民法典》第588条规定："当事人既约定违约金，又约定定金的，一方违约时，对方可以选择适用违约金或者定金条款。定金不足以弥补一方违约造成的损失的，对方可以请求赔偿超过定金数额的损失。"据此，即使Z应当对Y作出违约赔偿，也只需赔偿转售合同中规定的违约金或者定金中的一种，而不是两种同时赔偿。并且，《民法典》第585条规定："约定的违约金低于造成的损失的，人民法院或者仲裁机构可以根据当事人的请求予以增加；约定的违约金过分高于造成的损失的，人民法院或者仲裁机构可以根据当事人的请求予以适当减少。"Z与Y的900多万元人民币的违约金约定明显高于实际损失，因为，Z在本航次的倒签提单诉讼中要求H赔付的全部损失，以及Z在本航次伦敦仲裁申请中要求C赔付的全部损失也都只有520多万元人民币。Z为了夸大总的索赔金额，不惜采取欺骗法庭和我当事人的做法，实为法律与商业道德所不能容忍。退一步说，即使Z真的向Y既赔付了300万元人民币定金，又赔付了900多万元人民币的违约金，也是Z在对Y的所谓赔偿中的失职。因此，本公司对Z的此项所谓损失无须赔偿。

关于出售所谓的受损货物的价格损失问题，我的当事人认为：第一，Z出售货物的价格损失完全是由于当时国内豆粕市场严重的供大于求导致价格大幅下跌所致，而市场价格跌落是Z应当承担的商业风险，这种风险不应由承运人承担。第二，Z在南通港卸货不及时，好坏货物相混，加大了货损程度，其责任应由Z自己承担。第三，Z出示的各项降价销售书面资料完全是Z自己的自话自说行为，违反了公平、公正原则。因为，对受损货物的处理，Z要么应当邀请本公司参与，要么应当请求法院采取拍卖的形式，才能够保证出售价格的公正性，而Z并没能这样做，据此，本公司拒绝对所谓的价格损失承担责任。

综上，Z在本案例中提出的索赔金额完全是捏造的，因为，Z主张的1 200多万元人民币的所谓货损根本不存在，有充分证据显示，Z在销售从D轮卸下的货物时，良好品质的印度豆粕国内价格已经因为供大于求而下降到不到每吨1 500元人民币，而Z的所谓残损豆粕处理价格平均在每吨1 223元人民币。照此计算，即使不考虑货损的性质，Z的实际损失也只有260多万元人民币，大约只是Z总索赔额的零头，也就是说，Z凭空捏造了1 000多万元人民币的损失。如果再考虑货损主要是因为货物本身含水量过高导致的这一事实，则Z能向我的当事人索赔的金额几乎不足挂齿。至于Z向Y的所谓1 200多万元违约赔付更是凭空捏造的，既无法律依据，又无事实依据。因此，请求法院本着公平公正原则，依法驳回Z的起诉。

6.两审法院的判决及H的申诉

初审法院认真研究分析了Z的诉求和H的抗辩，审查了双方提供的各项证据后认为：D轮签发的提单能够证明 Z 与 H 之间运输合同的成立，双方的权利义务关系应当依据提单规定确定；Z 提供的卸货港的货物残损报告应当视为有效证据予以使用，被告人的货损系货物本身潜在缺陷的主张不予支持；货物损坏是承运人在装货港雨天装货和航行途中通风不够造成的；H 适用英国法的主张，因提单中没有专门条款将租船合同的法律适用条款并入提单，本院不予支持；H 的损失计算应当按照商业发票价格减去目的地跌落的市场价格计算的主张不予支持。据上于当年的 11 月 30 日判决：H 赔偿 Z 货物损失人民币 12 019 776 元，商检费人民币 49 445 元以及上述损失的相应利息，H 负担案件受理费和诉前财产保全费人民币 144 758 元。

H 不服初审海事法院的判决，向当地省高级人民法院提起上诉。H 在上诉中请求法院指定专家对豆粕的损坏原因进行重新鉴定，理由是，初审法院指定专家的检验报告称，该船货物 8 089.60 吨水分超标，豆粕受热过度，蛋白质消化率降低，为不合格饲料。但是，该报告同时又称，由于没有取得货物装船前、装船时和装船后的货物情况资料，不宜对货损原因下结论。原告提供的装货港品质检验报告称货物含水量为合格，而 D 轮在航行过程中船况良好，货舱处于水密状态，原告也无法提供船舶漏水的任何证据，那么，超标的水分从何而来？很明显，装货港口的关于水分含量的质量检验报告存在虚假。而初审法院不顾事实，武断地采纳了当地进出口商品检验局的残损报告，致使本公司成为无辜的货损责任承担者，是不公平的，请求法院驳回初审法院的不公判决。

上诉法院经过审理后认为，初审法院审理的事实清楚，适用法律正确，于本案发生后的 1999 年 7 月 20 日判决维持原判，案件受理费人民币 46 100 元由 H 承担。

H 不服省高级人民法院的终审判决，于 2000 年的 8 月 30 日向中华人民共和国最高人民法院申诉，请求最高法院查明本案货损的真正原因，公断本案。H 的申诉理如下：

（1）上诉法院没有查明涉案豆粕货损的真正原因，在事实没有查清的情况下作出错误的判决，依法应当予以纠正。

在上诉法院审理过程中，申请人多次向法院提出，分析豆粕货损原因涉及专业技术和专业知识，请求法院指定豆粕专家对豆粕货损的原因进行鉴定，但是上诉法院没有采纳申请人的意见，仅凭被上诉人的一方之词便作出判决。

为了查明豆粕货损的真正原因，申请人委托伦敦的豆粕专家从豆粕的产地印度开始，一直到中国的卸货港口，对全部运输过程进行了大量的系统调查，分析并提出了涉案豆粕货损的原因，这份报告经过公证和认证后，提交给了上诉法院。但是，上诉法院对这份技术性很强的鉴定报告不予采纳，这是完全错误的。

（2）上诉法院认为，申诉人无充分证据证明在运输过程中履行了妥善谨慎的管理货物义务，因此认定涉案豆粕损坏是承运人没有履行管理货物义务所致。这是不顾事实的错误判决。

涉案豆粕的货损是货物内在缺陷和自然特性所致，伦敦豆粕专家的鉴定报告充分证明了这一点。

原审法院因申诉人要求，委托 A 农业大学专家对豆粕货损的原因作出鉴定意见，申诉人提供了全部资料和受损货物样品，并为此支付了大笔鉴定费。但遗憾的是，A 农业大学提供的鉴定报告只有区区两页，并明确表示不便提出豆粕货损原因的鉴定结论。

初审原告提供的南通进出口商品检验局出具的检验报告，仅仅对货物的表面状况和货损程度提出了检验意见，没有对货损原因作出技术分析，这份检验报告是不足以作为定案依据的。

（3）上诉法院在南通进出口商品检验局的报告没有货损原因分析，A 农业大学又不愿对货损原因表达意见的情况下，拒绝采纳伦敦专家的货损原因鉴定意见是错误的。

申诉人在上诉法院审理中，要求被上诉人向法庭提供证明豆粕货损原因的技术鉴定报告，被申请人没有提供；申诉人要求南通进出口商品检验局检验人员出庭作证，提供豆粕货损原因的分析意见，二审法院不予采纳。二审法院应当知道，二审为终审判决，应当知道，不查明豆粕货损真正原因，对申诉人会造成怎样的伤害。

（4）上诉法院认为被上诉人的损失为国外采购价格减去残损货物销售价格，而无视国内豆粕价格每吨 800 多元人民币的价格自然下跌的做法是错误的。

但是，在申诉人提交了申诉状后，最高法院对本案的审理却如石沉大海，没了音讯。

7.尾声

根据本案二审法院的终审判决，Z迫使W根据前述的释放船舶保函向Z支付了78万美元，但Z认为尚有人民币6 878 575元无法执行，于是于本案发生后的第3年，即2000年，申请初审海事法院在中国惠州港又一次扣押了命运多舛的D轮（说D轮命运多舛一点不为过，因为同年11月29日，C在遭到Z的伦敦仲裁索赔后，在中国香港申请香港高等法院扣押了D轮，好在H有与Z的关于倒签提单和解协议的保护，Z以仲裁索赔额让步换取了D轮的释放），同时也发起了对货物保险公司的保险合同赔偿之诉，要求保险人赔偿其货物损失870万元人民币。最终迫使W向Z支付了人民币450万元，货物保险公司向Z支付了人民币198万元，所有当事人于当年的12月22日达成最终和解协议，D轮被释放。至此，这场持续了3年多的烽火连天的商战以Z从多方通过不同的合同关系总共获得了人民币1 295万元赔偿而宣告彻底结束。

8.讨论思考题

（1）提单持有人在提单项下是否具有索赔权？

（2）诉前保全包括哪些内容？应如何实施？

（3）提单项下货物索赔应做哪些准备？

（4）索赔金额应如何计算？

（5）如何才能将航次租船合同中的法律管辖和法律适用约定并入提单？

9.参考文献

［1］英国1992年海上货物运输法［EB/OL］．［2025-01-10］．http：//wenku.baidu.com/view/e0443f18964bcf84b9d57b0f.html.

［2］中华人民共和国海商法［EB/OL］．［2025-01-10］．中华人民共和国海商法_相关规定_中国政府网.

［3］中华人民共和国海事诉讼特别程序法［EB/OL］．［2025-01-10］．中华人民共和国主席令（第二十八号）　中华人民共和国海事诉讼特别程序法__

2000年第2号国务院公报_中国政府网.

[4] 司玉琢. 海商法［M］. 5版. 北京：法律出版社，2023.

[5] 杨良宜，杨大明，杨大志. 证据法：国际规管与诉讼中的证据攻防［M］. 北京：法律出版社，2020.

[6] 杨良宜. 合约的解释：规则与应用［M］. 北京：法律出版社，2015.

[7] 李勤昌. 国际货物运输［M］. 6版. 大连：东北财经大学出版社，2022.

[8] 李勤昌. 提单的若干概念及其法律问题［J］. 国际商务，2010（1）.

10.案例英文信息

Cargo Claim against Vessel D for Neglect in Caring for Cargo on Baord

Abstract： In international trade，a majority of cargo claim is lodged based on B/L，whereas in reality the right to claim under B/L is uncertain so far. Following the subject of Z Imp.& Exp.Co.'s cargo claim，this case describes the process of series of claim battle between Z and H shipping Co.，Z and the P & I Company，Z and the insurance company.The background is given at the beginning，following that are the detailed vivid stories of ship arresting，suit and defence at court of first instance and the appeal court，and complain at the Supreme Court. The case reveals the complication and difficulties in the cargo claim under a B/L in general.In the second part of case theoretical analysis and comments on each scenario are given.

Key words： cargo claim，obligation for caring cargo，arresting vessel，damage inspection

案例使用说明

一、教学目的与用途

本案例适用于"国际贸易实务"、"国际货物运输"和"国际物流"课程中关于货物索赔知识点的教学。案例的编写目的是，通过案例中描述的各争议焦点的讨论，旨在引导学生领会提单下货物索赔的相关法律规定并掌握索赔技能，培养学生处理提单项下货物索赔的实践能力。通过阅读、分析和讨论本案例资料，帮助学生思考和掌握下列五个具体问题：一是提单持有人的货物索赔权利确定；二是诉前保全的法律规定；三是货物索赔的程序；四是索赔金额计算的法律规定；五是商务索赔技巧。

本案例的概念难度、分析难度和陈述难度均适中，适用对象包括国际贸易专业、国际物流专业和国际商务专业的本科生、研究生和国际商务专业学位研究生。对于缺乏专业基础理论知识的本科生，可以根据教学大纲，有选择地引导阅读案例相关材料，重点分析提单下货物索赔的基本法律依据和基本程序；对于缺乏实践经验的研究生，可以引导其将掌握的理论知识运用于本案例每一个具体问题的分析，对案例中争论的几个焦点问题，作出自己的是非判断，锻炼其处理实际问题的能力。

本案例规划的理论教学知识点包括：

（1）提单持有人货物索赔权的法律依据；

（2）诉前证据保全和诉前扣押船舶的法律依据；

（3）索赔金额确定的法律依据。

本案例规划的能力训练教学内容包括：

（1）货损检验的正确组织；

（2）索赔证据的搜集；

（3）诉前保全的实施；

（4）索赔金额的计算及证据支持；

（5）整体索赔的筹划与组织。

二、分析思路

本案例的核心问题是Z贸易公司作为提单持有人在提单项下是否具有对承运人的索赔权问题，这是本案例教学的核心知识点。围绕这一核心知识点，建议案例的课堂讨论按照下列思路和顺序展开：

第一，引导学生讨论商业索赔的一般性思路。可以让同学们从日常生活中或曾经参与过的商业性质索赔经验中总结，最后引导学生从不同的经验中总结出商业索赔的一般性程序思路：确定索赔性质、索赔权的认定、损失认定和具体索赔实施。随后，将同学们认知的这一索赔一般性思路引导到本案的讨论中来，并结合本案例事实和课前发给大家的讨论思考题，具体讨论每一具体环节涉及的理论知识和需要解决的具体问题。

第二，从索赔性质认定角度，引导学生按照以下顺序讨论：本案例中的索赔是什么性质的？厘清这一问题有助于准确确定索赔对象和正确适用法律。导致货损的通常原因有哪些？厘清这一问题有助于分清本案例中货方和承运方的各自责任。导致本案货损的责任人到底是谁？是实际发货人还是承运人？厘清这一问题是对本案例中索赔人和承运人各自主张以及各级法院判决正确与否的判断基础。关于托运人和承运人的法律规定是什么？明确这一问题是判断本案索赔是否合理、合法的唯一依据。

第三，从索赔权认定角度，引导学生按照以下顺序讨论：（1）收货人是否具有索赔权？如果有，依据的合同关系是什么？（2）提单持有人是否具有索赔权？如果有，依据的合同关系是什么？（3）发货人是否具有索赔权？如果有，条件是什么？（4）承租人是否具有索赔权？如果有，条件是什么？依据又是什么？（5）在海上货物运输中，是否存在承运人向货方索赔的情形？如果存在，索赔的依据是什么？讨论上述问题的目的是让学生准确把握索赔对象，正确运用法律依据。

第四，从损失认定角度，首先引导学生讨论海上货物运输中可能发生的各种损失，包括市场差价损失、预期利润损失、转售合同损失；其次讨论损失的鉴定问题，包括何时何地进行鉴定、由谁鉴定；再次讨论残值的认定问题，包括残损货物的处理人、处理时间、处理方法等；最后引导学生回到相关法律规定上来。

第五，从向承运人索赔的角度，引导学生讨论具体索赔操作技能问题。这些问题应当包括采取法律诉讼还是仲裁？如何实施证据保全和扣押船舶？如何向承运人发出损失通知？如何准备索赔证据？如何准备诉讼或仲裁申请书？如何保护索赔时效？如何在索赔过程中正确运用法律和索赔技巧等问题。通过对这些问题的讨论，可以培养学生货物索赔的实战能力。

第六，从向保险人索赔角度，引导学生讨论除向承运人索赔之外，如何根据货物保险合同向保险人索赔的问题。该问题讨论可以包括向保险人索赔的意义，如果首先向保险人索赔应注意什么问题（这实际上讨论的是保险合同下被保险人的义务问题），索赔证据和方法等。

在完成本案例知识点教学任务后，还可以讨论收货人可否向卖方进行货物索赔以及如何索赔这一延伸问题。

三、理论依据及分析

1.关于提单持有人提单项下的货物索赔权

本案例中争议的第一个问题就是提单项下提单持有人是否具有货物索赔权问题。这是一个法律问题，回答这一问题需要回到相关法律规定上。

美国1916年《联邦提单法》对收货人和提单持有人概念分别作出明确界定。该法第42节规定："收货人是指提单中载明的应向其交付货物的人""提单持有人是指实际占有提单并同时享有提单下物权的人，但不包括通过承运人签发提单而持有提单的托运人。"

英国1992年《海上货物运输法》（替代了1885年《提单法》）对提单持有人作出详细规定。该法第5条第2款规定："本法所称的提单持有人是指以下各种人：（a）在提单上载明因而成为提单项下货物收货人的占有提单的人；（b）通过提单的交付而完成了提单的背书转让或在空白提单下通过其他方式完成了提单转让，因而占有提单的人；（c）因任何商事交易而占有提单的人，但该商事交易进行时，占有提单已不再赋予占有人对承运人主张提单下货物的权利，若非如此，该商事交易的进行将使提单占有人成为前述（a）、（b）两项所指的持有人。"同时，该法第1条第2款（a）项将提单限定为"不包括不能通过背书即可转让，或不能像空白提单那样无须背书，通过交付即可转让的单证，但包括收妥待运提单"。

现行的国际海上货物运输公约中，《海牙规则》和《海牙-维斯比规则》对这两个概念都没有明确作出界定。《汉堡规则》在第1条第2款对收货人作出界定，即"收货人是指有权提取货物的人"（consignee means the person entitled to take delivery of the goods），但没有对提单持有人的概念作出界定。《海商法》借鉴《汉堡规则》做法，在该法第42条对收货人概念作出与《汉堡规则》相同的界定，但同样没有对提单持有人的概念作出界定。

尽管相关法律对提单持有人和收货人的含义界定有所不同，但都承认提单持有人或者收货人（持有提单）在提单项下对提单承运人的货物索赔权。本案例中，Z是提单持有人，不论是依据《中华人民共和国海商法》或司法实践，还是参照国外相关法律或司法实践，对涉案提单项下的承运人H是具有索赔权的，H的主张于法无据。

2.提单持有人应如何实施诉前保全

海上索赔权利保全也称为海事请求保全，是指对海事请求具有管辖权的法院根据海事请求人的申请，为使其海事请求民事权利得以保障，对被申请人的相关证据、财产或行为所采取的民事强制措施。这些强制性措施通常包括：强行封存相关证据；强迫被申请人提供可信赖的担保；扣押义务人的船舶；要求义务人实施某种作为或不作为等。采取保全措施的目的是保证海事请求民事权利的顺利实现。

海事请求人申请证据保全应当在起诉前向保全地法院提出书面申请，说明所要保全的证据、该证据与海事请求的关系，以及申请理由。采取海事证据保全应当符合下列条件：第一，请求人必须是海事请求的当事人；第二，请求保全的证据对该海事请求具有证明作用；第三，被请求人是与请求保全的证据有关的人；第四，情况紧急，不立即采取证据保全就会使该海事请求的证据灭失或难以取得。

海事请求人申请扣押当事船舶的，应当向具有海事案件管辖权的法院提出书面申请。申请书应当说明拟扣押船舶的名称和船舶当前所处位置、扣押理由及相关证据、要求被执行人提供担保的种类和金额等项内容。海事法院在考虑接受扣船申请时，可以要求申请人提供担保，作为错误扣船给船舶带来经济损失时的赔偿担保。对申请人在申请扣船时是否必须提供担保，各国法律规定不尽一致。

由于船舶具有很强的流动性，世界各国法律几乎都规定，对船舶扣押的法律行为不受合同有关法律管辖权规定的限制，申请人可以在世界任一港口向当地的法院申请扣押船舶。

根据《中华人民共和国海事诉讼特别程序法》的规定，可以扣押的船舶是：第一，当事船舶，但船舶所有人对海事请求需负有责任，并且在实施扣押时是该船的所有人；或者该船舶的光船租赁人，但该光船租赁人需对海事请求负有责任，并且在实施扣押时仍是该船的光船租赁人。第二，可以扣押海事请求责任人所拥有的任何船舶，包括船舶所有人、光船租赁人、定期租船人或者航次租船人在实施扣押时的其他船舶。

在船舶被依法扣押后，被申请人一般会向申请人提供由银行或船舶保险公司或船舶保赔协会出具的赔偿保证书，在收到满意的担保书后，申请人应当立即向法院申请解除扣押，恢复船舶自由。如果被申请人没能提供上述担保，申请人应当在法律规定的扣押时限内（如我国法律规定，海事请求保全扣押船舶的期限为30日），提起诉讼或申请仲裁；否则，被申请人可以要求法院解除扣押。海事诉讼或仲裁开始后，上述时限不再适用。当扣押期届满，被申请人不提供担保，而且船舶不宜继续扣押的，申请人可以在提起诉讼或仲裁后向法院申请拍卖船舶。

本案例中，Z提出的豆粕货损索赔金额高达1 200多万元人民币，为了日后法院判决的顺利执行，Z很好地运用了有关诉讼前扣押船舶的法律规定，不失时机地申请有关海事法院扣押D轮，迫使H费了九牛二虎之力安排保险人提供担保。这种做法符合法律规定，也是行之有效的索赔措施，值得大家借鉴学习。

3.提单项下货物索赔应作的准备

提单项下的货物损失索赔应按照一定的程序进行，通常包括以下主要内容：

（1）及时发出事故通知

根据有关国际公约、国内法规或合同的规定，在发生海上货物损失时，收货人或其他货物索赔人应在规定的时间内向承运人发出货物损失通知书，声明保留货物损失索赔权。货物索赔人发出货物损失通知是有时间限制的。《海商法》第81条规定："货物灭失或者损坏的情况非显而易见的，在货物交付的次日起连续七日内，集装箱货物交付的次日起连续十五日内，收货人未提交书面通知的，适用前款规定。货物交付时，收货人已经会同承运人对货物进行联合检查或者检验的，无需就所查明的灭失或者损坏的情况提交书面通知。"各国的相关法律对索赔的时效规定有所不同，像本航次中Z对C在英国的仲裁，GAFTA 125仲裁规则就规定了从几天到一年不等的时效，Z就是因为错过了时效才在伦敦的仲裁中处于被动地位。而在本次货损索赔中，Z及时地通过扣押D轮向H发出了货损通知，为日后的正式索赔奠定了基础。

（2）准备索赔文件

通常，提单持有人或收货人在提出索赔时应提供以下文件：

①索赔函。索赔函是货物索赔人向承运人提出货物索赔的正式文件，该文件无固定格式，但应包括以下主要内容：索赔人的名称、地址；船名；装卸港口名称和船舶抵达卸货港的日期；提单号码及提单中的货物描述；货物灭失或

损坏的情况证明；索赔日期、索赔金额及索赔理由。

应当注意的是，索赔人按照法律规定向承运人提出的货物损失通知并不表示已经向承运人提出索赔，只有索赔人向承运人提出索赔函时，才表明索赔的正式开始。

②提单。提单是海上货物索赔中的重要依据。提单作为货物收据，表明承运人收到货物的数量和外表状况；提单作为运输合同，表明了承运人应当承担的责任、义务，是处理索赔的重要法律性依据。根据提单合同及相关法律规定，承运人必须对上述损失承担赔偿责任，除非承运人能够举证，根据提单合同及有关法律，它才可以免除赔偿责任。

③卸货报告、理货报告、货物溢卸（短卸）报告、货物残损单等卸货单证。上述各种单证是对船舶卸下货物的原始记录，由船方和理货人或装卸公司共同作出并会签。

④货物残损公正检验报告、重理单。当收货人和船方对货物的损坏程度、数量、损坏原因无法作出正确判断，或存在争议时，往往需要双方共同指定公正检验机构对残损货物进行检验，确定损坏程度、数量、价值，以及导致货物残损的原因等，并出具货物残损检验证书（inspection certificate for damage and shortage）。

⑤商业发票、装箱单、重量单等。商业发票是由贸易合同中的卖方开给买方的商业票据。它记载了货物的单价和货物总值，是索赔时计算索赔金额的直接原始依据。如果发票中记载的是货物的CIF价值，索赔金额应当按此价值计算；如果发票是以FOB、CFR价格开具的，计算时还应加上运费或保险费，但索赔人应提供运费或保险费收据，以资证明。装箱单和重量单通常是商业发票的随附单证，用以证明提单项下货物品种和数量的详细情况，因此是提单中货物记载的辅助性证明。

海上货物损失多种多样，当发生货物灭失或损坏时，应根据事故的具体情况，搜集、准备损失证明。除上述单证外，凡是能够确定货物损失的原因、损失程度、损失金额、货物损失责任的任何文件都应当准备齐全，与上述单证一起提供。

本案例中，Z在向法院提交的文件中包括了上述证明文件，从形式上看，证据基本齐全，为他们后来胜诉提供了基础性保障。但问题是，Z提供的货物残损检验报告是根据他们的单方面申请作出的，根据重大货损应进行联合检验的原则，此项检验报告的公正性受到质疑。最重要的是，从实质内容作客观分析，该项检验报告只对货物的外表状况进行鉴定，并据此作出货损原因推断，而没有对货物损坏的内在原因作细致的科学分析，这是这项检验报告最致命的缺陷，也是H不承认这项检验报告的证据效力的原因，也是H反复请求两审法院指定豆粕专家对货物损坏原因重新进行鉴定的原因。客观地说，H的要求是合理的。

4.索赔金额的正确计算

下面介绍海上货物运输索赔金额的确定原则，以及赔偿责任的免除等问题。

违约性损害赔偿金额应当按照运输合同或有关法律规定确定。因为货物的灭失或损坏情况千变万化，运输合同一般都只能规定确定损害赔偿的一般原则，而不便规定赔偿的具体金额。一般赔偿原则的确定是通过合同的法律适用条款实现的，例如合同法律适用条款规定：本提单适用《海牙-维斯比规则》，那么《海牙-维斯比规则》中关于赔偿金额的确定方法和承运人赔偿责任免除的规定就成为确定该提单下货物灭失或损坏赔偿的标准。

关于赔偿金额的标准，《海牙-维斯比规则》第2条（a）款规定："全部赔偿应参照该项货物，根据合同从船上卸载或应卸载的当时当地的价值计算。货物价值应按照商品交换价格确定，或如无此价格时，则按现时市场价格，或如无商品交换价格或现时市场价格时，则按该相似种类和质量货物的正常价值确定。"

《海商法》第55条规定："货物灭失的赔偿额，按照货物的实际价值计算；货物损坏的赔偿额，按照货物受损前后实际价值的差额或者货物的修复费用计算。货物的实际价值，按照货物装船时的价值加保险费加运费计算。前款规定的货物实际价值，赔偿时应当减去因货物灭失或者损坏而少付或者免付的有关费用。"这一规定与上述国际公约的规定基本相同，都是按照货物的CIF价格计算的。

根据上述法律及《民法典》的规定，在实际业务中，货物灭失或损坏赔偿金额应按下列原则计算：

货物灭失、短少的索赔金额以CIF发票价格作为卸货地的价格。在FOB价格条件下，则以发票价格加上保险费、运费和卸货费（如果没有包括在运费内）的总额作为卸货地价格。如果遇到两种货币折算，则按照船舶到达目的港之日的汇率进行换算。但是，如果托运人在托运时申报了货物价值，则应按照申报价值加上货物运费（包括装卸费）和保险费计算。

货物损坏赔偿金额应以货物受损前后目的港实际价值计算。其中，确定受损货物的残值十分重要。受损货物的残值可以按照当地市场的合理销售价格，或无此销售价格时，按照价格公正认定部门确定的价格确定。

计算总赔偿金额时，应当按照合同或法律规定，对合理的预期利润损失予以计算。对符合免责和赔偿责任限制条件的，应当按照法律规定予以扣除。对延迟交付造成的直接经济损失应予以计算。

在计算索赔金额时，还要贯彻因果关系原则。海上货物运输索赔中的因果关系原则是指加害方只对与其错误或过失有直接因果关系的损害承担赔偿责任的法律原则。因果关系有时呈链状形式存在，一个因果关系中的结果成为下一个因果关系中的原因，这种连续的因果关系，我们称之为因果关系链（chain of causation）。在一方违约或侵权导致连续损害后果的情况下，只要因果关系链没有打断，或者说没有插入新的介入因素改变这种因果关系链，加害方就必须对这种连续的后果承担责任。

在处理"多因一果"的损害赔偿时，还必须贯彻"近因原则"。近因原则是指在损害赔偿中要求最主要责任人对其过失引起的损失进行赔偿的法律原则。

此外，在向承运人的索赔中，还应遵循法律规定的承运人责任免除或赔偿责任限制的规定。例如，《海牙-维斯比规则》和《海商法》都规定，船长、船员等船上工作人员驾驶船舶或管理船舶疏忽导致的货物灭失或损坏，火灾导致的货物灭失或损坏，托运人疏忽、货物本身的潜在缺陷导致的货物灭失或损坏，承运人免除赔偿责任。上述法律还规定，即使承运人应当承担货物灭失或损坏的赔偿责任，也应将此种赔偿限制在一定范围之内，不必作出全部赔偿。

根据上述的货物损失计算原则和相关法律规定，本案例中豆粕的货损原因和Z的经济损失存在多种原因。豆粕在装船时含水量过高和豆粕易吸潮的自然特性可能是涉案豆粕变色、结块、变质的主要原因，在装货港口下雨时D轮船员关舱不及时也可能是部分货损的原因，航行途中D轮通风不当也可能是部分原因，豆粕市场价格下跌可能是Z销售损失的主要原因，也就是说，Z的所谓人民币1 200多万元损失可能是由多种原因导致的，也可能是由其中的主要原因导致的。正确的做法是，要客观公正地找出导致豆粕货损和Z的经济损失的主要原因，公平地计算损失和判定主要责任者。本案例中，Z的索赔金额计算、法院审理的依据和最终判决是很值得商榷的。

5.航次租船合同中的法律管辖和法律适用约定并入提单

在海上班轮货物运输中所签发的提单背面，一般都有管辖权条款和法律适用条款，但在航次租船运输中所签发的提单一般都为简式的租船合同提单（如CONGENBILL），此种提单没有管辖权条款和法律适用规定。而一些格式航次租船合同，如GENCON 1976年版本中，也没有这类规定，但合同双方一般都会通过追加条款对此作出约定。1994年版的GENCON合同的第19条对此作出规定。问题是，在租船合同并入提单后，仲裁条款、管辖权条款和法律适用条款是否也一并并入了提单呢？这是一个复杂的问题，引发了不同的解释，英国法院对此也进行过多次判决，本案例中也涉及这个问题。

对于这种被并入航次租船提单的诉讼管辖权、仲裁或者法律适用条款的效力，根据目前我国海商法学界普遍认同的观点及英国等国家的司法实践，如果航次租船合同下签发的提单中的并入条款只是使用了一般的用语，如"租船合同中的所有条款，均适用本提单，并视为并入本提单"等，则只有与提单主旨即与货物的装卸、运输、交付等有关的航次租船合同条款才能有效并入提单，而那些与提单主旨无关的条款，如诉讼管辖权、仲裁、法律适用条款等则不能有效并入提单。

要使这些与提单主旨无关的航次租船合同条款也能有效并入提单，应当在提单中用清楚、明确的文字对其予以说明。按英国的实践，如下三种情形可使航次租船合同中的仲裁条款有效并入提单：在提单并入条款中明确指明航次租船合同中的仲裁条款一同并入；将航次租船合同中的仲裁条款的序号在提单并入条款中言明；并入条款所引用的航次租船合同条款本身就包含了仲裁既用来解决租船争议又用来解决提单争议的内容。

《海商法》第95条也规定："对按照航次租船合同运输的货物签发的提单，提单持有人不是承租人的，承运人与该提单持有人之间的权利、义务关系适用提单的约定。但是，提单中载明适用航次租船合同条款的，适用该航次租船合同的条款。"

本案例中，H主张涉案提单并入租船合同，该租船合同中约定适用英国法律，在英国的GAFTA仲裁庭仲裁，该项约定应认定为并入了提单，因此，本提单下的任何争议应当在GAFTA仲裁，Z无权在中国法院进行诉讼，法院应当驳回 Z 的诉讼申请。但是上述分析说明，在租船合同提单下，租船合同中关于争议解决的司法管辖、法律适用和仲裁条款必须在提单中具体说明，否则不能认定这类条款已经并入提单，也就是说，这类条款对提单下的争议不适用。所以，H 的抗辩因没有法律根据而站不住脚。

四、关键要点

阅读本案例并正确回答讨论思考题，需要学生把握以下要点：

（1）货物损坏可能是卖方造成的，也可能是承运人造成的，应查明货损的原因，有的放矢地确定责任人。

（2）即使收货人不是租船合同的缔约方，其仍可以提单持有人的身份向承运人提出货物索赔。

（3）收货人在卸货港发现承运人责任货损，应首先考虑采取诉前保全措施。

（4）货物索赔前应当搜集充足的证据，可将货物保险人列为被告。

（5）索赔中应当合理计算索赔金额。

五、课堂教学计划建议

本案例可以作为专门的案例讨论课来进行。如下是按照时间进度提供的课堂计划建议，仅供参考。

对于本案例教学，建议在给出本案例前，教师用 50 分钟的课堂时间预先讲授相关知识，并在相关知识讲授完毕后，立即给出本案例素材和讨论思考题，然后根据思考题的数量将全班学生分成若干组，每一组分配一个问题，要求各组在课后阅读案例材料，根据所学知识对分配的问题作出分析性答案，并将主要分析依据和结论做成 PPT。然后准备 100 分钟全班同学听取汇报和教师评论。课中计划：

简要的课堂前言，明确主题：2～5 分钟

小组发言：每组 10～15 分钟，控制在 80 分钟内

引导全班进一步讨论并进行归纳总结：15～20 分钟

第三章

及时交货

M轮延迟交货引发的索赔

　　摘要：货物进口业务中，因为运输中货损和迟期交付从而引发收货人向承运人索赔的事例层出不穷，本案例正文描述的正是这样一个事件。案例以W贸易公司进口钢材延迟到港索赔为主线，在介绍了案件发生背景和基本事实的基础上，详细地描述了当事船舶在载货航程中主机事故频发导致货物严重延迟抵达和货舱不水密导致钢材损坏的主要情节，记叙了W贸易公司运用法律手段适时地对当事船舶采取证据保全、诉前扣押船舶和在法庭上慷慨陈词地向承运人索赔巨额损失的激烈场景，揭示了船舶不适航给收货人带来的巨大危害和承运人不履行船舶适航保证义务的严重后果。案例的使用说明部分对案例正文描述的主要情节进行了理论分析和评价，同时提供了案例使用指导。

　　关键词：船舶适航　货物索赔　证据保全　扣押船舶

案例正文

W贸易公司（以下简称W）是注册在大连市的拥有20多年历史的金属进出口公司。对于W，2002年的秋天是个名副其实的收获季节。这一年来，国内钢材市场因供货不足而价格大涨，公司倚仗多年在国际市场的纵横驰骋经验和扎实良好的客户关系，分别在10月、次年的1月和2月从罗马尼亚采购到了两万多吨不同型号的钢材，而后出售给了南方Z公司。经过初步测算，本次交易扣除包括FOB购货成本、海运费和保险费、进口卸货费、海关税费在内的各项成本，可大赚约3000万元人民币，可谓是赚得盆满钵满。

一切看起来都很顺利，2003年4月，W采购的12 700多吨不同规格的钢材在罗马尼亚装上M轮，正常情况下5月初即可抵达中国的黄埔港。可天有不测风云，M轮因主机故障，拖延至2003年11月10日才抵达黄埔港，比正常抵达时间足足晚了半年。其间，公司李总和他的同事如坐针毡，原有的喜悦早已荡然无存，因为国内市场钢材价格在不断下跌，而载货M轮的抵达却遥遥无期。照这样下去，W的这笔生意不仅赚不到钱，还必定要赔钱，并且还可能因无法交货而面临国内购货商的索赔。整个公司笼罩在低气压的氛围中，李总和公司主要负责人的办公室经常彻夜灯火通明，烟灰缸满了又倒、倒了又满，苦思冥想却又一时无计可施。

1.背景

让我们先来讲述这笔钢材进口业务跌宕起伏的进展吧。

2002年10月30日：W与罗马尼亚C公司签订买卖合同，约定购买1万吨线材，价格条件为FOBST CONSTANZA，242.50美元/吨，以信用证方式付款。

2003年1月16日：W与罗马尼亚L公司签订买卖合同，约定购买2 012吨不同规格的扁钢，价格条件为FOBST CONSTANTZA，单价分别为170美元/吨和240美元/吨，以即期汇票方式付款。

2003年2月3日：W与罗马尼亚C公司签订买卖合同，购买1万吨角钢，价格条件为FOBST CONSTANZA，275美元/吨，以信用证方式付款。

2003年2月10日：W与广州的Z公司签订了销售合同，约定由W销给Z公司线材1万吨，单价每吨4 000元人民币；角钢1万吨，单价每吨4 800元人民币；规格为40×10的扁钢527吨，单价每吨3 600元人民币；规格为50×10的扁钢1 485吨，单价每吨3 600元人民币。上述货物均应于2003年5月中旬前分批交货。合同还约定，W委托Z公司向广州的银行贷款400万美元用于信用证付款，由W提供担保并承担还本付息责任。为保证合同的履行，合同还分别约定了卖方不履行和延期履行货物交付的违约金，Z公司在合同签订后向W支付了400万元人民币定金。

2003年3月3日：W委托大连某银行向H银行罗马尼亚布加勒斯特分行开出信用证，金额5 175 000美元，信用证项下货物为线材和角钢共20 000吨。

2003年3月23日至4月12日：C公司和L公司在罗马尼亚康斯坦萨港将12 700多吨货物装上M轮。W支付运费478 970.07美元，支付保险费42 920.30美元。

2003年4月26日：大连某银行承兑了信用证部分款项共计2 804 888.41美元，W于同日向该银行付款，取得了班轮公司签发的1号提单。

2003年4月28日：W通过大连某银行以电汇的方式向卖方付款375 802.30美元，并通过中国驻罗马尼亚大使馆商务处外交人员从罗马尼亚L公司处取得了班轮公司签发的2号提单，该提单没有经托运人背书。

2003年5月20日：Z公司向W声明，W未能按照合同约定的交货期交付订购的钢材，正式宣布取消该项合同，并要求W双倍返还定金共计人民币800万元，支付合同金额10%的违约金95 243 200元人民币。

2003年11月15日：中国某理货公司出具了货物残损单，该单据显示共有615捆线材和165捆角钢发生锈蚀。

2003年11月19日：W将M轮卸载的部分钢材卖给广州某实业公司，其中线材2 200吨，单价为每吨3 200元人民币；角钢1 000吨，单价为每吨2 700元人民币；已锈蚀的角钢220吨，单价为每吨2 000元人民币。

2003年11月20日：W将部分钢材卖给广州某贸易公司，其中线材2 000吨，单价为每吨3 200元人民币；已锈蚀的线材327吨，单价为每吨2 000元人民币；角钢1 000吨，单价为每吨2 700元人民币；已锈蚀的角钢200吨，单价为每吨2 000元人民币。

2003年12月15日：根据W的申请，广东某商品检验局出具了检验证书，该检验报告表明，因受海水浸蚀，615捆327.18吨线材表面严重锈蚀，估损率为65%；165捆418.245吨角钢估损率为70%。

2003年12月15日：W将剩余的不同规格角钢200吨和3 700吨，分别以每吨2 000元人民币和每吨2 700元人民币，卖给广州黄埔某物资总公司。至此，W已将到港的钢材全部降价售出。

本来预计很赚钱的生意，因载货船舶不适航和严重迟期抵达，致使W遭受了巨大损失。经计算，钢材市场价格下跌损失17 650 000元人民币，由于不能及时偿还银行贷款的利息损失227 000美元，部分货物受海水腐蚀削价出售的损失1 825 136元人民币，加上其他损失，合计损失19 475 136元人民币和227 000美元。这还没计算400万元人民币定金赔偿和违约金赔偿。得知这一统计结果的李总心痛不已，夜夜失眠，员工的情绪也受到了极大影响。

2.命运多舛的M轮

M轮的船东为罗马尼亚海运公司R（以下简称R），该轮为普通杂货船，载重吨16 486吨，设计航速为14～15海里/小时。该轮装有两部四冲程船用主柴油机，通过齿轮减速离合器，双主机共同（或单机）驱动一条推进轴。装有一台可调距螺旋桨，螺距角负荷调控范围为0～90%，满负荷螺距角为最大距角的90%。该轮持有的各种证书均在有效期内。据M轮船长发给R的电报称，该轮上一航次仅使用右主机航行。下面我们来看看发生在M轮身上的诡异故事吧。

2003年3月17日：抵达康斯坦萨港的M轮向某修理公司提交了两份修理清单，要求该公司对包括主机在内的各种机舱设备及船舶其他部分进行修检，修检内容共68项。

3月23日8时：M轮开始装货。在装货过程中，对主机及其辅助设备和机舱的其他机器进行修检。

4月12日16时：装货完毕，船长签发了1号和2号提单。1号提单中记载装载线材8 605捆4 578.545吨，不同规格的角钢共2 407捆6 160.150吨；2号提单中记载装载40×10毫米的扁钢183捆510.83吨，50×10毫米的扁钢525捆1 489.34吨。两份提单的背面条款均载明1924年《关于统一提单若干法律规定的国际公约》（简称《海牙规则》）作为适用法律而并入提单。而后R收取了W支付的运费。

4月2、5、6、7、8、12、13、14、15、16、20、26日：对主机透平增压

扫气系统、主机阀门、主机进气管接头、主机进气管的排气管道、压载系统与主机冷却系统的连接阀、左主机气缸阀门、左右主机空气冷却器、主机淡水冷却系统进行了反复的检测与修理。

4月29日，5月1日、4日和13日：M轮多次试航均因机器故障未能成功。

5月13日：R的机务管理人员与M轮轮机长共同签署了船舶设备状况表，认为该轮状态已适于计划中的航行。

14日0时：M轮移泊康斯坦萨港外锚地。同日，取得港口当局签发的离港证。

14日20时至15日7时：又对主机进行修理。

15日7时：启动双主机，当螺旋桨负荷值为30%时，右主机透平增压器前的排气温度已超过600℃（最大允许值为550℃）。

15日10时20分：轮机长报告，左主机起火，温度升高。

10时22分：双主机停机，船长组织船员灭火。

16日8时：重新点火。

16日9时10分：左主机起火，右主机高温，用二氧化碳灭火。

16日12时30分：停右主机，靠左主机航行。

17日0时：停机漂流。

17日17时：重新启动右主机。

17日20时40分：停机漂流，之后又重新启动。

18日8时：驶抵伊斯坦布尔港。同日，船长在发给R的电报中称："桨距40%～50%，左主机的排气温度也是高的，在这种情况下，我们无法继续航行。"要求R给予指示。

5月19日：R指示使用单机航行，桨距0～35%，航行至塞得港进行修理。

5月27日：在伊斯坦布尔港锚地修理右主机，之后，以右主机单机航行。

5月31日至8月24日：抵达塞得港，并一直在该港修理主机。其间，R派公司总轮机长登轮参与修理船舶。

8月24日：在引水员和拖轮的协助下，使用左主机通过苏伊士运河。

8月28日：驶抵吉大港，重新修理主机。

9月1日：驶抵亚丁港，R请主机制造厂的工程人员登轮修理主机，但未能修复。之后，使用左主机继续航行。

10月6日8时至10月28日：驶抵新加坡锚地，并停泊修理右主机。

10月28日9时33分：起锚离开新加坡锚地，使用左主机单机航行。

11月10日：抵达目的港中国黄埔港锚地。后W持M轮船长签发的1号和没有经托运人背书的2号提单向R在黄埔港的船务代理公司办理了提货手续。代理公司对2号提单的合法性没有提出异议。

11月11日：中国船级社对M轮的主机和推进装置进行了技术状况检验，并出具了检验证书。该项检验证书认为，该轮右主机在康斯坦萨修理持续近一个月时间，船长没能提供任何证据足以证明船方曾向负责签发船舶证书的主管机关罗马尼亚船舶登记局（Romanian Naval Authority，RNR）报告右主机损害情况并申请修理检验，也没有提供修理后由RNR验船师签发的有关右主机经检验合格的报告，其船级证书也没有关于右主机经修理的签署。因此，没有任何证据可以证明M轮在5月15日开航前是处于适航状态。5月15日开航后，M轮右主机仅运转了3个小时便发生严重故障而不能维持正常使用，双主机船只能靠单机在非正常技术状态下航行。同时，该轮先后途经伊斯坦布尔、塞得港和新加坡三个港口都对右主机进行了修理，均无法修复。船长也没有提供各次修理曾经向RNR或任何其他公证机构申请检验的文件依据。因此，M轮从康斯坦萨至黄埔港的整个航程，其所持的船级证书和构造证书与原发证条件是不相符的。

3.W申请证据保全和扣押M轮

面临如此复杂的糟糕局面，李总与手下开始考虑应对的方式问题。他们从来没有遇到过这种复杂情况，开了多少次会也找不出切实可行的办法。这时，一位下属站出来说，他在大学时学过国际货物运输这门课程，依稀记得老师讲过的船舶适航这个概念，说好像可以找船东算账，可当李总问他具体如何操作时，他也一时讲不清楚。这时有人说，可以用《国际货物运输》教材拍R老板一砖，保证够厚够沉，大家听了都被逗笑了，可笑中又有一丝苦涩——现在不是考虑出气的时候，怎样能解决问题才是最重要的。此时另一个同事灵光一闪，他提醒李总，应当找一位懂海商法的律师来处理此事。李总采纳了这个同事的建议，出高价聘请了一位著名的海事律师，开始对R和当事船舶M采取行动。

2003年10月15日：W向海事法院申请证据保全。申请书称：2003年4月10日，被申请人R所属M轮装载申请人进口的1.27万吨钢材，从罗马尼亚康斯坦萨港运往中国黄埔港，预定抵达时间为 5 月 12 日，但至申请之日，M 轮尚未抵达，给申请人带来严重的经济损失。申请海事法院在 M 轮抵达黄埔港时，对其实施证据保全，封存其航海日志、轮机日志等相关文件。

11 月 11 日：海事法院裁定准予申请人的申请。同日，审判人员和聘请的验船师登上 M 轮，对该轮主机和推进装置进行检验，对船长和轮机长进行了询问并做了笔录，提取了该轮有关航次的航海日志、轮机日志、该轮在康斯坦萨港船长及高级船员的适任证书、船舶检测手册、验船报告、船级证书、船舶函电以及康斯坦萨港的离港签证。

11 月 16 日：W 以 M 轮不适航，以致货物延迟运到并发生严重货损为由，向海事法院申请扣押 M 轮，要求被申请人提供 300 万美元的担保。

11 月 17 日：海事法院裁定扣押 M 轮，并向该轮送达了扣船令，M 轮被依法扣押。

2003 年 12 月 15 日：广东某进出口商品检验局出具的检验证书显示，因受海水浸蚀，615 捆 327.18 吨线材表面严重锈蚀，估损率为 65%；165 捆 418.245 吨角钢估损率为 70%。

2004 年 5 月 7 日：中国船级社对 M 轮进行了航行试验，结果左主机启动正常，右主机需转车至某一二个位置才能启动。

2004 年 5 月 18 日：R 未能在规定的期限内提供担保，经 W 申请，海事法院强制拍卖了 M 轮。

4.W 与 R 法庭上的辩论

W 在海事法院正式起诉 R。

4.1 原告 W 的诉讼请求

原告 W 诉称，R 提供的船舶不适航，抵达黄埔港的时间比正常航行时间晚 6 个月，造成其损失，请求判令 R 赔偿货物市价损失 17 650 000 元人民币、由于不能及时偿还银行贷款的利息损失 227 000 美元，以及部分货物受海水腐蚀削价出售的损失 1 825 136 元人民币，合计 19 475 136 元人民币和 227 000 美元。此外，还请求法院判令 R 赔偿因货物晚到导致的国内转售合同定金损失 400 万元人民币，违约金损失 95 243 200 元人民币。

4.2 原告律师的代理词摘要

原告的律师认为，原告持有被告签发的提单，对被告有诉权。被告所属 M 轮在开航前和开航当时是不适航的，具体表现在：船员未配足，燃油未加足，证件未齐备，船舶主机一直未能处于可作本航次航行的状态，开航前因两台主机存在重大故障而多次试航不成功，但该轮仍然开航，以致船舶在航行途中不断出现故障，比正常航行时间晚半年抵达黄埔港。因 M 轮所载钢材延迟交付，使得原告的钢材销售合同被用户解除，原告收到钢材时，钢材市价下跌，原告蒙受了定金损失、违约金损失、降价处理的市价跌落损失及利息损失。还有部分钢材受海水侵蚀而降价处理，这些损失均应由被告赔偿。被告签发的提单注明适用《海牙规则》，因被告没有履行《海牙规则》规定的保证船舶适航义务，故无权享受责任限制，而且原告的索赔并没有超过《海牙规则》规定的每件 100 英镑的限额。

4.3 被告的答辩意见

被告 R 辩称，双方当事人并没有约定交付时间，故不存在延迟交付问题。承运船舶在开航前和开航当时是适航的，航行中出现故障是因船舶的潜在缺陷所致，属于承运人的免责事由，故请求驳回原告的诉讼请求。

4.4 被告律师的代理词摘要

被告代理律师认为：W 据以向港方提取货物并主张权利的 1、2 号提单记载的收货人为"凭指示（TO ORDER）"，但 2 号提单并没经有关方背书。根据提单转让的有关原则，W 不能根据 2 号提单主张任何权利。W 和 R 并未约定交货时间，R 也从未保证过船舶抵达的时间，因此，M 轮不存在延误交货问题。M 轮在开航前和开航时，持有全套有效的各种证书，船上也按规定配备了足够的人员，因此，在没有充分的、直接的、与上述事实相反的证据的情况下，M 轮在开航前是适航的。4 月 16 日，船舶装货完毕后，启动主机开往锚地，此时船舶的各方面包括主机均未出现异常，表明船舶装货完毕时是适航的。该轮在锚地保养完毕后，于 5 月 15 日 7 时开航，此时机器未出现异常。右主机在开航后几小时出现排气温度过高的现象，并不能推定船舶在开航时不适航。M 轮主机的故障，完全是无法预见的，是由其潜在缺陷造成的。康斯坦萨港港务监督向 M 轮签发了离港证，证明港口当局认为船舶是适航的。2004 年 5 月 11 日，中国船级社对 M 轮的试航报告也证明该轮的右主机并不存在明显的问题，主机的所谓故障是偶然的。因此，该轮在开航前及开航当时是适航的。W的损失是不存在的，请求的金额是不合理的。而且，在任何情况下，R有权享受运费限额的责任限制，责任限制金额为403 774.4美元。

M与R分别向法庭提交了各自的证据，围绕M轮在开航前和开航当时是否处于适航状态问题和M所谓的损失问题在多场庭审中激烈地交锋……

5.讨论与思考题

（1）何谓延迟交付？延迟交付产生的主要原因有哪些？

（2）海上货物运输中延迟交付的法律规定是什么？

（3）何谓船舶不适航？船舶不适航的主要表现有哪些？

（4）船舶不适航的法律后果是什么？

（5）本案例中收货人的索赔范围和金额是否合理？

（6）本案例中承运人的船舶适航抗辩是否成立？

6.参考文献

［1］海牙-维斯比规则［EB/OL］.［2025-04-10］. https：//wenku.so.com/d/2f3095c038eb703c4fa525b2a94a24cf? src=ob_zz_juhe360wenku.

［2］英国1992年海上货物运输法［EB/OL］.［2025-01-10］. http：//wenku.baidu.com/view/e0443f18964bcf84b9d57b0f.html.

［3］中华人民共和国海商法［EB/OL］.［2025-01-10］. 中华人民共和国海商法_相关规定_中国政府网.

［4］1999年国际扣船公约［EB/OL］.［2015-08-10］. http：//www.un.org/chinese/documents/decl-con/docs/12-8.htm.

［5］中华人民共和国海事诉讼特别程序法［EB/OL］.［2025-01-10］. 中华人民共和国主席令（第二十八号）　中华人民共和国海事诉讼特别程序法__2000年第2号国务院公报_中国政府网.

［6］司玉琢. 海商法［M］. 5版. 北京：法律出版社，2023.

［7］杨良宜，杨大明，杨大志. 证据法：国际规管与诉讼中的证据攻防［M］. 北京：法律出版社，2020.

［8］杨良宜. 合约的解释：规则与应用［M］. 北京：法律出版社，2015.

［9］李勤昌. 国际货物运输［M］. 6版. 大连：东北财经大学出版社，2022.

7.附录

一审法院判词节选

审理本案的合议庭认为：W、R一致同意以《海牙规则》作为解决本案纠纷的法律。W与R双方选择法律适用的意思表示不违反中国法律，应确认其有效力。但是，该公约对违约损失的计算没有明确规定，因此，有关赔偿范围及损失的计算应适用中华人民共和国法律。

W与罗马尼亚卖方签订购买钢材的合同，并在付出货款后，取得M轮船长签发的提单。尽管2号提单未经背书，但W提货时，R的代理人并未提出异议，故W有权就提单项下货物的延期运到所遭受的损失向R提出索赔。

根据《海牙规则》的规定，承运人有义务在开航前和开航当时恪尽职守，使船舶适航，妥善地配备船员、装备船舶和供应物品，以及使货舱、冷藏舱和船舶其他载货处所适于并能安全收受、运载和保管货物，承运人还应当适当而谨慎地装载、操作、积载、运输、保管、照料和卸下货物。班轮公司作为承运人，在接受托运后，应合理地指派在开航前和开航当时处于适航状态的船舶，以保证船舶具备完成预定航次安全航行的能力。货物装船完毕后，应适当而谨慎地运输，在合理时间内开航并完成预定的航次。M轮在本案争议航次的上一航次，主机已发生故障。R明知该轮主机必须经过有效的修理，才能恢复良好状况，以保证正常运行，但是，在船舶还没有进行任何修理的情况下便开始装货，对M轮的修理一直进行到船舶装货完毕后的一个月。在此期间，M轮多次试图启航均告失败。虽然该轮开航前取得了港口有关当局的离港签证，但取得签证后，船舶又进行了修理。主机启动后，负荷仅增至额定负荷的30%时，右主机的排气温度已超过允许的最高值，接着又发生左主机起火事故。船舶离开康斯坦萨港后的航行时间里，M轮船员对船舶左、右主机及辅助机械进行了长时间的修理，仅在中途塞得港的修理就长达3个月，但均未使船舶恢复正常状态。可见，M轮在离开康斯坦萨港时船舶推进装置已处于极其不良状态，相关机械设备的故障是存在的，而且是严重的。如此严重的故障，不可能在船舶刚刚启动而逐渐增加负荷的过程中突然发生。可以认定，M轮在开航前和开航当时并未处于适航状态。虽然M轮持有全套有效的各种证书，但船舶是否适航或者说是否具备安全航行能力是一个事实问题，应以船舶的实际状况为准。中国船级社检验发现 M 轮本航次所持的船级证书和构造证书与原发证条件不相符。R 主张，M 轮于 1993 年 5 月 15 日开航前和开航时持有全套有效的各种证书，船舶是适航的，缺乏事实和法律依据，理由不能成立。R 明知船舶主机存在故障，不能正常航行，没有履行保证船舶适航和合理速遣的义务，没有采取有效措施保证在合理的时间内将货物运到目的港，船舶比正常时间晚到 6 个月，给货主造成重大的经济损失。R 应对 W 所遭受的货损损失、货物市场损失、银行利息损失以及因索赔发生的费用损失承担赔偿责任，而且无权享受赔偿责任限制。W 索赔的货损损失、市场差价、银行利息损失合理，应予认定。违约金损失与 R 的过失无直接的因果关系，不予认定。

依据 1924 年《关于统一提单若干法律规定的国际公约》第 3 条和《中华人民共和国民法通则》第 111 条、第 112 条、第 145 条的规定，现判决：

一、R 赔偿 W 的货物市场损失 15 330 000 元人民币、货损损失 1 830 000 元人民币，贷款利息损失 205 000 美元，以及上述款项自 2003 年 12 月 1 日起至付款之日止按中国人民银行同期流动资金贷款利率计算的利息。

二、R 赔偿 W 为诉前证据保全、诉前财产保全及申请拍卖 M 轮而缴付的申请费、执行费人民币共计 15 000 元。

拍卖 M 轮发生的拍卖费用 120 900 美元和扣船期间执行监护发生的执行费用 107 520 美元，由 R 负担。

驳回 W 的其他诉讼请求。后来，二审法院驳回了 W 对经济损失索赔的其中两项：市场损失和违约金损失。

8.案例英文信息

Claim for Late Arrival at Discharging Port of Vessel M

Abstract： Claims by cargo receivers for late arrival of cargo against carriers happens endlessly in international trade，so is in this case.Following the subject of claim by receiver W Co. for late arrival of steel products，this case firstly introduces the background and facts of this claim，then describes in details the frequent main engine breakdown of the carrying vessel which caused the late arrival of the goods，the leakage of sea water into the cargo holds which leaded to the damage of the goods， depicts vividly the scenarios of the preservation of evidence， the vessel arresting and the struggling in the courts， reveals the serious consequence of unseaworthiness of carrying vessel to the cargo receivers.

Key words：seaworthiness of ship， cargo claim， evidence preservation， arresting vessel

案例使用说明

一、教学目的与用途

本案例适用于"国际贸易实务"、"国际货物运输"和"国际物流"等课程中关于承运人延迟交付货物索赔知识点的教学。案例的编写目的是，通过对案例中描述的各争议焦点的讨论，引导学生领会延迟交付货物的相关法律规定，培养学生处理延迟交付货物损失索赔问题的实践能力。通过阅读、分析和讨论本案例资料，帮助学生思考和掌握下列具体问题：一是延迟交付违约的构成条件是什么？二是延迟交付的法定责任是什么？三是延迟交付损失应如何计算？四是诉前扣押船舶的法律规定是什么？五是如何进行延迟交付索赔？

本案例的概念难度、分析难度和陈述难度均适中，适用对象包括国际贸易、国际物流和国际商务专业的本科生、研究生和国际商务专业学位研究生。对于缺乏专业基础理论知识的本科生，可以根据教学大纲，有选择地引导阅读案例相关材料，重点熟悉延迟交付的概念和船舶不适航的概念与具体内容，掌握延迟交付索赔的基本法律依据和基本程序；对于缺乏实践经验的研究生，可以引导其将所掌握的理论知识运用于本案例中每一个具体问题的分析，对案例中争论的焦点问题，作出自己的是非判断，锻炼其解决实际问题的能力。

本案例规划的理论教学知识点包括：

（1）延迟交付违约的构成条件；

（2）延迟交付违约的法律后果；

（3）延迟交付赔偿责任限制的例外；

（4）船舶不适航的含义及法律后果。

本案例规划的能力训练教学内容包括：

（1）对承运人延迟交付货物的判定能力；

（2）延迟交付索赔证据的搜集能力；

（3）延迟交付索赔的操作能力；

（4）船舶不适航索赔的操作能力。

二、分析思路

本案涉及延迟交付、船舶适航保证、索赔范围和金额的合理确定问题，因此，建议课堂讨论按照以下思路进行：

首先，引导学生在一般意义上讨论承运人延迟交付货物和保证船舶适航义务的基本内容。具体地，关于延迟交付，讨论它的概念是什么？产生的原因是什么？延迟交付的后果是什么？法律对延迟交付赔偿有何规定（包括赔偿限额及其例外）？关于船舶不适航，讨论它的概念是什么？主要表现有哪些？导致的后果通常有哪些？赔偿的法律规定是什么？

其次，引导学生讨论本案索赔性质的二重性。延迟交付导致的损失内容是什么？船舶不适航导致的损失内容是什么？

再次，引导学生讨论本案例中索赔人损失的认定问题，具体包括延迟交付损失的范围与金额和船舶不适航导致损失的范围与金额。

最后，引导学生讨论索赔的技术性问题。具体包括两种索赔的时效有何不同？可以采取何种索赔手段？如何搜集相关证据？

三、理论依据及分析

1.问题的性质与讨论意义

案例中纠纷的核心问题是海上货物运输中的承运人延迟交付货物问题。那么，什么是延迟交付？这个概念直到现在国际上仍然没有统一。

（1）《汉堡规则》中对延迟交付的定义

1978年《联合国海上货物运输公约》（以下简称《汉堡规则》）在第5条第2款中第一次在国际范围内对延迟交付作出明确定义："如果货物未能在明确议定的时间内，或虽无此项议定，但未能在考虑到实际情况对一个勤勉的承运人所能合理要求的时间内，在海上运输合同规定的卸货港交货，即为延迟交付。"该条第1款还明确规定："除非承运人证明他本人、其受雇人或代理人为避免该事故发生及其后果已采取了一切所能合理要求的措施，否则承运人应对因货物灭失或损坏或延迟交货所造成的损失负赔偿责任，如果引起该项灭失、损坏或延迟交付的事故，如同第四条所述，是在承运人掌管期间发生的。"

（2）《海商法》中延迟交付的概念

《海商法》第50条规定："货物未能在明确约定的时间内，在约定的卸货港交付的，为延迟交付。"由此可见，《海商法》主要采用了《汉堡规则》中关于延迟交付定义的原则，但只引入了《汉堡规则》第50条第2款关于延迟交付规定的前半段，对此款规定的后半段，即"或虽无此项议定，但未能在考虑到实际情况对一个勤勉的承运人所能合理要求的时间内，在海上运输合同规定的卸货港交货，即为延迟交付"却没有引入。也就是对未明确约定货物交付时间的延迟交付没有作出明确规定，致使在海事审判实践中出现了不少问题。

（3）讨论的意义

现实中，对延迟交付损失进行索赔存在困难，更为糟糕的是由于运输延迟所引起的损失和费用一般为保险的除外责任。比如《中国人民保险公司海洋运输货物保险条款》（1981年修订版）就规定被保险货物因运输延迟所引起的损失或费用为保险人除外责任。《海商法》第243条规定：除合同另有约定外，保险人对由于航行延迟、交货延迟而造成的货物损失不负赔偿责任；英国1906年《海上保险法》也规定"如无合法理由，自延迟显为不合理时起，保险人责任即予免除"。另外，《协会货物条款》（Institute Cargo Clause，I.C.C.）（A）一般除外责任第5点也规定：除外责任包括"延迟直接造成的损失、损害或费用，即使该延迟是由承保风险引起的"。因此，研究如何就延迟交付向承运人索赔就显得十分重要。

本案例中，R就一直坚持自己在租船合同中从未保证货物何时抵达黄埔港，法律也没有船舶应当在何时抵达卸货港口的规定，因此，拒绝承认货物延迟抵达导致的市价损失。W对此也十分明了，自己投保的海上货物险也不包括货物延迟抵达的经济损失，因此，必须以船舶不适航为由向承运人主张损失赔偿。

2.延迟交付成因及其责任确定

海上货物运输具有距离长、环节多、风险多等特点，所以导致延迟交付的原因也各种各样，但是对于常见的原因，可以归结为以下几种：

（1）船舶的原因

船舶本身的原因主要涉及"适航"问题，包括船体本身、船员配备、船用设备和供应品的配备以及载货舱室的状况等都应能够保证该航次运输任务的顺利完成。如果船舶不适航，很可能造成海上事故、航速不足或中途修理等，进而延误航程，造成运输延迟，导致货物的延迟交付。本案例中，W 正是抓住了 M 轮不适航的大量证据，向法院主张因此导致的钢材的市价损失。在这个问题上，R 的辩驳是很苍白的，也是站不住脚的。

（2）承运人不当操作的原因

操作环节出现问题可能存在于装货港、中转港、卸货港及海上航程中。其中，在装货港和中转港最容易出现延迟出运的问题，尤其是班轮运输，延迟出运的现象很多。导致延迟出运的原因很多，例如承运人出于商业上的考虑，接受订舱的货量、箱量太大，不得已而甩货、甩箱。对于货物运达卸货港后发生的延迟交付情况，往往是因为承运人或其代理人的操作失误或不适当地留置货物所造成的。航行过程中的不当操作主要是发生不合理绕航。本案例中不存在上述问题。

（3）港口方面的原因

港口是海上货物运输的端点和枢纽，港口的正常运营是保证运输质量的关键因素之一。比较常见的港口原因导致的延迟交付有以下两种：一是港口拥挤。承运人只要能证明港口拥挤是其所不能控制的，并对此没有任何过错，那么承运人对延迟交付损失不负赔偿责任。二是港口工人罢工，发生战争或类似战争事件。由此导致的延迟损失，承运人一般不负赔偿责任。本案例中也不存在上述问题。

3.延迟交付的责任归属

当在卸货港口发生了延迟交付，并给收货人带来了损失的时候，收货人索赔前首先要确定延迟交付的原因，并由此来判断相关的责任。

（1）承运人违反合同约定义务的责任

无论是《海牙规则》《汉堡规则》《海商法》，还是英美普通法，都允许承托双方在合同中约定条款来增加自己的责任（例如，《海牙规则》第5条和第6条、《海商法》第45条、《汉堡规则》第23条第2款）。部分航次租船合同约定了承运人保证货物抵达卸货港口的时间，在这种情况下，如果载货船舶没能在约定的时间内抵达，就视为承运人违约。本案例中，承运人没有在租船合同中作出这项保证，因此，在庭审中 R 以此对 W 的延迟交付的经济赔偿主张进行了反复抗辩。

（2）承运人违反法定义务而承担延迟交付责任

在航运实务中，承托双方在通常情况下不会明确约定货物的交付时间，此时处理承运人延迟交付问题就要看运输合同所适用的法律规定了。

《汉堡规则》和《海商法》规定承运人应当在"合理时间"内交付货物。瑞典海商法、澳大利亚海上货物运输法、俄罗斯联邦海商法典和挪威海商法典中也有类似的规定。这些法律适用的难点之一是如何确定"合理时间"的问题。

在英美普通法中，如果双方当事人未就运输合同的履行时间作出约定，那么承运人应当依照合理速遣的要求采取措施确保货物在合理的时间内交付。普通法中将合理速遣与提供适航船舶、不得不合理绕航并列，作为承运人的一项重要的默示义务无须在运输合同中明确约定。这项义务渐渐为国际航运界所接受，成为国际航运界的一个公认惯例，而为合同当事人所普遍运用。对于船舶在装货港或中途港不合理滞留或航速减慢造成的延迟到达，普通法中一般用合理速遣的原则来调整。合理速遣主要包括以下两方面的内容：一是船舶在港口装载货物以及船舶开航离港时，应迅速而毫不拖延地进行。这是一个谨慎的承运人所必须做到的，否则，便是违反了这一默示义务，例如，船员上岸，迟迟未归，导致船舶延迟开航，就是违反了合理速遣的义务。二是船舶在航行过程中，承运人有义务采用通常、习惯上或合同中约定的航线，快捷而毫不延迟地直驶合同约定的目的港。

尽管我国的《海商法》未对"合理时间"作出详细解释，但从对承运人的基本义务规定中也可以找到答案。延迟交付往往是承运人没有履行其法定义务造成的，所以当出现延迟交付时，货方要尽量查明原因，看是否可以从承运人违反基本义务入手进行索赔。

第一，《海商法》第47条规定了承运人在船舶开航前和开航当时使船舶适航的义务。如因船舶不适航导致货物延迟抵达，应当承担赔偿义务。

第二，《海商法》第48条规定了承运人管货义务的七个环节，其中包括应当妥善、谨慎地装载、搬移、积载、运输、保管、照料和卸载所运货物。如果因为承运人在这些环节当中的过错致使货物延迟交付，承运人应当负赔偿责任。

第三，《海商法》第49条规定了承运人不得进行不合理绕航义务。该规定也是该法第48条关于承运人妥善、谨慎运输货物义务的具体化。即使运输合同对货物的交付时间没有约定，若承运人有不合理绕航行为，并导致货物不能在按照具体情况对一个勤勉的承运人所能合理要求的时间内交付的，海事法院会判决承运人应对因不合理绕航所造成的事实上的延迟损失承担赔偿责任。

本案例中，W的索赔主张正是基于上述法律规定和M轮主机故障构成其不适航的事实，向R提出赔偿主张的。应当说，W的这一主张是正确的，因为，M轮比正常时间延迟到港长达六个月之久，远远超出了"合理时间"的范畴，M轮不适航也是客观存在的。

4.延迟交付的损失与索赔范围的确定

（1）延迟交付造成的损失具体内容

延迟交付造成的损失包括物质上的损失和经济上的损失。

物质上的损失是指货物本身的灭失或损坏，从而使货物丧失使用价值或者使用价值降低。这主要发生在承运人承运易腐烂变质货物的情况下，由于运输的延迟，很可能造成承运货物的腐烂或变质。通常易造成物质上损失的货物有新鲜蔬菜和水果、粮谷类货物、饲料等。本案例中，目的港的检验表明，部分钢材受到海水浸蚀而贬值，此项损失不是因为航程延长货物本身变质导致的，而是M轮货舱漏水导致的，即因为M轮不适航导致的，对此，根据相关法律规定，R必须作出赔偿。

经济损失是相对于物质损失而言的，是指货物物质上没有发生任何变化，但是由于延迟交付，遇上货物市场价格跌落，造成时间利益上的损失或违约赔偿损失。如市场差价损失、使用利益损失、货款的利息损失和对第三人的违约金损失等。常见的经济损失包括以下几种：

一是市价损失。商品价格受供求关系的影响波动频繁，这种波动在带有季节性特征的货物（如假日消费品等）或受供求市场影响较大的货物（如钢材、有色金属、石油等）方面尤为突出。此类货物的延迟交付，很容易使货主错过良好的销售机会，从而带来市价损失。本案例中，W就对由于货物延迟抵达使其遭受的市价损失提出了损坏赔偿，其要求是合理的。

在对市价损失进行索赔时，首先要确定市价损失的大小。虽然对延迟交付造成的市价损失大小的确定属于事实认定的范畴，但是根据已有的案例，在判断时还是有一些被普遍接受的标准的。市价损失应以目的港货物应交付或应合理交付之日与货物实际交付之日的差价计算，而且参照的市价不是个别合同中的价格，而是目的港市场上同一种商品的平均价格。如果目的港不存在这类货物的市场价格，那么应以距目的港最近地区此类货物的市场价格为标准。本案例中，W 在计算市价损失时，按照自己的销售合同价格与货物实际抵港时的价差计算市价损失的做法是不妥当的。

二是使用利益损失。如果货方购买的货物不是为了转售，而是为了自己使用或者进行生产加工，比如工厂购买的原料、设备等，那么承运人的延迟交付很可能会导致工期推迟、停工待料、放弃其他合同机会等损失，这种损失就是使用利益的损失。本案例中不存在上述损失。

三是利息损失。利息损失是承运人违反运输合同的时间义务，延迟交付引发的自然结果。在本案例中，原告对延迟交付引起的利息损失作出赔偿请求。确定利息损失的关键在于明确计息的本金数额及起算时间。关于利息计算的本金，《海商法》第55条规定："货物的实际价值，按照货物装船时的价值加保险费加运费计算"。另外，还可以参照《海牙-维斯比规则》的规定，即参照货物根据海上货物运输合同交付或者本应交付的当时当地的正常价值计算，并规定货物的正常价值按照货物的交易价格确定，或者，如无此种价格，按照其市场价格确定；如无交易价格和市场价格，参照相同种类和质量的货物的正常价值确定。对于利息损失的利息率的确定，应视货款的来源而定，如系贷款，应以银行贷款利率作为利率，否则应以存款利率作为利率。本案例中，W 向国外支付的货款是从银行借来的，货物延期抵达6个月，让 W 承受了这期间的利息损失，对此项损失，W 有权对 R 进行索赔。利息损失计算中的本金应当是W 对外实际支付的金额，利息应当按照 W 的借款利息计算。

四是利润损失。利润是指货方当事人在取得货物后运用其从事生产经营活动而产生的财产增值利益。在货物延迟交付的情况发生时，货方不能按时取得合同规定的应按时交付的货物，造成其生产经营活动中断或者从事该活动的基础和条件丧失，从而导致利润损失。根据《民法典》第584条的规定，损失索赔可以包括正常利润。本案例中，W 的利润应当是国外钢材采购的人民币成本与国内销售价格的差额。

五是责任损失。承运人延迟交付的货物可能是收货人与第三方订立的买卖合同的标的，因货物的延迟交付造成收货人无法按时履行同第三人之间的合同，导致收货人被置于相对困难的境地：他可能因违约而向第三方支付违约金，甚至面临着被解除合同的危险，商业信誉也有可能因此受到损害。这种损失是承运人在订立运输合同时无法预料的。因此，除非在运输合同中有明确约定，否则不应当属于可以赔偿的范围。在本案例中，W没有向R告知它的转售合同的违约金和定金的约定情况，因此，R不应赔偿W所要求的高额违约金和定金，但法院应当裁定R对此项损失给予合理的赔偿。

（2）延迟交付损失索赔范围的确定

对于延迟交付引起的物质损失的赔偿，《汉堡规则》和我国《海商法》都对此作出规定。《海商法》第55条规定："货物灭失的赔偿额，按照货物的实际价值计算；货物损坏的赔偿额，按照货物受损前后实际价值的差额或者货物的修复费用计算。货物的实际价值，按照货物装船时的价值加保险费加运费计算。"本条规定的实际价值也就是CIF价格。美国的做法也是如此。因此，本案例中对被海水侵蚀那部分钢材的损失就应当按照《海商法》规定的方法计算。

对于延迟交付造成的经济损失的赔偿问题，明确规定承运人赔偿责任以及赔偿范围的法律很少。《汉堡规则》虽然是第一个明确承运人的延迟损失赔偿责任的国际海上货物运输公约，规定了承运人应当对延迟经济损失负责，但是它没有明确规定承运人对延迟经济损失的赔偿范围，而将这一问题留给各国的海商法解决。

《海商法》对延迟交付和承运人对延迟经济损失的赔偿都作了明确规定。该法第50条第3款规定："除依照本章规定承运人不负赔偿责任的情形外，由于承运人的过失，致使货物因迟延交付而遭受经济损失的，即使货物没有灭失或者损坏，承运人仍然应当负赔偿责任。"但是同《汉堡规则》一样，《海商法》对延迟经济损失的赔偿范围没有作出相应的规定。因此，在法院的审判实践中不能从《海商法》中找到确定延迟经济损失赔偿范围的明确的法律依据，而只能根据法院查明的案件事实和相关的法律条文作出认定。

综合以往的案例，我们注意到，法院在确定损失范围时普遍遵守以下几个原则：一是合理预见原则。《民法典》第584条规定的损害范围是"不得超过违约一方订立合同时预见到或者应当预见到的因违约可能造成的损失"。在本案例中，对于W提出的市价损失，R在事实上是难以预料的，因此，从公平原则出发，不应予以赔偿。二是近因原则。三是积极减少损失原则。

5.承运人对延迟交付的免责和责任限制问题

对于已经发生的延迟交付损失，承运人并不一定承担赔偿责任，即使是承运人的责任导致的，承运人也可能享受一定的赔偿责任限制，而不必对全部损失进行赔偿。

（1）对承运人延迟交付责任的约定免责

在有些提单或者合同中，承运人直接加入免除责任的条款，例如声明：承运人不保证能在特定的时间把货物运至卸货港或交付地点，也不保证能满足任何特定市场的需要，并且承运人在任何情况下都不承担延迟交付造成的直接损失、间接损失或者相关的经济损失。但是，在国际公约和法律的约束下，以及法院的解释中，这样的条款很难发生效力，除非承运人及其代理人不存在疏忽或过失并且延迟交付存在合理原因。

（2）对承运人延迟交付责任的法定免责

为了保护承运人，《海牙规则》规定了17条承运人可以免责的事项，《海商法》的第51条把免责事项归纳为12项。所以，承运人在发生延迟交付时可以根据上述事项免责。《汉堡规则》第5条第5款规定：如果承运人能够提出足够的证据证明灭失、损坏或延迟交付是由于运输活动物所固有的任何特殊风险造成的，也可以不负赔偿责任。

但是，承运人享受免责事项是有条件的：一是要尽到适航义务，否则对因此给货主造成的损失不能主张免责；二是承运人在履行有关义务中没有主观过错。《海商法》第47条的适航义务，第48条妥善、谨慎地管理货物的义务以及第49条不得进行不合理绕航的义务，都是援引免责事项的前提条件，或者能证明虽然承运人未履行上述义务，但与货物灭失或损害的发生之间不存在因果关系。本案例中，承运人R明显没有履行保证船舶适航义务，因此丧失了法定免责权利。

（3）承运人延迟交付责任的限制

承运人的赔偿责任限制一般来自两个方面：一方面是法律法规赋予的单位赔偿责任限制和海事赔偿责任限制；另一方面来自合同和提单中合法的责任限制条款。但是并非在任何情况下承运人都能享受责任限制的权利。《海牙-维斯比规则》《汉堡规则》《海商法》都规定，货物的灭失、损坏或者延迟交付是由于承运人的故意或者明知可能造成损失而轻率地作为或不作为造成的，承运人不得援用限制赔偿责任的规定。本案例中，由于承运人R没有履行保证船舶适航义务，明知M轮主机状态无法正常履行航次任务，但还是指令其承运本航次的货物，因此，同样丧失了赔偿责任限制权利。

6.索赔人在延迟交付索赔中的义务和责任

延迟交付发生后，索赔人除了需要确定损失和承运人责任外，要成功进行索赔，还必须履行一定的义务。货方的义务和责任至少应包含以下几个方面：

一是尽量减少损失的义务。所谓减少损失义务，是指法律规定一方违约后，另一方有义务及时采取措施，防止损失扩大。

二是在有效的时间内进行索赔和诉讼的义务。《海牙规则》《汉堡规则》《海商法》都对收货人提出索赔通知的时间作出明确规定，例如《海商法》第82条规定："承运人自向收货人交付货物的次日起连续六十日内，未收到收货人就货物因迟延交付造成经济损失而提交的书面通知的，不负赔偿责任。"但是，上述原则只是针对延迟交付造成的经济损失而言，而对延迟交付造成的物质损失（灭失或损坏）并不适用。所以，即使收货人没有在60日内提出延迟交付造成损失的书面通知，收货人也不必认为完全没有了对损失的索赔权。

三是诉讼中承担的举证义务。当索赔诉讼作为一种可选择的最终解决争议的方式时，举证责任便成为一项重要的诉讼规则而为人们所普遍接受。海上货物运输索赔举证责任与民事举证责任有不同之处，这主要是因为海事法律调整的对象和范围不同，以及民法和海商法的责任基础不同。

延迟交付损失索赔中的举证涵盖两个方面的内容：一方面是索赔方对延迟交付事实认定的举证；另一方面是对延迟交付损失范围的举证。对于举证责任，货方还应该清楚法律对承运人的举证责任的规定。《海商法》未直接规定违约归责原则，但通过对相关条文的分析可以看出，在我国，对承运人实行的是不完全过错责任。在海上货物运输索赔诉讼中，当承运人处于被告的地位时将承担法定的，或依举证责任原则而分配的举证责任。这包括对索赔人提出的承运人未尽法定义务的抗辩反驳的举证义务。

四、关键要点

阅读本案例并正确回答讨论思考题，需要学生把握以下要点：

（1）货物索赔不仅仅是买卖合同双方的相互索赔问题，更多情况下是收货人根据海上运输合同向承运人索赔的问题。

（2）《海牙-维斯比规则》以及相关国内法下承运人的及时交付货物义务的规定是对承运人延迟交付货物索赔的法律依据。分析和回答思考题时，应根据这些法律规定来作出是非判断，而不是主观臆断。

（3）确定承运人延迟交付货物导致的损失，应当根据《民法典》《海商法》的相关规定来确定。

（4）承运人能否主张免责和赔偿责任限制，应根据《海牙-维斯比规则》《海商法》和案例事实来确定。

（5）索赔方在延迟交付案件中所应当承担的义务应当依据民法的减少损失义务、《民法典》和《海商法》的相关规定来确定。

五、课堂教学计划建议

本案例可以作为专门的案例讨论课来进行。如下是按照时间进度提供的课堂计划建议，仅供参考。

对于本案例教学，建议在给出本案例前，教师用50分钟的课堂时间预先讲授相关知识，并在相关知识讲授完毕后，立即给出本案例素材和讨论思考题，然后根据思考题的数量将全班学生分成若干组，每一组分配一个问题，要求各组在课后阅读案例材料，根据所学知识对分配的问题作出分析性答案，并将主要分析依据和结论做成PPT。然后准备100分钟全班同学听取汇报和教师评论。课中计划：

简要的课堂前言，明确主题：2～5分钟

小组发言：每组10～15分钟，控制在80分钟内

引导全班进一步讨论并进行归纳总结：15～20分钟

第四章

责任区间

K公司天津港集装箱堆场货损索赔纠纷

摘要：国际贸易风险无时不有，无处不在，风险责任纠纷不断。本案例以K公司出口不锈钢丝网遭遇天津港"8·12"瑞海公司危险品仓库特别重大火灾爆炸事故导致货物全损事件为主线，在描述了涉案货物损毁的触目惊心过程后，重点描述了K公司为货损责任分担陷入的纠纷与困惑：一是K公司与X公司就可否援引不可抗力而终止合同的争议与困惑。二是K公司与L公司就后者将货物堆存在具有巨大风险的集装箱堆场，是否应当因未履行谨慎处理义务而承担货物灭失赔偿责任的争议与困惑。三是K公司与承运人M公司就后者是否已经接管货物因而应当承担货物灭失赔偿责任的争议与困惑。案例揭示了国际贸易实务不同业务环节中风险责任划分的复杂性。案例的使用说明对案例正文描述的主要争议与困惑进行了理论分析和评价，并给出教学建议。

关键词：货损纠纷　不可抗力　货代责任　承运人责任期间

---

1. 本案例描述的是一个真实的事件，案例编者"有幸"亲历事件全程。案例对于不可抗力事件法律后果、货物风险责任分担、货运代理责任、运输合同下承运人管理货物责任等知识点教学具有较高使用价值。由于企业保密要求，案例描述中对有关当事人做了必要的掩饰性处理。
2. 本案例只供教学使用，无意明示地或暗示地褒奖或贬低涉及公司的相关行为。

案例正文

1.引言

2015年6月28日，K贸易公司（以下简称K公司）与新西兰X贸易公司（以下简称X公司）签订一批价值70多万元人民币的不锈钢丝网出口合同。货物生产完成后，K公司委托工厂将该批货物从河北省安平县工厂运抵天津港S公司经营的东疆货场，经海关查验后装入集装箱等候装船。然而，3天后，即8月12日，距离该货场仅600米的瑞海危险品仓库发生了震惊世界的天津港"8·12"瑞海公司危险品仓库特别重大火灾爆炸事故。消防人员被大火吞噬的新闻、难以扑灭的熊熊烈火，以及成堆的被爆炸冲击波严重扭曲损毁的集装箱画面在各电视台连天地滚动报道。

这真是天上飞来的横祸。K公司在震惊之余，也在想方设法打探自己那价值70多万元人民币货物的境况。无奈，因为货场被武警部队封锁，十几天未得到一丁点消息。集装箱堆场一幕一幕的惨状充斥人们大脑，K公司在做最坏的打算了。冷静下来后，K公司想到的第一件事是货物损失风险是否已经转移给了X公司，以及尝试援引不可抗力终止合同履行。于是在事故发生的第15天，将自己的想法告诉了X公司。因为最终用户催货，X公司收到K公司信息后要求其继续履行合同，而对爆炸事故中的货损风险划分避而不谈。

K公司将涉案货物的出口代理业务委托给了天津L国际货运代理有限公司（以下简称L公司），包括接收货物、货物进出集装箱堆场、报关、订舱、装船等事宜。K公司想到的第二个问题是，天津新港有多个集装箱堆场，如果L公司选择远离瑞海危险品仓库的集装箱堆场，或许自己的货物就不会被爆炸殃及，那么，L公司是否应当因选场不当而需要承担货物灭失赔偿责任呢？

K公司想到的第三个问题是，此次海运订舱性质为集装箱班轮运输，按照常规，托运人将载货集装箱运进承运人指定的集装箱堆场，承运人即应承担起货物的妥善保管义务。那么，在K公司自己没有与M集装箱班轮公司（以下简称M公司）订立运输合同的情况下，抑或是，即使直接与M公司签订运输合同，M公司是否应当承担货损赔偿责任呢？如果这几个问题的答案都是肯定的，那么，K公司就可以大松一口气了，它多么希望是这样啊！

2.背景

K公司是大连市一家进出口公司。公司业务二部经理C女士在2004年国际贸易专业本科毕业后，进入这家公司工作，积累了比较丰富的外贸工作经验，并被公司升职为业务二部经理。该业务部的一项主要业务就是金属丝网出口，经过20余年的努力，销售网络基本形成，其中就包括新西兰的X公司。

X公司是K公司培育较早的生意伙伴，双方在合作中诚实守信，关系良好，业务规模达几百万美元，从未发生过大的业务纠纷，个别小的问题都能通过友好协商顺利解决，X公司还指定K公司为中国市场的独家供货商。

2015年6月28日，K公司与X公司又签订了本年度的第3笔不锈钢丝网出口合同。合同货物包括不同规格的不锈钢编织网和不锈钢电焊网，CFR贸易条件，由买方办理保险，集装箱整箱运输，装货港口为天津新港，卸货港口为新西兰的奥克兰港，交货期为2015年8月13日前；合同总金额84 690美元，30%货款在合同签订后电汇预付，其余货款在货物装船取得提单后，电汇至K公司指定账户。合同还约定了货物检验条件、卖方需提交的单证和仲裁条款，但如同以往的合同，没有约定不可抗力条款和法律适用条款。具体合同条款参见附录。

3.天津港"8·12"特大火灾爆炸事故中货物在装船前杳无音信

根据出口合同约定，K公司与河北省安平县的一家生产商签订了该批丝网的供货合同，买方的30%预付款也拨付给了工厂。工厂在合同签订后，一如既往地紧张生产，在合同约定的8月7日完成了该批货物的生产。K公司立即委托工厂安排将该批货物通过当地物流公司用卡车运到天津新港指定货场。为货物报关出运，K公司委托天津L公司办理该批货物的订舱、装箱、报关和装船工作。后者指定了天津S集装箱场站（以下简称S）接收货物和装箱，并将该信息通报给K公司。L公司也根据买卖合同的交货期，选定了M班轮公司（以下简称M公司）承运该批货物至新西兰，并签订了运输合同。

8月9日，该批货物运抵S场站，10日，在海关监督下完成装箱，并堆存在S场站，等候班轮公司入港指示。一切进行得都很顺利，就等载货班轮抵港，便可装船出运了，70%余下货款也将很快入账，K公司在酷暑中紧张地忙碌了一个多月后，终于可以松一口气了。

然而，就在K公司准备享受酷暑之后的秋高气爽之际，灾难降临了。

8月12日23：30左右，位于天津滨海新区塘沽开发区的天津东疆保税港区瑞海国际物流有限公司所属危险品仓库发生易燃易爆物品大爆炸。现场火光冲天，在强烈爆炸声后，高数十米的灰白色蘑菇云瞬间腾起。随后爆炸点上空被火光染红，现场附近火焰四溅。第一次爆炸发生在8月12日23时34分6秒，近震震级约2.3级，第二次爆炸发生在30秒钟后，近震震级约2.9级，据官方报道，两次爆炸总能量相当于450吨TNT当量。爆炸核心区留下的直径约为60米的深水坑内，氰化物平均超标40多倍，浓度最高处超标甚至达800多倍，有毒污水、泥土、被炸毁的建筑物、烧毁的车辆和包括集装箱在内的各种被毁货物花费了一个多月时间都没有处理完毕。事故造成大量人员伤亡。据事故最终统计，爆炸致165人遇难，8人失踪，死亡人员中大部分为公安消防人员。

事故还造成304幢建筑物、12 428辆商品汽车、7 533个集装箱严重受损。在集装箱堆场，有的集装箱被严重烧毁，有的集装箱被爆炸产生的强大冲击波扭曲变形，3大堆损毁集装箱垛成3座"集装箱废钢山"，平均高度10余米。国际海上保险联盟（IUMI）货物委员会主席Nick Derrick在一份声明中称，这次爆炸或许导致10亿美元损失，对海上保险业造成重大冲击。

K公司的业务经理C女士有熬夜的习惯。8月12日晚上，她如往常一样在电脑上翻阅各种信息。突然，电脑屏幕上出现了一则惊人新闻，天津港货场发生大爆炸，字数虽然不多，但足以让她瞪大眼睛。接下来的视频中熊熊燃烧的大火和腾空而起的蘑菇云让她震惊不已。原子弹爆炸般的威力，这得夺去多少人的生命，损毁多少财产啊！瑞海货场离S货场有多远？自己的货柜怎样了？这种震撼和忧虑令她彻夜无眠。

第二天早晨8点刚过，C女士便迫不及待地联系L公司，试图了解一些有用的信息。无奈，事故现场大火还在燃烧，还不时地发生小规模爆炸，有毒气体不断向外扩散，威胁着周围地区的生命安全。国务院、天津市政府事故处理领导小组下令封锁了东疆货场整个区域，组织各方力量灭火救人，清理有毒危化品和被其污染的污水、泥土、货物，整个过程持续了40多天。在这段时间里，C女士除知道自己的货物距离爆炸货场只有600多米外，再有一条信息就是"还在封锁，无法进入"。她在为遇难的生命祈祷之余，也在为自己的货物安全祈祷，媒体的遇难人数滚动报道加剧着她的焦虑，新西兰客户焦急地等待货物加剧着她的焦急，让她领会到了什么是度日如年。

4.新西兰买方等不及了

爆炸事故发生后，K公司原本请X公司保持耐心，待政府灭火、救人和危化品污染清理结束后，了解了合同货物的状况后再协商如何处理，X公司也表示理解。但40多天过去了，X公司等不及了。原来，X公司订购的这批货物除部分自己用于工程外，另一部分是为他人订购的。这些人等不下去了，纷纷要求X公司要么立即重新生产，要么取消合同并返还定金并赔偿损失。

X公司将这一情况告知了K公司，请求理解其面临的困难处境，并要求在最短的时间内重新组织生产他人订购的货物并尽快出运，否则X公司面临的损失将由K公司承担。

K公司担心的事情终于来了。本来公司只向生产商支付了30%货款作为定金，其余货款等收汇后再付。目前的麻烦是，欠工厂的余款早该偿还了，而货物在天津货场到底怎样仍然杳无音信。如果货物全损，则意味着近70多万元人民币灰飞烟灭，公司要自掏腰包偿还工厂货款和退回X公司的预付货款。在尚欠着大笔余款的情况下，再去要求工厂重新制作这部分货物，怎么张嘴去说呢？还有，即使解决了这部分货物，那么另一部分货物将来怎么办？而且不用等太久这个问题就会接踵而至。到底该怎么办呢？

5.K公司与X公司关于不可抗力和风险分担的争议与困惑

为解决"到底该怎么办"的问题，K公司试图从合同关系上寻找办法。

K公司从总经理到业务员都是国际贸易专业毕业生，老师们教过的专业知识并没有遗忘殆尽，他们想到了"不可抗力"。这么大的爆炸事故还不是"不可抗力事件"吗？肯定是！那么，问题可能就基本上解决了。

于是，经过一番讨论后，K公司向X公司发出了如下意见：

（1）尽管合同货物因重大爆炸事故滞留天津港给贵公司带来麻烦，但该事故是本公司在签订合同和履行合同过程中所无法预见和无法克服的，属于不可抗力事件。根据相关规定，在此种情况下，可以免除本公司的继续履行合同义务，因此，本公司无法满足贵公司的重新制作部分货物要求。如果贵公司仍需要这部分货物，应当重新签订合同，并向我方支付30%的定金，我们将全力以赴尽快安排这部分货物的生产和运输。对该事故给贵公司带来的麻烦再次表示歉意。

（2）关于滞留在天津新港的货物，我们认为，我公司已经履行了交货义务。货物报关和装入集装箱后堆存在集装箱堆场，应当认为货物已经交给了承运人接管，按照贵我双方的贸易条件，应当认为货物的风险已经转移到贵公司。根据《海商法》第46条的规定，承运人对集装箱运输的责任期间应当从装货港接收货物时起至卸货港交付货物时止的货物处于承运人掌管之下的全部期间。因此，该批货物灭失、损坏和延迟交付导致贵公司的损失，应当由贵公司向承运人提出。此外，贵我双方贸易条件为CFR，这意味着由贵公司购买该批货物的运输保险，因此，贵公司还可以就货物灭失向保险公司要求赔偿。

收到K公司上述意见后，X公司也有些丈二和尚摸不着头脑。如果真的像多年真诚合作伙伴所说的那样，那不等于说发生在万里之遥的天津大火烧到了处于大洋洲的自己头上了吗？当年美国在日本投放的原子弹也没能殃及我们呀！X公司静下心来研究了双方的合同，又翻阅了相关法律条文，然后向K公司发出了如下立场：

"贵公司的电子信函收悉。经过仔细研究，我们认为无法接受贵公司的意见。第一，双方合同中没有关于不可抗力及其法律后果的约定，因此，贵公司无权基于不可抗力主张解除合同，而应当继续履行交货义务。贵公司在爆炸事故发生15天后才通知我们，违反了法律规定的及时通知事故义务，由此贵公司也应当丧失了提出免责的权利。第二，即使不可抗力事件成立，贵公司欲主张免责，也需要证明该批货物灭失后，再也无法安排替代货物，才能主张解除合同。但事实上贵公司完全可以重新组织生产，因此本案件不属于法律规定的免责条件。在本案件中，也只能允许贵公司延期履行合同，但也不能遥遥无期。目前，货物滞留天津新港已经40多天，货物损毁与否仍无法知晓，因此，贵公司有义务重新组织生产该批货物并尽快发运。第三，我们无法接受贵公司的货物风险已经转移到我方的说辞。双方合同约定的贸易条件是CFR，根据INCOTERMS2010的解释，只有贵公司将货物装到承运船舶后，风险才能转移到我公司，而事实上现在货物并未装船，该批货物灭失或损坏的风险仍由贵公司承担。第四，即使我公司购买了海上货物运输险，由于货物尚未装船，我方对该批货物尚不具有可保利益，因此，保险公司也是不会赔偿我们的。综上所述，我们坚持要求贵公司迅速组织该批货物重新生产并尽快装运，否则，导致的一切后果只能由贵公司承担。"

收到X公司上述函电后，K公司对X公司的主张一时也提不出充足的反驳理由，公司上下陷入一片茫然，这仗不好打。

在对上述问题僵持不下的情况下，总经理提出，尽管公司目前可能面临几十万元的经济损失，但在商业经营中，最重要的还是客户关系。目前X公司提出的问题不解决，会为客户关系维持埋下巨大隐患。于是提出，先按照X公司的要求，安排最急需的半个货柜丝网的生产和发运，后半个货柜货物看情况再说。

9月13日，K公司向河北的生产商支付了部分货款，要求他们迅速组织半个货柜丝网的生产。工厂十分理解K公司的困境，加班加点，很快完成了生产，并替K公司将货物运抵天津港，K公司同时安排货运代理公司订好了舱位，支付了800多美元的运费后，将该批货物发往奥克兰。

9月25日，鉴于爆炸事故中的那箱货仍然杳无音信，X公司要求K公司交付另半箱货物，出于同样的考虑，K公司又向工厂支付了全部货款，重新生产了这部分货物发往奥克兰。

此后不久，爆炸货场完成清理工作并重新开放。K公司提心吊胆几十天的事情还是发生了，经过核查，起初等待装船出口的那个集装箱已经全部损毁。至此，K公司因爆炸事故不但损失了70多万元人民币的货物，还为重新发运货物额外支付了1 900多美元的海运费和两笔代理费，尝到了国际贸易风险带来的苦头。

6.K公司与L公司的责任分担争议与困惑

10月31日，L公司致信K公司称，鉴于K公司的损失，大爆炸损毁的那个集装箱的代理费、装箱费等就免收了，但之后托运的两个集装箱的相关费用共计3 000多元人民币应当支付。K公司本来还在想如何与L公司交涉那70多万元人民币损失赔偿，结果它自己倒上门催债了。借此机会，K公司致信L公司称，L公司接受了我公司委托，在接收货物后，本应承担保管照料货物义务，包括指定安全的堆场、集装箱查验、妥善地装箱等义务。但事实上，L公司没有履行上述义务，错误地将货物堆存在毗邻危险品货场的危险场所，以至于货物在大爆炸中全部损毁。因此，L公司应承担全部货损赔偿责任。

对于K公司的主张，L公司回复称，在履行本次委托业务中，本公司已经尽到应尽义务，从接收货物、订舱、拖箱到货物装箱，均未发生货物损毁事故。指定的S堆场系经政府多部门批准设立的，具有合格资质和营业执照，是正规的集装箱场站经营人。因此，本公司在委托集装箱场站经营人问题上不存在过错。货物损毁系意外事故所致，爆炸事故也与本公司没有任何关系。因此，本公司不应承担贵公司的经济损失。出于对K公司利益考虑，L公司也尝试与S场站协商，请其考虑对K公司的损失作出赔偿，或者请求其责任保险人作出赔偿，但S场站经营人对此没做任何答复。L公司也将此情况通报了K公司。

对于L公司的回复，K公司表示不能接受，要求要么L公司对K公司作出赔偿，要么L公司要求S作出赔偿。为此，K公司与L公司在随后的日子里进行了多次友好协商，但始终未果，谈判陷入胶着状态。K公司也有通过法律途径解决问题的想法，但考虑到集装箱堆场选址以及批准均与L公司无关，S场站也是化学品货场爆炸的受害者，同时，S堆场内集装箱因大爆炸损失几十亿元，受害货主众多，即使起诉胜诉，S场站也可能寻求破产保护。如果这样，不但无法获得赔偿，还得搭进去诉讼成本和时间成本。至于对化学品货场经营人的侵权诉讼，获偿的机会就更渺茫了。这些"可能与不可能"让K公司陷入漫长的煎熬之中。

7. K公司与M公司关于承运人管理货物责任区间之争

K公司在与X公司和公司的两场斗争中均未取得实质性进展的情况下，思考向承运人M公司索赔的可能性。经过一段时间的酝酿，K公司与M公司的索赔之争开始了。

集装箱运输属于班轮运输性质，在业务环节上，承运人一般采用装货港集装箱堆场收货，卸货港集装箱堆场交货的货物交接方式。因此，有关法律规定，承运人管理货物的责任区间是从收到货物时开始到交付货物时为止。

K公司认为，本案损毁货物就是采用集装箱运输的，而且受损货物是在集装箱堆场内由L公司安排工人将丝网装入M公司所属集装箱的。因此，从丝网在堆场装入M公司的集装箱内那一刻起，M公司就应当承担起管理货物的责任，该责任的核心内容就是保证货物安全。遗憾的是，M公司未能保证该批货物的安全。于是，K公司以上述理由向承运人M公司发出了索赔函。

事实上，并非只有K公司向M公司托运货物，堆场内许多受损集装箱也都是向M公司托运的。M公司的法务部陆续收到了多位货主的索赔函，也就是说，M公司受到了群体攻击。

M公司毕竟是国际上数一数二的集装箱班轮公司，拥有一百多年的历史，在处理货主索赔上可谓身经百战，斗争经验极其丰富。在收到K公司的索赔函后，M公司法务部打官腔简短回复称：对于K公司的货物灭失表示遗憾，但此次爆炸事件属于不可抗力性质，根据相关法律，本公司无须承担任何责任。此外，K公司并非运输合同的托运人，因而无权向本公司索赔。

M公司的回函虽然简短，但言简意赅，立场清楚。K公司遇到了在前两场争斗中同样的头疼问题，一时又难以找到解药。

8.尾声

天津港"8·12"瑞海公司危险品仓库特别重大火灾爆炸事故弥漫的硝烟已经散去，但大爆炸中165人遇难带给人们的痛心疾首却久久无法散去，惊天动地、震耳欲聋的大爆炸给人们带来的心理冲击久久无法散去，大爆炸造成近70亿元人民币的财产损失给人们带来的压抑心情久久无法散去。还有，大爆炸引发的各类国内外商业纠纷也久久无法平息，正常的交易秩序遭到破坏，久久无法修复。K公司70多万元人民币的损失，由于种种原因也不了了之。

痛定思痛，案例中惊心动魄的大爆炸场景是否再次唤醒人们对"国际贸易风险无时不有无处不在"这一警句的深刻认识呢？K公司与X公司关于不可抗力事件的不同认识，K公司与L公司货运代理合同的责任之争，K公司与M公司关于货物照料责任起讫界限的纠纷，所有这些矛盾产生的根源到底在哪里？是否可以事前采取措施予以规避？或至少通过合同约定将风险责任划分清楚呢？研读本案例，应该吸取哪些教训呢？

9.参考文献

［1］杨良宜，杨大明，杨大志. 合约的履行、弃权与禁反言［M］. 北京：法律出版社，2018.

［2］司玉琢. 海商法［M］. 5版. 北京：法律出版社，2023.

［3］李勤昌. 国际货物运输［M］. 6版. 大连：东北财经大学出版社，2022.

［4］李勤昌. 提单的若干概念及其法律问题［J］. 国际商务，2010（1）.

［5］李勤昌. 海上货物索赔对象难以认定的原因研究［J］. 国际贸易问题，2004（10）.

［6］杨良宜. 合约的解释：规则与应用［M］. 北京：法律出版社，2015.

［7］王淑梅. 海上货物运输合同纠纷案件裁判规则［M］. 北京：法律出版社，2021.

10.附录

爆炸损毁的金属丝网买卖合同
SALES CONTRACT

NO.: SXSC15WM003

DATE：2015-06-28

The seller：DALIAN K IMP.& EXP.GROUP CO.，LTD.

Address：×××RENMIN ROAD，DALIAN 116001，CHINA

The buyer：× Pest Proof Fencing Company

Address：×××Sala Street，Rotorua 3010，New Zealand.

This Sales Contract is made by and between the Sellers and the Buyers whereby the Sellers agree to sell and the Buyers agree to buy the under - mentioned goods according to the terms and conditions stipulated below：

Name of Commodity & Specification	Quantity	Unit Price CFR Auckland, NZ, by Sea	Total Amount
Stainless steel 304 woven mesh 8 mesh × 0.7MM, 1M × 30M/roll	20 rolls	USD 306.00/roll	USD 6 120.00
Stainless steel 304 woven mesh 6 Mesh × 0.8MM, 1M ×30M/roll	60 rolls	USD 309.00/roll	USD 18 540.00
Stainless steel 304 woven mesh 6 mesh × 0.8MM, 100MM × 800MM/PC	550 Pcs	USD 8.60/pc	USD 4 730.00
Stainless steel 316 welded mesh, green PVC coated, 6.5MM × 25.5MM × 1.15MM, 1.22M × 30M/roll	140 rolls	USD 395.00/roll	USD 55 300.00
Total: Say US Dollar eighty four thousand six hundred and ninety dollars only.			USD 84 690.00

1.The accuracy of the sizes of the welded mesh:

Hole size: +/− 0.1MM.

Roll size: width +/− 0.02M, length +/− 0.02M

Wire thickness : +/− 0.01MM

2.Time of shipment: Sea freight.The shipment shall be delivered within 45 days from contract signing date.

3. Packing: Waterproof paper for each roll. Sea freighted rolls are packed on pallets.All the meshes to be labeled with buyer labels （attached）.

4.Insurance: To be effected by the Buyers.

5.Origin & manufacturers: CHINA.

6.Shipping marks: N/M.

7.Loading port: Tianjin Xingang Port, China.

8.Port of discharge: Auckland, New Zealand.

9. Term of payment: 30% of total contract value shall be paid by Buyer as deposit within 3 working days after signing this contract.Balance of 70% shall be paid by Buyer after delivery and receiving copy of shipping documents.

10.T/T beneficiary: DALIAN K IMP.& EXP.GROUP CO., LTD.

Address: ×××RENMIN ROAD, DAIAN 116001, CHINA

Beneficiary Bank: City Bank, Dalian Branch

Bank Add.: ××× ZHONGSHAN SQUARE DALIAN 116001 CHINA

Swift Code: BK×××××810; TELEX NO.: 8××××CLB CN

A/C No.of Beneficiary: ×××××××××××

11.Documents requested: Commercial Invoice, Packing list, Full set of clean on Board Bills of Lading, Quarantine Declaration, Inspection Certificate issued by SGS China.

12.Inspection on specifications and sampling for testing should be done for the Stainless Steel 316 Welded Mesh, Green PVC coated, 6.5MM × 25.5MM × 1.15MM Mesh, by SGS China before loading.The buyer will pay for the cost of the SGS testing directly to SGS.And here below is the acceptable range of the chemical contents （%） of the Material and the accuracy of the sizes of the goods:

Chemical	C	Si	Cr	Mn	Ni	Mo
Standard	≤ 0.08	≤ 1	16 ~ 20	≤ 2	10 ~14	2 ~3
Tolerance	0.01	0.05	0.2	0.04	0.15	0.1

The accuracy of the sizes of the goods:

The hole size: width 6.5MM +/− 0.2MM, length 25.5MM +/− 0.2MM.

The roll size: width 1.22M +/− 0.02M, length ≥30M.

Wire thickness （before PVC coating）: 1.15MM +/− 0.01MM

13. Arbitration: Any dispute arising from the execution of, or in connection with this Contract should be settled through negotiation.In case no settlement can be reached, the case shall then be submitted to the Foreign Trade Arbitration Commission of the China Council for the promotion of International Trade, Peking, for settlement by arbitration in accordance with the Commission provisional Rules of procedure, The award rendered by the Commission shall be final and binding on both parties.

THE SELLER: THE BUYER:

DAIAN K IMP.& EXP.GROUP CO., LTD.   X PEST PROOF FENCING COMPANY

11.案例英文信息

The Disputes on K Company's Cargo Damage Incurred at CY in Tianjin Port

Abstract： In international sale of goods，risks exist at any time and in any context，thus liability disputes often present. Taking the total loss caused by the "8·12" explosion at Tianjin Port of K Company's stainless steel wire mesh for export as the principal line，this case firstly describes the shocking scenario of the "8·12" dangerous goods explosion accident and its adverse effect to the mesh，then focuses on the describing of the disputes and confusions faced by K Company for the compensation of the damage：they are：the dispute and confusion between K Company and X Company on whether the accident is a Force Majeure in nature；the dispute and confusion between K Company and L Company over whether the latter should bear the responsibility of the cargo loss for reason of piling the cargo into the risky CY，and lastly，the dispute and confusion between K Company and M Company on whether the latter has taken over the goods and therefore should bear the compensation responsibility for the loss of the goods. The case reveals the complexity of risk liability division in international trade practice. In the instruction section of the case，theoretical analysis and evaluation are made on the main disputes，teaching suggestions are also provided.

Key words： cargo damage dispute，force majeure，freight forwarder liability，liability period of carrier

案例使用说明

一、教学目的与用途

本案例适用于国际商务专业硕士和国际经济与贸易专业本科生的"国际贸易实务与惯例""国际货物运输""跨境电商物流""国际货运代理"等课程中货物索赔知识点教学。案例编写的目的是，通过对案例描述的各争议焦点的讨论，引导学生领会与国际商务相关的不同合同下不可抗力免责、风险责任划分，以及管理货物责任划分的相关法律、惯例规定，掌握索赔依据与技能，培养学生预防和处理货物索赔的实践能力。

本案例的概念难度、分析难度和陈述难度均适中。对于缺乏实践经验的研究生，可以引导其将所掌握的理论知识运用于本案例每一个具体问题分析，通过自主学习、团队合作，对案例中争论的焦点问题作出是非判断，培养他们运用理论知识处理实际问题的能力。对于缺乏专业基础理论知识和实践经历的本科生，可以根据教学大纲，有选择地引导阅读案例相关材料，重点分析货物索赔的基本法律依据和基本程序。

二、讨论思考题

1.K公司是否有可能采取措施避免爆炸带来的货损风险？国际贸易中能否找到买卖双方都满意的最佳风险管理办法？

2.你如何理解合同中约定不可抗力条款的重要意义？如何妥善处理货物索赔和客户关系维护的矛盾？你如何评价K公司在发生不可抗力事件后仍按照X公司要求，重新组织发货的行为？

3.L公司在货代合同下是否存在谨慎处理义务？L公司是否需要承担K公司的货损赔偿责任？不同合同下，妥善和谨慎履行义务的要求是不同的，能否找到一般性的"妥善和谨慎模型"，供我们在实践中参考？

4.运输合同下K公司与M公司的货物风险承担如何划分？你如何评价双方的争议？在法律尊重双方特别约定的条件下，对于班轮运输合同，推而广之，对于所有商业合同，如何才能通过特殊约定将自己承担的风险最小化？

三、背景资料

1.全球保险市场货损索赔动态

国际贸易中风险无时不在、无处不在，这个结论可从多方得到验证。间接的证据是国际海上货物运输保险费收益逐年增加，背后的逻辑是货主支付保险费是"用脚投票的"，若不是货物损失逐年增多，理性的货主谁都不会无故增加保险费支出。直接的证据是保险公司赔付率（赔偿支出在保费收入中的占比）不断上升。根据国际海上保险联盟（IUMI）发布的2021年全球海上保险报告，全球保险市场的赔付率一直居高不下。图4-1显示，2011—2021年，欧洲保险市场的货物保险赔付率长期保持在50%～70%，列出的典型恶性事故，就包括天津港"8·12"瑞海公司危险品仓库特别重大火灾爆炸事故。

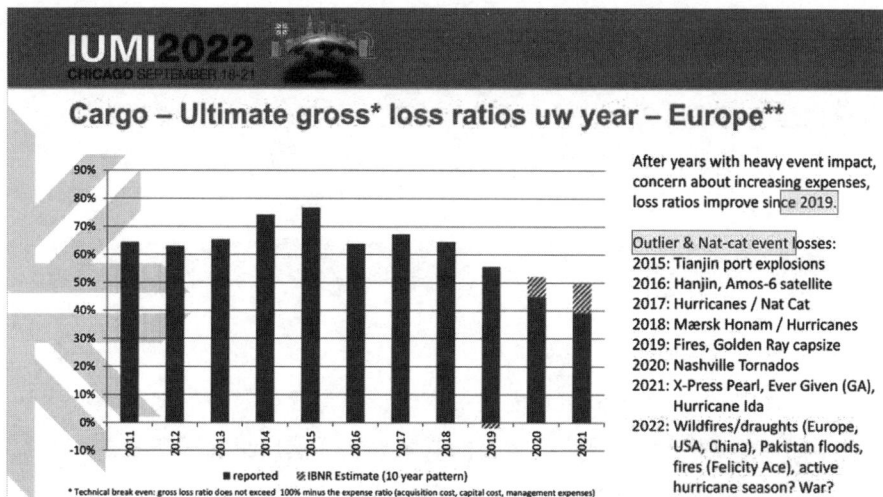

图4-1 欧洲货物保险市场赔付率

图4-2显示亚洲货物保险市场的赔付率也一直保持在40%～60%，其中也提及了天津港事故的影响。

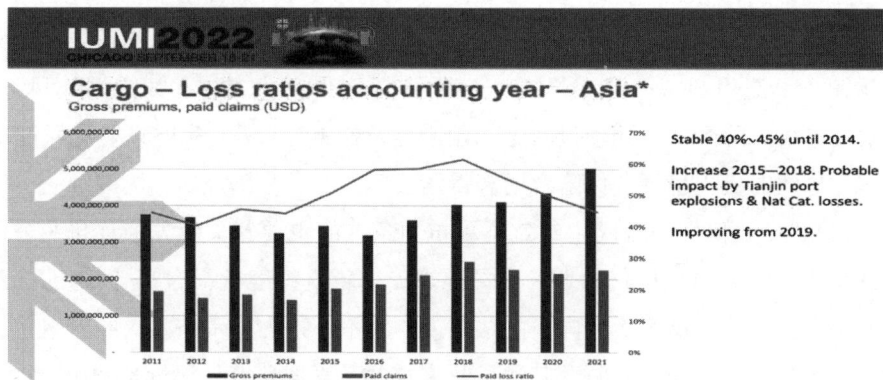

图4-2 亚洲货物保险市场赔付率

2.我国民法体系的变更——《民法典》的诞生

天津港"8·12"瑞海公司危险品仓库特别重大火灾爆炸事故发生时，我国的民法体系仍处在单行法状态，当时有《中华人民共和国婚姻法》《中华人民共和国继承法》《中华人民共和国民法通则》《中华人民共和国收养法》《中华人民共和国担保法》《中华人民共和国合同法》《中华人民共和国物权法》《中华人民共和国侵权责任法》《中华人民共和国民法总则》。2020年5月28日，第十三届全国人民代表大会第三次会议表决通过了《中华人民共和国民法典》，自2021年1月1日起施行，前述各单行法同时废止。《民法典》分为总则、物权、合同、人格权、婚姻家庭、继承、侵权责任及附则，共计7编1 260条，之前单行法有关规定纳入了法典。编撰成为法典后，除了少部分调整外，大部分内容基本没有变化，只是结构和条款序号统一排列。我们要加快熟悉《民法典》，以《民法典》为准绳来规范我们的民事行为，争做守法好公民。

四、分析思路及教学要点

1.本案例思考题的讨论思路

总体思路：首先从案例中找出与每个讨论思考题相对应的案例素材，认真阅读案例相关材料，挖掘提炼出相关的基本事实，然后再运用所学专业知识或利用线上线下资源，对争议焦点作出有理论或法律依据的判断。

具体思路：

（1）"K公司是否有可能采取措施避免爆炸带来的货损风险？"问题的推荐思路是：首先，考虑主合同——在K公司与X公司的买卖合同下，通过选用贸易术语减少卖方风险。本案例中，卖方只要听从INCOTERMS的推荐，在集装箱运输下，选用FCA、CPT或CIP，就可避免案例中卖方的天津港爆炸风险。其次，考虑保险合同，即使没有选用刚刚提及的3个术语，卖方只要选择CIF，大爆炸导致的货损也可从保险合同获得赔偿。

（2）"你如何理解合同中约定不可抗力条款的重要意义？如何评价K公司在发生不可抗力事件后仍按照X公司要求，重新组织发货行为？"问题的推荐思路是：首先，考虑买卖合同下的法定或约定不可抗力免责条款，结合案例正文双方争议情景，作出判断。其次，从客户关系管理角度，评价K公司的重新发货行为。最后，通过不可抗力规定相对于合同受阻原则的优越点，培养学生民族自信和民族自豪感。

（3）"L公司在货代合同下是否应当承担谨慎处理义务？妥善谨慎应到什么程度？"问题的推荐思路是：首先，回到案例正文，找到货运代理委托合同关于委托事项的约定，明确L公司的合同义务。其次，找到相关法律法规，收集国内外有关受托人妥善、谨慎履行受托义务的参考案例，结合本案例作出判断。

（4）"运输合同下托运人K公司与承运人M公司的货物风险承担如何划分？如何评价该合同下当事人的争议？"问题的推荐思路是：首先，弄懂集装箱海上运输的特点和《中华人民共和国海商法》有关承运人责任区间在两种情形下的不同规定，对案例争议作出一般性判断。其次，再回到案例中，弄清楚涉案运输合同是否作出特别约定，再对该问题作出具体判断。

2.本案例规划的理论教学知识点

（1）买卖合同下不可抗力免责的法律规定或合同约定，两大法系有关规定的差异点。

（2）货运代理合同与运输合同下双方义务的本质性区别。

（3）集装箱货物运输合同下承运人的责任起讫一般性原则与特殊约定。

（4）商业合同履行过程中第三人侵权的责任认定原则。

3.本案例规划的能力训练点

（1）一笔货物出口业务中相关的合同关系判别能力。

（2）不同合同关系中风险责任的划分约定识别能力。

（3）多个合同下同时发起索赔的组织能力。

（4）货物索赔的实战能力。

五、理论依据及分析方法

1.国际货物买卖合同下的风险承担原则

对于思考题"K公司是否有可能采取措施避免爆炸事故货损风险责任？"问题的讨论，实际上是讨论货物买卖合同下货物灭失或损坏的风险划分问题。对此，东西方合同法主流原则是，以货物交付（不论是实际交付还是象征性交付）为界线，交付前由卖方承担，交付后由买方承担，双方另有约定除外。

在国际贸易中，货物交付地点有多种，风险划分点也就相应的有多种。例如在卖方仓库交付、在卖方所在地生产商仓库交付、在卖方所在地的交通枢纽站交付、在出口国港口交付、在买方港口交付、在买方所在地指定地点交付等。又因为在各个交货地点，还存在卖方是否要负责将货物装上运输工具的问题，就出现了"承运人指定交付地点"和"运输工具上"两个风险划分点。

为方便人们确定风险划分点，国际商会编撰了"国际贸易术语解释通则"，目前为2020年版（Incoterms2020），其中解释了11种贸易术语，确定了7个货物风险划分点，由买卖双方协商选择。

　　建议对本问题采用线上线下混合的"问题导向法"（PBL）进行教学：课前线上解决案例研读和掌握Incoterms2020的风险划分方法，课中分组讨论问题解决方案，归纳出该类问题的一般解题思路，课后线上提交布置的有关案例分析报告，检查知识应用能力，同时培养自主学习习惯与能力。

　　2.合同履行中的"三不能情形"免责法律原则——不可抗力与合同受阻

　　对于合同中约定不可抗力条款重要性问题的思考，核心问题是弄懂不可抗力与合同受阻法律原则及其差异。不可抗力（force majeure）这个法律概念来源于法国民法典，大陆法系国家法律一般都有不可抗力的规定。我国《民法典》第180条规定："因不可抗力不能履行民事义务的，不承担民事责任。法律另有规定的，依照其规定。不可抗力是不能预见、不能避免且不能克服的客观情况。"（简称"三不能情形"，编者注）。第563条规定：因不可抗力致使不能实现合同目的，当事人可以解除合同。第590条规定："当事人一方因不可抗力不能履行合同的，根据不可抗力的影响，部分或者全部免除责任，但是法律另有规定的除外。因不可抗力不能履行合同的，应当及时通知对方，以减轻可能给对方造成的损失，并应当在合理期限内提供证明。"

　　"三不能情形"是一个概括性的规定，一般指严重的自然灾害、意外事故和大规模社会动乱。这类事件不必写在合同中，只需约定适用法律即可。易产生纠纷的是对合同履行影响不那么明显的，又没作出明确约定的事件。所以，一个约定明确、具体的不可抗力条款非常重要。本案相关争议起因就是买卖合同没约定这样的条款。可否解除合同义务的判断标准还得看事件对合同履行的影响程度，这应多去查阅以往的法院判例加深理解。

　　英美普通法中没有不可抗力的概念，取而代之的是"合同受阻（frustration）"。它是在合同签订后，在合同任何一方无过失的情况下，发生了不可预见的严重突发事件，令合同无法履行的情形。例如卖方的特定货物被大火烧毁，又无法从他处另行采购，导致无法向买方交货，或无法向承租人交付运输，导致买卖合同和运输合同履行受阻，依据普通法，双方的合同义务可自动解除，卖方也无须作出赔偿。

　　在问题的分析方法上，建议引导学生理解不可抗力和合同受阻两个概念的异同点。大陆法系下，不可抗力条款或者通过法律适用条款来援引不可抗力规定，都需要在合同中明确约定。而合同受阻因为是默示法律规定，适用时只有合同终止与继续履行两个结果，不包括不可抗力条款下可以延迟履行的情形，所以，想要通过合同受阻原则终止合同履行是比较困难的。合同受阻只有在比较极端的情况才能成立，大部分履约困难情形，即使继续履行要增加很大成本，都不能令合同终止。所以，为了增加合同的肯定性、可操作性、更考虑到每一个交易情形的差异性，在合同中订立一条明示的、内容全面的不可抗力条款就非常必要。因为该条款自愿约定，所以应根据业务风险特点，将必要的阻碍事件列入其中。这一点是学生讨论要达到的高阶目标。同时，也应让学生明白，我国《民法典》明示的不可抗力规定优越于英美法合同受阻原则，增强了民族自信心与自豪感。

3.委托合同下受托人责任判定原则

本案例涉及当L公司作为货代委托合同下的受托人，应否履行谨慎处理义务，是否应当承担因集装箱堆场选择不当而导致的货损的问题。对此，我们应首先到《民法典》中寻找答案。

《民法典》关于代理关系的第164条规定："代理人不履行或者不完全履行职责，造成被代理人损害的，应当承担民事责任。"

《民法典》关于委托关系的第929条规定："有偿的委托合同，因受托人的过错造成委托人损失的，委托人可以请求赔偿损失。"

《民法典》关于保管关系的第892条规定："保管人应当妥善保管保管物。"第897条规定："保管期内，因保管人保管不善造成保管物毁损、灭失的，保管人应当承担赔偿责任。"

《民法典》关于仓储关系的第917条规定："储存期内，因保管不善造成仓储物毁损、灭失的，保管人应当承担赔偿责任。"

上述规定规范了多种形式委托合同关系，其中一个共同的立法理念是，在委托合同下，受托人应当无过错地，或者说，恪尽职守地完成受托事项而不让委托人遭受损失。

本案中的L公司是一个从事国际货物运输代理业务的企业，简称"货代企业"。货代企业接受进出口货物发货人、收货人或其代理人的委托，以委托人名义或者以自己的名义办理有关业务，赚取代理费或佣金，此种为典型的委托代理行为。也有的货代企业接受进出口货物发货人、收货人或其代理人的委托，签发运输单证、收取运费，履行运输合同承运人义务，此种为独立经营人或称无船承运人行为。此时，"代理"二字已经失去了法律上的代理意义。

本问题的分析方法，建议按照厘清案件事实、确定行为本质、对照法律规则、结合业务特点、判断问题是非的思路引导学生展开讨论。案例中，K公司委托L公司的业务包括：订舱、货物进场、货物装箱、报检报关、检验、领取运输单据等。那么，对于L公司在代理业务过程中是否履行谨慎处理义务，就要引导学生根据上述法律规则和货运代理业务性质，对照实际代理业务行为进行分析判断。

延伸的思考问题是，如果L公司在货代合同下具有谨慎处理业务义务，那么，它应承担哪些方面的妥善、谨慎处理义务？妥善、谨慎到什么程度？对此，我国《民法典》没有具体规定。但是，《中华人民共和国海商法》第48条规定："承运人应当妥善地、谨慎地装载、搬移、积载、运输、保管、照料和卸载所运货物。"参照该条规定可以看出责任范围和责任程度的一般性立法思想：一是妥善、谨慎程度应当结合业务特征以保证货物安全为原则。根据普通法和我国司法实践，妥善是指采用的技术性方法得当，谨慎是指责任心上的恪尽职守。二是责任范围以责任人可以控制的业务环节为界限。可以照此推断L的妥善和谨慎处理责任。

4.K公司与M公司纠纷的处理原则与分析方法

与题目中问题相关的法律原则主要有：

我国《民法典》第832条规定："承运人对运输过程中货物的毁损、灭失承担赔偿责任。但是，承运人证明货物的毁损、灭失是因不可抗力、货物本身的自然性质或者合理损耗以及托运人、收货人的过错造成的，不承担赔偿责任。"

我国《海商法》第48条规定："承运人应当妥善地、谨慎地装载、搬移、积载、运输、保管、照料和卸载所运货物。"第46条规定：承运人对集装箱装运的货物的责任期间，是指从装货港接收货物时起至卸货港交付货物时止，货物处于承运人掌管之下的全部期间。在承运人的责任期间，货物发生灭失或者损坏，除本节另有规定外，承运人应当负赔偿责任。

上述规定都是针对承运人义务而言的。

从集装箱班轮运输业务角度看，不论是海上集装箱班轮运输还是中欧班列集装箱运输，都是采用装运港/始发站集装箱堆场接受装箱货物、装船/装车、运输、卸船/卸车、目的港/终到站集装箱堆场交货的运输环节，承运人的货物管理照料责任要覆盖其掌管货物的全部期间。本案例采用的是集装箱海上班轮运输方式，那么，集装箱货物进入装货港承运人指定堆场后，M公司就应该承担责任。但是，我国《民法典》第832条也作出了不可抗力造成的货损承运人不承担赔偿责任的规定，争议的焦点最后可能落在承运人在指定堆场问题上是否履行了谨慎处理义务。

本问题的分析方法，仍然建议按照厘清案件事实、确定行为本质、对照法律规则、结合业务特点、判断问题是非的思路引导学生展开讨论。

本案例还涉及两个重要的延伸问题：风险管理和客户关系管理。前者涉及风险的预防，后者涉及客户开发与关系维护，二者都是国际贸易、国际商务管理中的深层次问题，建议针对专业特点，引导学生对这两个高阶性问题进行适当讨论，有关原理和方法，有专门的教科书可供参考。

六、教学组织建议

本案例可以作为案例讨论课使用。以下教学组织建议仅供参考。

1.PBL导向案例教学组织模式

为贯彻成果导向教育（OBE）教学理念，可以实施如图4-3所示的线上线下、课前课中课后全方位的问题导向案例教学组织模式。

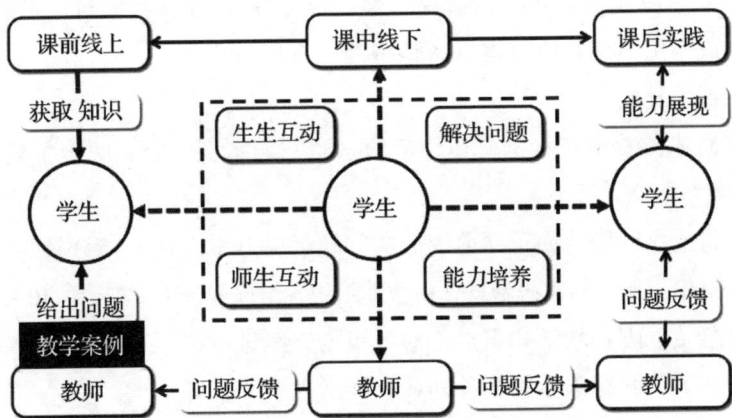

图4-3　问题导向案例教学组织模式

2.班级组织与教室布置

案例讨论课的班级人数不宜过多，应控制在30人左右，4～6人为一个小组。教室的桌椅布局应让所有课堂参与者以组为单位围坐四周，使其容易听到和看到各发言人为宜。教室中应配有投影仪、白板、写字笔，教师端电脑、各学生组一台电脑，装有 Office 办公软件即可。为方便学生更好地参与案例讨论，教师可在课前提醒学生准备小组的座位名牌，营造轻松的讨论气氛。有条件的可在超星平台线上建课，将案例教学资料上传平台，学生使用学习通进行线上学习讨论和提交问题或作业。

3.教学内容与问题选取

本案例案情复杂，涉及问题较多。本科生教学建议一次教学针对教学知识点任务选取 1~2 个问题进行学习讨论，国际商务硕士研究生可选取全部涉案问题进行学习讨论，培养全方位的解决复杂问题能力。

4.过程组织与时间安排

全案例讨论分为课前线上、课中线下和课后线上三个阶段，其中，课前线上规划 100 分钟，课中线下 100 分钟，课后线上 50 分钟，总计 250 分钟。具体步骤和时间分配建议如下：

（1）课前计划

教师提前 1~2 周将案例正文和案例使用说明中的讨论思考题线上发给学生。根据讨论思考题，学生用 50 分钟独立阅读案例正文，掌握相关事实，通过线上线下自学方式，找出解决问题的法律依据，提出 1 000 字左右的案例阅读报告，其中应包括问题初步解决方案。小组用 50 分钟线上讨论形成统一认识，并形成小组最终解决方案以备课中线下全班讨论之用。

（2）课中计划

案例概述：教师作案例概述，带领学生回顾案例内容，明确主题。5~10 分钟。

小组讨论：回顾与完善课前形成的问题解决方案。10~15 分钟。

班级讨论：围绕讨论思考题，由教师组织各组逐一讨论、辩论。40~50 分钟。

评价总结：围绕教学知识点，对各组的方案进行梳理总结。15 分钟。

问答环节：回答学生的相关问题。10 分钟。

（3）课后计划

为检验学生学习效果，安排课后线上案例分析作业环节。课后作业一要遵循学以致用原则，案例编写应保持与课上讨论的问题同类，解题依据同类，但可适当提高高度和宽度。建议阅读 20 分钟，线上学生自主讨论完成作业并线上提交 30 分钟。

第五章

倒签提单

D 轮倒签提单引发的商业大战

摘要：案例正文描述的这场由 D 轮倒签提单引发的商业大战发生在 20 世纪末的中国。交战的一方是当时的 Z 国有大型进出口公司，另一方是大连市的 H 海运公司，战事还波及卖方 C 和其印度兄弟公司。交战各方为了维护各自的经济利益，在长达 3 年多的时间里进行了多场烽火连天的激烈交锋。案例介绍了这场商战的贸易和运输背景，细致地描述了 D 轮倒签提单的过程、Z 进出口公司作为提单持有人在目的港对 D 轮实施证据保全和司法扣押的细节、H 海运公司与索赔人 Z 进出口公司之间的博弈、卖方 C 与 Z 进出口公司在伦敦仲裁庭围绕买卖合同下是否迟期交付货物的战斗，以及 H 海运公司与倒签提单保函出具人的争斗等重要情节，揭示了倒签提单行为的危害性。案例的使用说明部分对案例正文描述的各场交锋进行了理论分析与评价，同时提供了案例使用指导。

关键词：倒签提单　证据保全　船舶扣押　交货期

1. 本案例描述和分析的商业大战是一个真实的事件，编者是当年的主要参与者。尽管事件发生在 20 世纪末，但鉴于事发至今的相关法律规则没有发生实质性变化，因此案例对当今的倒签提单问题的教学仍具有使用价值。由于企业保密的要求，案例中对有关当事方做了必要的掩饰性处理。
2. 本案例只供教学之用，并无意明示地或暗示地褒奖或贬低案例中涉及的公司的相关行为。

案例正文

本案例描述和分析的是一场倒签提单索赔之战。20世纪末，Z进出口公司（以下简称Z）因进口豆粕国内市场价格下跌损失惨重，于是抓住H海运公司与卖方C国际贸易公司（以下简称C）和其印度兄弟公司延迟交货并倒签提单的证据，在长达3年多的时间里，分别向H海运公司、C国际贸易公司进行索赔，并多次扣押当事船舶，每场交锋都进行得十分激烈。

1.背景

豆粕本是大豆榨油的副产品，但因为其富含蛋白质和粗纤维而成为饲料加工的重要原料。豆粕的交易量如此之大，以至于世界上主要农产品交易所都把它作为重要的交易标的，中国的大连商品交易所就有豆粕的期货交易。中国的畜牧饲养业规模很大，需要大量的饲料。因为国产豆粕无法满足饲料加工业的需求，每年需要从巴西、印度、美国等大豆主产国大量进口来补充。在国内豆粕交易市场上，每当豆粕供货出现短缺，豆粕价格就会快速上涨，这为那些信息灵通的豆粕进口商们带来了商机。

1997年的下半年，中国豆粕市场上又出现了供货紧张局面，豆粕价格开始上扬。饲料加工企业感到了压力，担心价格继续上涨，便开始大量订购豆粕，结果导致市场价格在短短的几个月内持续上涨，比国际市场价格高出30%还多。商人对市场的嗅觉总是灵敏的。看到了豆粕市场的这种变化，国内有能力的农产品贸易公司便开始到国外抢购豆粕。

Z在当年是一家国有大型公司，总部设在北京，常年经营饲料进口业务，拥有一批精明强干的业务人员，在国内外积淀了广泛的交易网络，豆粕市场的这种悄然变化Z当然不会没有察觉。Z通过各种渠道从印度市场陆续订购了数万吨豆粕。Z初步估计，这数万吨豆粕按照当时两个市场的差价计算，出售后净利润可达数千万元人民币。由于中国的大量采购，印度豆粕供应也出现了紧张局面，导致合同交货期大致都在数月之后。但Z仍依稀看到了数月后的可观利润入账，其中就包括Z与卖方C的1.1万吨印度豆粕合同。

C的母公司是一家专门从事农产品进出口的大型跨国公司，是世界四大粮食和饲料交易商之一，业务范围几乎囊括全球的各类农产品贸易，在世界主要农产品进出口国设有许多分公司，C注册在新加坡，是其母公司众多子公司之一。1997年的11月6日，Z与C签订了一份合同号为S0187的豆粕采购合同。合同约定，C向Z销售散装印度片状黄豆粕，数量11 000吨（增减10%），价格为CFR每公吨278.5美元，结算方式为不可撤销的即期信用证，装货港为印度的维沙卡帕特南，卸货港为中国南通，交货期为1998年的1月15日至2月15日，其他条款依照GAFTA 100格式合同，仲裁按照GAFTA 125规则执行。事实上，C销售的豆粕是从母公司下属的印度P公司（以下简称P）购买的，后者是这笔交易的实际发货人。12月8日，Z根据合同约定通过国内某银行向C开出了金额为3 063 500美元的即期付款信用证。

2.D轮在维沙卡帕特南莫名其妙地倒签提单

D轮是在大连注册的H海运公司（以下简称H）所属的一艘普通杂货船，载重吨为15 000多吨，有5个货舱，有过运营欧洲、中南美和印度港口的经历。H并没有Z那样的市场嗅觉，也不那么关心豆粕市场的大起大落，日复一日、年复一年地从事着自己的国际海运业务。C的贸易量很大，对于船东来说它就是一个超级货主，以至于每次与其进行运输合同洽商时总是处于被动地位。C对于自己的这种超级地位当然是清楚的，因此，凡是其交易的货物都是自己负责运输。与Z的豆粕买卖也是这样，于是便有了H与C的1万多吨的豆粕运输合同，D轮及其船东H也因此卷入了后来那场噩梦般的激烈商战当中。

C与Z签订了11 000万吨豆粕销售合同后，于当月10日，与H签订了D轮的该批货物运输合同，受载期为1998年1月10日至2月10日，其他主要相关条款与其买卖合同一致。1998年2月9日，D轮按照运输合同约定抵达印度的维沙卡帕特南港并靠泊开始装货。据后来该轮船长说，全部货物本来可以在2月15日装完，但天气的干扰延长了装货时间，直至16日16时，全部货物才装船完毕。之后，港口当局下达了书面指令，令D轮立即启航离港。期间，发货人P将编号为No.1的大副收据交由该轮大副签字。P出示的大副收据显示，托运人为P，收货人为凭指示，通知方为Z，承运船舶为D轮，装货港为维沙卡帕特南，卸货港为中国南通，货物为散装印度片状黄豆粕，重量10 479吨，清洁已装船，日期为2月15日。D轮大副发现日期错误，要求更改为2月16日，此外，装货时还发现部分货物为褐色而非黄色，准备在大副收据上作出批注。

P随即向大副出具了以下内容的倒签提单和清洁提单保函，要求保留装货日期为2月15日，并不要加注部分货物为褐色的批注。

To：M/V D

Goods：Indian yellow soybean meal，10 479 MT

Bill of Lading No.：01

Port of loading：Visakhapatnam，India

The above goods were shipped on the above vessel by Messrs C，but the on board date is 16th February，1998，and the color of part of the goods is brown instead of yellow.We request you to date the Mate's Receipt and the Bills of Lading as 15th February，1998，and not remark the brown color on both the Mate's Receipt and the Bills of Lading.

In consideration of your complying with our above request，we hereby agree as follows：

（1）To indemnify you，your servants and agents and to hold all of you harmless in respect of any liability，loss，damage or expenses of whatsoever nature which you may sustain by reason of issuance of Mate's Receipt and B/L in accordance with our request.

（2）In the event of any proceedings commenced against you or any of your servants of agents in connection with issue of Bill of Lading in any place to provide you or them on demand with sufficient funds to defend the same.

（3）If the ship or any other ship or property belonging to you should be arrested or detained or if the arrest or detention thereof should be threatened to provide such bail or other security as may be requested to prevent such arrest or detention or to secure the release of such vessel ore property and indemnify you in respect of any liability，loss，damage or expenses caused by such arrest or detention whether or not such arrest or detention or threatened arrest or detention may be justified.

（4）The liability of each and every person under this indemnity shall be joint and several，and shall not be conditional upon your proceedings first against any person，whether or not such person is party to or liable under this indemnity.

（5）This indemnity shall be construed in accordance with English Law and each and every person liable under this indemnity shall be at your request submit to the jurisdiction of High Court of Justice of England.

    Yours faithfully

    C International Trading Pty Ltd

按照常理，托运人的倒签提单和清洁提单请求应当向当事船舶的所有人或经营人提出，船上任何人员无权决定。但是，P却微妙地选择了向D轮的大副提出，而时任大副却既没有向船长请示，更没有向船东H请示，莫名其妙地接受了托运人的保函，签发了日期为2月15日的清洁大副收据。由于港务当局催促船舶开航，船长委托当地的船舶代理严格按照大副收据签发提单，随即驾驶D轮起航了。满载的D轮进入公海定速航行后，除了值班驾驶员在谨慎地驾驶着船舶外，包括船长在内的其他人员都很快地进入了"梦乡"。没人想到，大副的这一看上去不起眼的行为后来在H与Z、H与P、Z与C之间将会引发怎样的激烈复杂的交战，会给D轮及其船东H带来怎样的恶果。

3.Z在南通港对D轮申请证据保全和扣押

商人的头脑并不总是精明的，也有糊涂的时候。几个月过后，当多家贸易公司在国外抢购的十几万吨豆粕开始陆续抵达中国港口时，国内的豆粕价格将发生怎样的变化大概连不那么懂得经济学的普通百姓也能看明白。市场规律是客观的。随着进口豆粕陆续抵达中国港口，国内豆粕价格开始出现下滑，随着人们对更多装载豆粕船舶将抵达的预期不断增加，豆粕价格下滑进一步加剧。至D轮3月5日抵达南通港时，市场价格下滑到不但消灭了Z的预计利润，据后来Z向H索赔的数据，还使其倒搭进去520多万元人民币。这样的结局Z是没有想到的，几个月前的喜悦荡然无存。这就如同炒股一样，股市上涨时股民们纷纷入市，被套牢时就纷纷感叹早知如此何必当初，市场无情应当是他们的共同感受吧！

到底是大公司里不乏高人。就在大家不知如何是好之时，一位平时不出众的业务员说了一句话："找律师问问吧。"总经理眨巴眨巴眼睛说："对呀，快把咱们的法律顾问请来。"公司的法律顾问很快来到了公司办公室（后来了解到，该法律顾问是某海事大学海商法专业的高才生）。律师了解基本情况后开始分析，价格的不利变化是市场风险，愿赌服输是普遍的商业法则，看来这买卖合同白纸黑字是赖不掉的。如果……如果……有了，学校里老师教过的，试试看，可能有转机。于是一个绕开买卖合同而从运输合同下手的解决方案经过大家商定后便开始实施了，由此也掀开了 Z 与 H 的交战序幕。

3 月 12 日，这位律师带着 Z 的委托向某海事法院（该法院对南通港具有管辖权）提交了对 D 轮实施证据保全的申请。海事法院审理后认为，该申请符合相关法律规定，当日便批准了此项申请并下达了对 D 轮实施证据保全的裁决书。裁决书主要内容如下：

"D 轮签发的提单表明，D 轮已于 2 月 15 日从印度装货出港，但申请人通过有关方面查知，该轮在 2 月 16 日仍在装货，表明该轮倒签提单。为此，申请人向本法院提出证据保全申请，要求对被申请人所属的 D 轮的船舶证书、航海日志、大副收据、租船合同、装卸时间事实记录、工班表及相关理货单据等予以证据保全。本院认为，申请人的申请符合法律规定，依据《中华人民共和国民事诉讼法》第 74 条的规定，裁定如下：准许 Z 提出的诉前证据保全申请，从即日起，对被申请人 H 所属的 D 轮的上述证据予以证据保全。"

3 月 13 日海事法院法官登上 D 轮，向该轮船长宣读了法院的裁决，并将船舶的上述证书带走复印封存。该轮的航海日志清楚地显示，该轮的确是 2 月 16 日装船完毕。Z 对这一发现如获至宝，因为，略知倒签提单法律后果的人都知道，Z 的赔本生意就要出现转机了。

获取了 D 轮倒签提单的证据之后，Z 马不停蹄地（估计相关文件早已事先准备好了）于证据保全的当日又向海事法院提出诉前扣船申请，海事法院又高效率地快速审理，于当日便下达了民事裁定书，裁定扣押 D 轮，要求该轮船东 H 向海事法院提供 1 200 万元人民币的担保（注：起初申请显示的市场差价损失为 520 万元人民币，不知申请人凭什么追加的，法院又是凭什么裁定的），同时将扣船令送达 D 轮。此后，尽管货物已于 3 月 17 日卸完，但由于 H 无力提供法院要求的巨额担保金，D 轮一直处于被扣押状态。相关法律规定，船舶扣押后，申请人应在 30 天内提起诉讼，否则，法院将裁定释放被扣船舶。鉴于 D 轮船东 H 一直没有提供担保，释放船舶日期已经逼近，Z 于 4 月 14 日向海事法院提出拍卖 D 轮的申请，海事法院也随即作出拍卖 D 轮的裁决。

4.H 与 Z 的博弈

D 轮被扣押后的当天，H 立即通过电话与 Z 沟通，商讨问题解决之策。主管船舶运营业务的副总经理李先生首先向Z承认D轮倒签提单的事实，但同时强调倒签提单是应Z的发货人P书面要求所为，并且提单也只是被倒签了16个小时而已。请求Z考虑双方同为国有公司，放H一马，转向买卖合同的卖方C索赔，并表示愿意为Z向C索赔提供证据帮助。H的提议被Z拒绝了，无奈，第二天H的总经理与该副总经理飞到北京与Z当面协商。

Z的总经理首先出面欢迎船东代表的到访，然后安排具体负责人和公司的律师与船东代表在公司的会议室具体协商。简单寒暄之后，协商很快进入正题。H的李经理首先就D轮船长未向公司请示，擅自同意托运人P的请求而倒签提单给Z带来的不便表达了歉意。随后，对Z向H主张赔偿提出质疑，认为Z的所谓市场差价损失是市场风险导致的，应当由市场的参与者Z自己承担，并请问对方，船长倒签提单16个小时会给Z公司带来多少经济损失？如果能够计算出这16个小时市场下跌的经济损失，船东愿意就此作出赔偿。

Z的律师马上反驳道，D轮船长倒签提单，给Z带来的损失根本不是16个小时内货物市场价格下跌多少的问题，而是倒签提单掩盖了P和C延期交付货物的事实，致使Z丧失了在信用证项下拒绝支付全部货款的权利。如果提单实事求是地签发为2月16日，Z则可以C违反合同交货期和信用证下交单不符为由取消这笔交易，那样的话，我的当事人就不会面临目前的市场损失。但贵公司的倒签提单行为使得C能够在严重违约的情况下划走信用证下的全部货款，使我的当事人不得不接受该船货物。经初步计算，我当事人的市场差价损失为：（2 550元/吨－2 050元/吨）×10 479吨＝5 239 500（元人民币）；因延迟交货违约而须赔付国内买家300多万元人民币。另外，卸货中还发现货物运输途中存在不同程度的损坏，初步估计平均贬值50%，待正式检验结果出来后告知。

H的李经理的本科专业就是国际贸易，当然不会不懂其中的道理。他立刻明白，自己目前的诡辩是糊弄不了Z的，遇到明白人了！于是，同总经理商量后向Z提出，愿意就倒签提单一事向Z支付5万美元赔偿，然后帮助Z根据买卖合同向C索赔。这一提议同样遭到了Z的拒绝，双方的谈判不欢而散。

返回公司后的一段时间里，H仍然积极主动地与Z沟通，劝说Z接受自己的建议，但一直没有得到积极的回馈。H对整个事件重新做了评估后，于3月27日给Z发去如下传真：

"对于贵公司在贵我双方北京商谈中提出的倒签提单损失问题，我们的意见是：

（1）关于市场差价损失

我们仍然认为贵公司声称的市场差价损失是一个相当长时期内的价格不利变动导致的，并不是 D 轮倒签提单导致的。具体地说，是从贵公司与 C 签订豆粕买卖合同之时起至该船货物抵达南通港时止这个时期内，价格下跌导致的，与倒签提单没有任何关系。贵公司以倒签提单 16 个小时为由要求船东承担全部市场差价损失是在利用租船合同转嫁商业风险，有违诚实信用原则。

（2）关于贵公司国内转卖合同的所谓违约赔偿问题

贵公司的国内买卖合同对货物交货期如何规定以及违约金多少与租船合同没有任何关系，因此也就与船东没有任何关系。本航次的运输合同没有船舶应当何时抵达南通港交付货物的约定，当事船舶也不存在不合理绕航的事实，当事船舶和船东已经尽到了合理尽速派遣船舶的法定义务，不存在任何违反法律规定或违反运输合同约定的行为，因此，船东对 Z 的国内转卖合同中的所谓违约后果不应承担责任。

（3）关于所谓的货损问题

当事船舶和船东作为承运船舶和承运人在装货港口只负责观察货物的外表状况，并无法定的或约定的义务也无能力检查货物的内在品质。D 轮的船舶各项检验证书表明，D 轮在装货前和在维沙卡帕特南开航当时，始终处于适航状态，船上的工作记录证明，船员在船舶航行中始终履行了妥善、谨慎地管理货物的义务。货物的颜色变深、发霉变质很可能是由于货物本身含水量过高导致的，是货物本身的潜在缺陷，而根据相关法律规定，船舶、船东对由此导致的货物损失不承担责任。

希望贵公司综合考虑各种因素，接受我公司向贵公司提供 10 万美元担保的建议，申请法院释放 D 轮，而转向卖方索赔。到目前为止，我公司因船舶被扣押已损失几十万元人民币，这是由于贵公司无理要求我们提供无法满足的高额担保造成的，对此项损失，我们保留向贵公司索赔的权利。"

对于 H 的上述传真建议，Z 回复表示仍无法接受，并告知 H，如果仍不能提供足额担保，将于 4 月 14 日向海事法院申请拍卖 D 轮。收到 Z 的回复后，H 非常焦急，绞尽脑汁思考如何破解这一灾难性局面。拍卖船舶……拍卖船舶……有了！4 月 10 日，H 李经理再次飞到北京与 Z 面谈。李经理直截了当地告诉 Z，D 轮目前设有银行抵押，银行贷款尚有 350 万美元没有偿还，而该轮目前的市场价值不过280万美元。如果拍卖船舶，按照《中华人民共和国海商法》的船舶优先权规定，Z将收不到分文。仍然希望Z考虑船东的建议，接受船东提供的10万美元担保，向海事法院申请释放D轮。H承诺协助Z向卖方C提起诉讼。对此提议，Z没有马上表示意见。

H的这一步棋着实给Z增加了不小的压力。他们在算计着，经过紧张的私下讨论后，Z提出，船东提高担保额到15万美元，并承诺协助Z向卖方C索赔，此为释放D轮的条件。对Z将担保额提高到15万美元的主张船东表示了拒绝。谈判再次处于僵持状态。

为了向H施加压力，Z于4月14日向海事法院提交了拍卖船舶申请，海事法院当即作出拍卖裁决。局势的急转直下令H措手不及。H原本判断，Z在了解船舶抵押的事实后，应当能够接受船东的提议，不会作出出力不讨好的事情来，而Z为多收取5万美元却使出了这样一个阴招！

考虑到被扣船舶与日俱增的船期损失，15万美元相对1 200万元人民币担保金毕竟还算是一个小数目，H最后同意了Z的要求。但H提出，在Z向卖方C索赔成功后，应将15万美元担保归还H，因为法律是不允许索赔人通过打官司赚钱的。毕竟一个大型国有贸易公司，不能不顾法律原则，Z思考后表示同意，于是李经理当天再次奔赴北京，双方签署了和解协议。随即，Z向海事法院提交了撤销拍卖船舶和释放D轮的申请。海事法院作出裁定，撤销拍卖船舶裁定，同时解除对D轮的扣押，D轮获得了自由。至此，在这场双方的博弈中D轮船东H总算暂时松了一口气。但整个事件还远没有结束。

5.Z与C的违约之战

在从H和D轮的身上暂时榨不出更多油水的情况下，Z组织实施了另一场战斗，即依据买卖合同向C索赔倒签提单损失。

Z委托某国际知名律师行I的中国事务所全权处理此事。I在了解买卖合同和装货港装货的基本情况后，着手开展相关证据的搜集工作。I明白，印度公司P与C同属一个跨国公司，要从P取得证据会相当困难。于是，I的律师来到H公司，调取D轮在维沙卡帕特南的大副收据、航海日志、提单副本、倒签提单保函、港口指令等证据，又向在家休假的时任船长和大副询问了D轮在维沙卡帕特南装货的具体情况，并一一作了笔录。已经搜集到的证据足以表明，P

和C明显违反了买卖合同关于交货时间的约定，延期交货，构成了根本性违约。但他们为了掩盖违约事实，请求D轮大副倒签大副收据，导致船舶代理倒签提单。经向委托人Z请示后，决定正式启动对C的索赔仲裁。

根据Z与C签订的GAFTA的格式合同和仲裁规则，Z的律师I于1999年3月向设在伦敦的GAFTA仲裁委员会提交了仲裁申请。该仲裁委员会后来的临时裁决书显示，Z以C和P倒签提单掩盖迟期交付货物的事实和到港货物存在品质缺陷为由，要求C赔付Z 736 988美元的市场差价损失，按照当时的汇率计算，约相当于610万元人民币。

仲裁庭组成后对双方提交的文件作了认真的审核，并组织了两场开庭，现场聆听双方的质证。对于索赔人Z的指控，答辩人C也提交了大量的文件，证明D轮当年在维沙卡帕特南的最后装货日是2月15日，而非2月16日；索赔人提供的船舶航海日志有伪造的嫌疑；所谓的货物质量问题也与答辩人无关，因为装货港的检验报告清楚地表明，货物在装船时是符合买卖合同约定的。因此，答辩人拒绝索赔人的索赔；最重要的是，GAFTA 125仲裁规则第2：2（C）条规定，索赔人应当在卸货完毕后的连续21天内向答辩人发出仲裁通知，并在随后的7天内指定仲裁员并通知答辩人，否则丧失索赔权利，而申请人发出仲裁通知和仲裁员指定的实际日期均超过了规则规定的最后期限。据此，答辩人请求仲裁庭拒绝索赔人的仲裁申请。

客观地讲，GAFTA 125规则2：2（C）条规定的21天时效确实太短了，对于复杂的本案而言，21天的时效稍纵即逝。但规则就是规则，看来Z是顾此失彼了。事情发生后Z将全部精力都放在对D轮采取措施上，忽略了买卖合同的索赔及索赔时效问题。好在英国法律追求公平原则，根据英国仲裁法，即使是过了仲裁时效，索赔人如果能够证明不进行仲裁对他是严重的不公平的话，法庭可以裁决允许他继续申请仲裁。这条法律规定救了Z。Z的律师I向仲裁庭请求本案的继续仲裁权，经过反复辩论，仲裁庭肯定了Z的继续仲裁权，又经过另一轮仲裁，最终仲裁庭支持了Z的主张。

6.H与P和C的倒签提单保函之战

H根据和解协议向Z支付了15万美元后，立即着手和P实施倒签提单保函索赔之战。前文提到，P为取得倒签提单向D轮提交了赔偿保函，承诺D轮或其船东等相关利益方因倒签提单遭到索赔时，由他们承担赔偿责任。那么，C为什么也成为被告了呢？事情是这样的。D轮在维沙卡帕特南装货后共签发了9份大副收据，其中只有两份是2月16日装完货的，即这两份大副收据是被倒签了，其余大副收据下的货物都是2月15日之前装上船的。因此，在维沙卡帕特南签发的9份提单中，只应有两份日期是倒签的。这意味着，即使Z对H的倒签提单索赔是合理的，其索赔也只能基于被倒签的两份提单的货物数量索赔损失，那样的话，索赔金额就大大降低了。9份提单被P交给了C，后者为了与Z的信用证单据要求相符，向H提交了一份赔付保函，要求H同意其将9份提单合并成一份提单（也就是后来Z向H索赔的那份提单），并承诺承担由此产生的一切责任。H认为，C也应当承担倒签提单的法律后果，因此，将其也列为起诉的对象。

H在新加坡注册了一家公司，作为D轮的注册船东。考虑诉讼的方便，H依据前述两份赔付保函在新加坡法院提起了对P和C的诉讼，请求法院判令两被告履行保函承诺，赔偿Z向其索赔的豆粕市场差价损失，以及D轮被扣押期间的船期损失及其他相关损失。

在法庭上，P和C分别采取了极其聪明的做法予以抗辩。P辩称，提单的日期只被倒签16个小时，完全是为了贸易上的方便。再者，英国普通法和新加坡法院的相关判例表明，法院不应受理依据倒签提单保函提起的诉讼请求。C则辩称，他合并提单所依据的9份提单日期均为2月15日，他没有倒签任何提单，因此H对他的赔付要求没有任何理由。法院查证了所有证据后，依据法院先例，最后驳回了H的诉讼请求，H在新加坡的这场战斗以失败而告终。

7. Z的另一场战斗——非倒签提单之战

Z的这场战斗并不是依据倒签提单而发起的，因而与本案例主题不大相关，但因其属于同一序列，规模之大，程度之激烈，不但H及D轮再次卷入其中，D轮保赔保险公司和货物保险公司也身陷其中。所以本案例还是将其列入其中，但案情介绍会压缩，以期能够让读者对提单下承运人的管理货物义务有所理解。

Z的前述几场战斗结果并未能够如其所愿。对D轮的扣押由于银行抵押权的存在使其从H处只拿到了15万美元，对C的仲裁索赔之战还在进行之中，何时结束，结果如何都还是个未知数。因此，Z决定另辟蹊径，对H和D轮发起另一场战斗——管货疏忽之战，由此把D轮的保赔保险公司和货物保险公司也卷入了战斗。

根据海上运输相关法律的规定，提单承运人应尽到妥善和谨慎地管理货物的义务，承运人未履行或未全部履行该项义务导致货物损坏的，应当负赔偿责任。前文提到，Z在D轮在南通卸货时发现，部分货物颜色变为褐色，还有部分货物发霉变质，并在扣押D轮时向H通报了这一情况。这实际上是Z为目前的这场战斗埋下的伏笔。

Z在准备和搜集了证据之后，便向H打响了这场承运人管货疏忽之战。就在向海事法院申请解除对D轮扣押后不久的1998年4月23日，Z又向海事法院提交了扣船申请，请求法院判令被申请人H提供人民币830万元的担保以释放被扣押船舶。

Z这次申请扣船的事实和理由是：被申请人H签发的01号清洁提单表明，D轮于1998年2月15日已经装完货物10 479吨，货物品质良好。申请人遂付款赎单，取得该正本提单。在该轮的卸货过程中发现货物发生损坏，部分货物严重碳化，已完全丧失使用价值；部分货物变色，发生贬值。申请人认为，H作为承运人未能尽到妥善谨慎管理货物义务，致使货物在其掌管期间发生损失，应当承担全部赔偿责任。

4月24日，海事法院收到Z的扣船申请后同样进行了快速审理，经审查后认为，申请人的申请符合法律规定。依照《中华人民共和国民事诉讼法》第93条、第251条第2款的规定，裁定准许申请人的诉前财产保全请求，从即日起扣押被申请人所属的D轮，责令D轮船东向法院提供人民币830万元的担保。同时，海事法院下达了扣船令，于当日在南通港又一次对D轮予以扣押。D轮再次失去了自由。与此同时，Z在海事法院提起了对H的诉讼。

这次诉讼不仅涉及H，还涉及D轮的英国保赔保险公司，因为其是H的船东责任保险人，也涉及某中国财产保险公司，因为它是这批货物的海上运输险的承保人，并为释放D轮提供了担保。这场战斗持续了两年之久，双方在法庭上你来我往，多次激烈交锋，案件甚至申诉到了中华人民共和国最高人民法院。最终，Z取得了这场战斗的最后胜利，从两家保险公司那里获得了1 200多万元人民币的赔偿，这远远超出了他们当初的想象，可谓战果辉煌。据悉，与此同时，Z又从对C的仲裁中获得了40多万美元的赔偿，可谓锦上添花。谁说不能通过打官司赚钱？Z真的做到了。至此，这场由D轮倒签提单引发的商业大战基本结束了。

8.讨论思考题

（1）了解倒签提单的法律性质对买卖合同履行有何意义？

（2）如何界定倒签提单的性质和法律后果？

（3）提单持有人应如何实施证据保全？

（4）提单持有人应如何实施船舶扣押？

（5）买方遇倒签提单可否向卖方索赔？

（6）如何认定倒签提单保函的法律效力？

9.参考文献

[1] 英国1992年海上货物运输法［EB/OL］.［2025-01-10］. http://wenku.baidu.com/view/e0443f18964bcf84b9d57b0f.html.

[2] 中华人民共和国海商法［EB/OL］.［2025-01-10］. 中华人民共和国海商法_相关规定_中国政府网.

[3] 中华人民共和国海事诉讼特别程序法［EB/OL］.［2025-01-10］. 中华人民共和国主席令（第二十八号）　中华人民共和国海事诉讼特别程序法__2000年第2号国务院公报_中国政府网.

[4] 司玉琢. 海商法［M］. 5版. 北京：法律出版社，2023.

[5] 杨良宜，杨大明，杨大志. 合约的履行、弃权与禁反言［M］. 北京：法律出版社，2018.

[6] 杨良宜. 合约的解释：规则与应用［M］. 北京：法律出版社，2015.

[7] 王淑梅. 海上货物运输合同纠纷案件裁判规则［M］. 北京：法律出版社，2021.

[8] 李勤昌. 国际货物运输［M］. 6版. 大连：东北财经大学出版社，2022.

[9] 李勤昌. 提单的若干概念及其法律问题［J］. 国际商务，2010（1）.

[10] 李勤昌. 海上货物索赔对象难以认定的原因研究［J］. 国际贸易问

题，2004（10）．

[11] 李勤昌. 海运提单持有人索赔权问题研究 [J]. 黑龙江对外经贸，2005（5）．

[12] 李勤昌. 论海运提单的运输合同属性 [J]. 世界海运，2002（5）．

10.案例英文信息

A 3-Year Commercial Fight for Ante-dating B/L by MV D

Abstract： This commercial war described in this case was incurred by ante-dating B/L issued by MV D. It happened at the end of last century in China. One of the participant was Z Imp.& Exp.Co.， a large state-owned company at that time， the other was H Shipping Company in Dalian city in China. Seller C and his brother company were also involved. The war consist of several fights within nearly three year. This case introduces the background of that war firstly， then describes vividly the details of how the ante-dated bill of lading was issued， how the bill of lading holder applied for evidence preservation and arrest of the carrying vessel， the game playing between the claimant and the shipowner and the fight in arbitration in London between the claimant and their seller and the fight between shipowner and LOI issuer. The description reveals the perniciousness of ante-dating the B/L. The second part of this case is of theoretical analysis and comments by the writer.

Key words： ante-dated B/L， evidence preservation， arrest vessel， delivery period

案例使用说明

一、教学目的与用途

本案例适用于"国际贸易实务"、"国际货物运输"和"国际物流"课程中关于倒签提单知识点的教学。案例的编写目的是，通过案例中描述的各争议焦点的讨论，引导学生领会倒签提单的相关法律规定和掌握索赔技能，培养学生处理倒签提单索赔问题的实践能力。通过阅读、分析和讨论本案例资料，帮助学生思考和掌握下列六个具体问题：一是倒签提单产生的原因；二是倒签提单的法律性质和法律后果；三是倒签提单诉前保全的法律规定；四是倒签提单索赔的程序；五是索赔金额计算的法律规定；六是商务索赔技巧。

本案例的概念难度、分析难度和陈述难度均适中，适用对象包括国际贸易专业、国际物流专业和国际商务专业的本科生、研究生和国际商务专业学位研究生。对于缺乏专业基础理论知识的本科生，可以根据教学大纲，有选择地引导阅读案例相关材料，重点分析提单下货物索赔的基本法律依据和基本程序；对于缺乏实践经验的研究生，可以引导其将掌握的理论知识运用于本案例每一个具体问题的分析，对案例中争论的几个焦点问题，作出自己的是非判断，锻炼其处理实际问题的能力。

本案例规划的理论教学知识点包括：

（1）倒签提单产生的原因；

（2）倒签提单的法律性质和法律后果；

（3）倒签提单诉前证据保全和诉前扣押船舶的法律依据；

（4）倒签提单索赔金额确定的原则；

（5）倒签提单索赔的操作程序。

本案例规划的能力训练教学内容包括：

（1）倒签提单证据的搜集能力；

（2）诉前证据保全和扣押船舶保全的实施能力；

（3）索赔金额的计算及证据支持能力；

（4）买卖合同中卖方迟期交货问题的妥善解决能力；

（5）整体索赔的筹划与组织能力。

二、分析思路

本案例的核心问题是倒签提单下的索赔问题，这是本案例教学的核心知识点。围绕这一核心知识点，建议案例的课堂讨论按照下列思路和顺序展开：

第一，引导学生讨论本案例的核心问题——倒签提单的法律性质和法律后果。围绕这一核心问题，引导同学讨论以下问题：一是倒签提单的定义。提单行为有很多，例如倒签提单、预借提单、交换提单、电放提单、拆分或合并提单，甚至伪造提单等，每一种行为的内容和法律后果不尽相同，因此，弄清倒签提单的定义是确定行为人责任及索赔人索赔权利的基础。二是倒签提单行为人的鉴别。倒签提单可以由发货人提出申请，由承运人实施，也可以由承运人自己实施，还可以在承运人不知情的情况下，由发货人申请，装货港口的船舶代理人实施。更有甚者，可能是发货人自己实施的（形同伪造提单）。讨论这一问题的意义在于，它是索赔人正确确定索赔对象的唯一依据。三是倒签提单的原因，弄清这一问题有利于学生理解在国际货物贸易中卖方履行及时交货义务的重要性。四是倒签提单行为的识别，掌握这一知识有助于判断是否为倒签提单行为。五是倒签提单的法律性质和法律后果。掌握这一知识的意义在于它是索赔人提出索赔的法律基础。在上述具体问题讨论的基础上，引导学生针对本案例中的倒签提单行为进行具体分析。

第二，引导学生对索赔人的索赔权展开讨论。围绕这一问题，引导学生按照顺序讨论下列问题：（1）收货人是否具有索赔权？如果有，依据的合同关系是什么？（2）提单持有人是否具有索赔权？如果有，依据的合同关系是什么？（3）发货人是否具有索赔权？如果有，条件是什么？讨论上述问题的目的是让学生掌握如何正确判断倒签提单下的索赔人及其权利，防止错误索赔和反驳承运人的不当抗辩。

第三，从损失认定角度，引导学生讨论倒签提单可能给提单持有人带来的各种损失，以便在索赔中正确确定索赔金额。应具体讨论市场差价损失、预期利润损失、转售合同违约索赔等是否均可向倒签提单行为人进行索赔。还应伴随讨论各类损失的鉴定问题，包括由谁进行鉴定，何时何地进行鉴定，最后引导学生回到相关法律规定上来。

第四，从向承运人索赔的角度，引导学生讨论倒签提单索赔的具体操作技能问题。讨论应当包括：采取法律诉讼还是仲裁？如何实施证据保全和扣押船舶？如何向承运人发出损失通知？如何准备索赔证据？如何准备诉讼或仲裁申请书？如何保护索赔时效？如何在索赔过程中正确运用法律和索赔技巧等问题。通过对这些问题的讨论，可以培养学生倒签提单索赔的实战技能。

第五，从向卖方索赔的角度，引导学生讨论倒签提单索赔的具体操作技能问题。讨论应当包括：在倒签提单案件中，除向承运人索赔外，可否向卖方索赔，索赔的法律基础是什么？证据是什么？索赔方式是什么？如何保护索赔时效？本案例中索赔人的教训是什么？通过对这些问题的讨论，让学生掌握倒签提单索赔的第二条途径，以及索赔的实战技能。

通过在上述五个问题的讨论中完成本案例知识点教学任务后，还可以引导学生深入讨论两个延伸问题：一是买卖合同的卖方在因各种原因无法按时交付货物的情况下，可否通过倒签提单继续交付货物？二是在信用证结算中，银行本身可否因提单倒签而止付，或买方可否因提单倒签而要求议付行或开证行止付信用证？

三、理论依据及分析

1. 倒签提单的产生及对买卖合同的影响

倒签提单是在签发提单时，承运人应托运人的要求，将提单的签发日期提前到信用证或买卖合同规定的装船日期。其主要特征是，提单的签发日期早于货物实际装船日期。

倒签提单除极个别的是由于承运人疏忽签错日期之外，绝大多数是应托运人要求而签发的。倒签提单的目的是贸易合同的卖方（实际托运人）为了提单上载明的日期与贸易合同及信用证规定一致，以便在表面上看来履行了合同的交货义务，从而能在信用证下顺利收汇。

《联合国国际货物销售合同公约》及各国的合同法都将卖方交货义务视为合同的重要义务，卖方不能交货或不能按时交货构成根本性违约，买方可以索赔损失甚至取消合同。即使是在货物运抵目的港情况下，如果买方能证明卖方未在合同约定的装运期完成装货，也有权拒收货物。

在信用证支付方式下，根据国际商会制定的《跟单信用证统一惯例》，卖方议付时所提交提单的签发日期必须与信用证规定的装运期一致，如果不符，银行将会拒绝接受该提单，信用证支付方式可能作废，银行信用将会变为商业信用，卖方回收货款的保障程度被降低。正是这种原因，卖方作为货物托运人便在实际装船日晚于规定的交货期时，要求承运人违背事实地填写了提单签发日。

本案例中，C的印度公司延迟交付货物仅为16个小时，但仍然构成延迟交付，因为延迟交付的定义就是货物交付的实际时间超过了合同约定的时间，而没有定义超过了多少时间才算延迟交付。P以及C本来应当本着诚实信用原则及时地将此告知Z，并通过延展合同和信用证的交货期来解决问题。但如果C这样做，在法律上就构成事先违约，Z在市场变得不利的情况下可能就会取消合同，这是C不愿意看到的。因此，C便采取了倒签提单的办法欺瞒Z，对船东H同样也采取了欺瞒的办法。倒签提单的请求本应向承运人提出，但C却向法律意识淡薄且在装货过程中已经忙得昏了头的大副提出，充分显示了他们的"聪明才智"。但是，C的倒签提单行为是违法的，在后来Z在英国提起的仲裁中败诉说明了这一点。

2.倒签提单的法律性质和法律后果

（1）倒签提单的法律性质

从法律性质上看，倒签提单行为是违法的，它同时具备违约性和侵权性。

根据有关法律，一项违约行为必须具备以下要件：第一，违约行为是以合同的有效存在为前提的，没有合同或当事人订立的合同无效，则不存在违约行为基础。第二，违约行为的当事人违反的是自己设立的并针对特定当事人的义务，即违反的是约定义务。第三，违约行为侵害的对象是因合同产生的债权。第四，违约行为的主体是特定的，仅限于合同的当事人。倒签提单的违约性表现在它违反了买卖合同和提单合同约定的义务。就买卖合同而言，卖方有义务按合同及信用证规定的装运日期完成货物装运。《联合国国际货物销售合同公约》及《民法典》都规定，卖方必须按合同规定的日期交货。如果卖方不履行按时交货义务，将构成根本性违约，买方可以解除合同并索赔损失。倒签提单行为背后隐藏的是卖方迟期交货的事实。

就提单合同而言，根据多数国家法律及有关国际公约，提单在转让后，构成承运人与提单持有人间的运输合同。根据《民法典》履行义务人应当遵守诚实信用原则的一般性规定，承运人作为合同一方当事人，应当按照货物装载完毕的日期签发提单。承运人违背事实，虚假签注提单日期，明显构成违约行为。上述两种合同下的违约，侵害了作为合同当事人的买方或提单持有人的合同债权。

倒签提单使买方丧失了撤销合同权利。因倒签提单，致使买方依据虚假的信息继续履行合同，使得卖方在单证相符形式下顺利收得货款，买方最终丧失了及时拒付权利及撤销合同的权利，丧失了对货款的所有权。因此，对造成此种损害的违约行为，应当追究当事人的违约责任。

倒签提单还具有侵权性质。根据民法一般原则，侵权行为的构成有四个要件，即损害事实、行为的违法性、违法行为与损害事实有因果关系、行为人的主观性。认定承运人倒签提单构成侵权是因为：第一，倒签提单行为下的损害事实是相当清楚的。倒签提单掩盖的是迟期交付货物，迟期交付货物必定导致货物迟期抵达目的港，要么导致买方延迟使用，要么导致其错过销售季节，要么导致其对分销合同违约，这都将最终导致买方经济损失。第二，倒签提单行为也是违法行为。诚实、守信是民事行为的最基本原则之一。承运人与托运人合谋，罔顾事实，虚填提单日期，是对善意提单持有人的欺诈行为。第三，在倒签提单下，买方的损失与倒签提单行为有直接关系。本来，在迟期交货情况下，买方有权拒绝接收货物，在市价下跌时，便可避免经济损失。但承运人倒签提单剥夺了买方拒收货物的权利，货款在信用证下被卖方议付，使买方承担了市场差价损失和其他风险。第四，倒签提单是承运人主观有意的行为。承运人在倒签提单时，一般都知道这一行为的违法性及可能造成的不良后果，因而都会要求托运人向其出具保函，保证承运人因此遭受索赔时，托运人予以赔偿。由此可见，倒签提单属承运人主观故意犯错。

（2）倒签提单的法律后果

就运输合同而言，倒签提单可导致承运人面临违约之诉或侵权之诉。《民法典》第186条规定："因当事人一方的违约行为，损害对方人身权益、财产权益的，受损害方有权选择请求其承担违约责任或者侵权责任。"受害人不论提起何种诉讼，倒签提单行为都会给承运人带来一系列严重的法律后果。

首先，承运人将丧失赔偿责任限制权利。在提单合同下，承运人根据《海牙规则》或有关提单法律，享有赔偿责任限制权利。《海商法》第59条规定：经证明，货物的灭失、损坏或者迟延交付是由于承运人的故意或者明知可能造成损失而轻率地作为或者不作为造成的，承运人不得援用本法第56条或者第57条限制赔偿责任的规定。可见，承运人主张赔偿责任限制权利是有前提条件的，即在其履行提单合同义务时不应存在过错。承运人倒签提单，明显属故意行为，该行为使其丧失了上述权利。

其次，承运人可能面临不同的赔偿责任。由于倒签提单可以认定为侵权性质，而侵权责任与违约责任在现行法律制度下存在差别，诉权人就可能选择有利于自己的诉因提起诉讼，使得承运人面临不同的赔偿责任。例如，《民法典》第584条规定："当事人一方不履行合同义务或者履行合同义务不符合约定，造成对方损失的，损失赔偿额应当相当于因违约所造成的损失，包括合同履行后可以获得的利益；但是，不得超过违约一方订立合同时预见到或者应当预见到的因违约可能造成的损失。"该规定最后一句等于为责任人设置了最高赔偿限额，即对承运人无法预见到的损失，即使该损失是由倒签提单行为导致的，承运人也无须作出赔偿。这常常成为承运人的抗辩理由，使被害人无法获得全部损失赔偿。的确，实践中对"预见到或者应当预见到"较难确定。例如，对因货物迟期抵达，导致收货人对转售合同违约所承担的议定的违约赔偿及转售利润，承运人应否预见到？对转售利润应当预见到多少？如承运人主张无法预见，受害人很难对此作出相反举证。但在侵权责任下，当受害人举证证明自己的实际损失时，承运人则难以作出相反举证，因此，赔偿额很可能大于违约责任的赔偿额。

最后，托运人向承运人出具的保函对收货人无效。托运人请求倒签提单时，一般需向承运人出具保函，保证由此引起的承运人任何损失，托运人都予以赔偿。但是，由于倒签提单属合谋欺骗行为，法律不会支持该保函对收货人的效力，承运人将无法得到保函的保障。

通过上述分析可见，倒签提单是一种欺诈性违约、违法行为，会给贸易合同的买方带来损失，也会使承运人背上沉重的法律责任。运输实务中存在着大量的倒签提单做法，应当改变。本案例中，Z对H的诉讼法院之所以能够接受，就是因为H的倒签提单行为既违约又违法。Z在伦敦对C的仲裁，本来Z已经错过了仲裁规则规定的仲裁时效，但仲裁庭考虑到C倒签提单行为的严重违法性，还是接受了Z的仲裁申请。各国法院或仲裁庭对倒签提单案件的审理均表明，倒签提单是违法和违约的，发货人和承运人必须对此行为导致收货人的损失承担赔偿责任。因此，倒签提单绝不是解决卖方延迟交付货物的一剂良药。

3.倒签提单证据获取的良方——海事证据保全

证据保全是海上索赔权利保全，也是海事请求保全的内容之一。海事请求保全是指对海事请求具有管辖权的法院根据海事请求人的申请，为使其海事请求民事权利得以保障，对被申请人的财产（包括证据材料）或行为所采取的民事强制措施。由于海事请求保全与一般的民事请求保全相比具有特殊性，国际上有专门的立法对海事请求保全这种法律行为进行规范。如1952年5月10日签订的《统一扣押海运船舶若干规定的国际公约》，我国也于1999年12月25日通过了《中华人民共和国海事诉讼特别程序法》，对海事请求保全及其审判程序作出专门规定。

海事证据保全是指法院根据海事请求人的申请，对有关海事请求的证据予以提取、保存或者封存的强制措施。船舶上的航海日志、轮机日志、电台日志或其他文字记录通常是在发生货物灭失或损坏事故时确定承运人责任的重要证据。但是船舶的流动性强，对船舶上保存的这些证据如果不能及时提取，极可能被篡改、销毁，或在船舶离港后很难找到。因此，对船上的海事证据依法进行保全，对保障海事请求人权益非常重要。

海事请求人应当在起诉前向保全地法院提出书面申请，说明所要保全的证据、该证据与海事请求的关系，以及申请理由。采取海事证据保全应当符合下列条件：第一，请求人必须是海事请求的当事人；第二，请求保全的证据对该海事请求具有证明作用；第三，被请求人是与请求保全的证据有关的人；第四，情况紧急，不立即采取证据保全就会使该海事请求的证据灭失或难以取得。

本案例中，Z的律师深知海事证据保全的重要性，对海事证据保全的法律规定也非常熟悉，所以，在他的委托人Z化解商业风险的过程中，正确地运用法律武器，及时地向当地海事法院提出了对D轮的证据保全申请，正是这一武器的使用，迫使H向Z提供了15万美元的现金担保，并承诺协助其向C进行索赔。由此可见，海上货物运输中的收货人在发现自己的权利受到承运人侵害时，应当注意使用证据保全的方式，它是证据搜集的一剂良方。

4.保证海事索赔顺利实现的重要方式——扣押当事船舶

（1）船舶扣押的种类

海事保全程序中的船舶扣押分为诉讼前的扣押、诉讼中的扣押和仲裁保全扣押。

诉讼前的扣押属诉前保全措施，它是指在实体争议开始解决之前通过法律程序对船舶实施强制留置措施，其目的是迫使被申请人提供足够担保，保证将来海事请求权利的实现。本案例中Z对D轮的扣押就属于诉讼前的保全措施，这是法律赋予的权利。

诉讼中的扣押是指在实体争议已经交由法院审理，对船舶实施的强制留置措施，其目的是使实体争议的判决得以执行。

仲裁保全扣押是指为了使仲裁裁决得以实现，或者在仲裁开始之前，由申请人向海事法院申请扣押船舶，或在仲裁进行过程中由申请人向仲裁机构申请，再由仲裁机构向海事法院申请，由法院对船舶实施扣押。但是，不管为何目的扣押船舶，都必须向海事法院提出申请，由海事法院进行。

（2）船舶扣押的申请

原告向具有海事案件管辖权的法院申请扣押船舶时，需提出书面申请。申请书应当说明拟扣押船舶的名称和船舶当前所处位置、扣押理由及相关证据、要求被执行人提供担保的种类和金额等项内容。海事法院在考虑接受扣船申请时，可以要求申请人提供担保，作为错误扣船给船舶带来经济损失时的赔偿担保。对申请人在申请扣船时是否必须提供担保，各国法律规定不尽相同。目前，在英国及与英国法律相似的国家，法院在接受扣船申请时一般不要求申请人向法院提供担保，只要法院审查申请人提交的文件，认为扣船理由充足时即可发出扣船令；其他国家的法院为保护船方利益，一般都谨慎地要求申请人提供担保。提供担保的要求增加了申请人申请扣押船舶的难度。但是，由于船舶具有很强的流动性，世界各国法律几乎都规定，对船舶扣押的法律行为不受合同有关法律管辖权规定的限制，申请人可以在世界任一港口向当地的法院申请扣押船舶。申请人可实行"择地诉讼"（forum shopping），选择诸如英国、新加坡以及中国香港等不要求提供担保和法律程序简单的地点向法院申请扣船。本案例中，Z 的几次扣船申请都是符合《中华人民共和国海事诉讼特别程序法》规定的，因此，海事法院在收到 Z 的扣船申请时，很快就作出裁决。

（3）船舶扣押的范围

根据《中华人民共和国海事诉讼特别程序法》的规定，可以扣押的船舶是：第一，当事船舶，但船舶所有人对海事请求需负有责任，并且在实施扣押时是该船的所有人；或者该船舶的光船租赁人，但该光船租赁人需对海事请求负有责任，并且在实施扣押时仍是该船的光船租赁人。第二，可以扣押海事请求责任人所有的任何船舶，包括船舶所有人、光船租赁人、定期租船人或者航次租船人在实施扣押时所有的其他船舶。

（4）船舶扣押的后续措施

在船舶被依法扣押后，被申请人一般会向申请人提供由银行、船舶保险公司或船舶保赔协会出具的赔偿保证书，在收到满意的担保书后，申请人应当立即向法院申请解除扣押，恢复船舶自由。如果被申请人没能提供上述担保，申请人应当在法律规定的扣押时限内（如我国法律规定，海事请求保全扣押船舶的期限为 30 日），提起诉讼或申请仲裁；否则，被申请人可以要求法院解除扣押。海事诉讼或仲裁开始后，上述时限不再适用。当扣押期届满，被申请人又不提供担保，而且船舶不宜继续扣押的，申请人可以在提起诉讼或仲裁后向法院申请拍卖船舶。本案例中，Z对上述法律规定吃得很透，在法律规定的扣押结束期之前，不失时机地在法院提起了诉讼。

5.买方遇倒签提单可否向卖方索赔

从程序上看，倒签提单发生在货物运输合同的履行环节，承运人违反诚实信用法律原则，伪造了提单上的货物装船日期，构成承运人违约行为。但是，发生倒签提单的原因又是买卖合同的卖方未能在约定的交货期内完成货物交付，为了掩盖这一事实，请求承运人倒签提单，这明显构成卖方的严重违约。因此，买方或提单持有人完全可以依据买卖合同向卖方提起违约诉讼。在查明承运人倒签提单后，买方或提单持有人有两条诉讼渠道可以选择：一是选择根据提单合同向承运人提起诉讼；另一条渠道是依据买卖合同向卖方提起诉讼。实践中应在发现倒签提单带来损失后，在这两个方面均作好诉讼或仲裁准备，防止出现本案例中的错过仲裁时效现象。本案例中，Z首先选择了依据提单向承运人H提起倒签提单之诉，如果能够达到索赔目的，就可以不考虑依据买卖合同向卖方提出索赔要求。但遗憾的是，D轮设有银行抵押，使其无法达到全部索赔目的，于是，Z便发起了对C的买卖合同下的倒签提单仲裁。倒签提单之诉总是有以上两种选择的，因为船舶价值较大，又在眼皮底下很容易实施扣押，因此，应当学习Z的做法，首先选择对当事船舶采取措施。

6.如何认定倒签提单保函的法律效力

前文述及了倒签提单的法律性质。在倒签提单行为中，一般来说，发货人都会向承运人出具一份赔付保函，承诺在承运人因此行为遭到他人索赔时，赔付承运人此项损失。但是由于倒签提单的欺诈性质，从各国的司法实践看，法院一般都不承认这种保证的法律效力。在保证人不履行保证承诺时，承运人欲诉诸法律向保证人提出损失赔偿，一般是无法得到法院支持的，因此，倒签提单保函对承运人而言，在绝大多数情况下属于画饼充饥。

四、关键要点

阅读本案例并正确回答讨论思考题，需要学生把握以下要点：

（1）倒签提单在实际业务中司空见惯，但法律难容，买方也难容。

（2）倒签提单构成对买方的欺诈，因此实施人必须承担法律后果。

（3）买方遇倒签提单，可对船舶实施证据保全。

（4）买方遇倒签提单，可以依法扣押当事船舶。

（5）倒签提单也是卖方违反合同行为，买方可以进行违约诉讼。

五、课堂教学计划建议

本案例可以作为专门的案例讨论课来进行。如下是按照时间进度提供的课堂计划建议，仅供参考。

对于本案例教学，建议在给出案例前，教师用50分钟的课堂时间预先讲授相关知识，并在相关知识讲授完毕后，立即给出本案例素材和讨论思考题，然后根据思考题的数量将全班学生分成若干组，每一组分配一个问题，要求各组在课后阅读案例材料，根据所学知识对分配的问题作出分析性答案，并将主要分析依据和结论做成PPT。然后准备100分钟全班同学听取汇报和教师评论。课中计划：

简要的课堂前言，明确主题：2～5分钟

小组发言：每组10～15分钟，控制在80分钟内

引导全班进一步讨论并进行归纳总结：15～20分钟

第六章

共同海损

H海运公司的共同海损分摊索赔

摘要：共同海损既是一种特殊的海上损失，又是海商法中一种特殊的法律制度，该项法律制度和共同海损理算规则是处理海上货物运输风险分担的重要法律原则和国际惯例。本案例正文以H海运公司就其所属G轮发生的共同海损索赔为主线，在介绍了案件发生的背景基础上，详细地描述了G轮共同海损事故的发生情节、各项共同海损费用的产生和处理过程，重点叙述了H海运公司对G轮发生的共同海损费用的详细理算意见，刻画了H作为承运人与美国收货人ADM就该项索赔展开的针锋相对的激烈交锋场景，揭示了共同海损事件的复杂性以及处理共同海损的原则。案例的使用说明部分对案例正文描述的主要情节进行了理论分析和评价，同时提供了案例使用指导。

关键词：共同海损　拖带费用　GA担保　船舶适航

---

1. 本案例描述和分析的H海运公司的共同海损索赔是一个真实的事件，案例编者是当年事件的主要参与者。尽管事件发生在20世纪初，但鉴于事发至今的相关法律规则没有发生实质性变化，因此案例对共同海损问题的教学仍具有使用价值。为了锻炼案例读者的实战能力，案例正文中的部分资料保持了当年的英文原本。由于企业保密的要求，在本案例中对有关当事方做了必要的掩饰性处理。
2. 本案例只供教学之用，并无意明示地或暗示地褒奖或贬低案例中涉及的公司的相关行为。

案例正文

本案例描述的是一起共同海损费用纠纷事件。2001年6月，H海运公司所属的G轮从越南承运美国ADM公司的大米去往海地太子港，航程途中船舶主机曲轴断裂，船东安排了拖带，产生20多万美元的费用。船东宣布共同海损并自己对这项费用作了初步理算。船东要求收货人ADM公司分摊共同海损费用，但后者拒绝承认共同海损的成立。双方为此发生了争议。

1.背景

1.1 G轮的基本情况

G轮是在中国大连注册的H海运公司（以下简称H）所属的一艘普通钢制的可全球航行的杂货船，船舶主要规范如下：

MV G

Nationality：ST Vincent and the Grenadines

Port of registry：Kingstown

Built：1977

16 220 MT DWT on 9.25M

G/N 9806/6023

LOA/BM：149.8/21M，Height 36.4M

Crane：6×10MT

5HO/HA

Hatch size：No.1）12.6×7.8M；No.2）12.75×10.4M；No.3）12.75×10.4M；No.4）17.25×10.4M；No.5）12.75×10.4M.

Grain/Bale capacity：Total：20 406/22 304 CBM；No.1）3 247/2 957 CBM；No.2）4 289/3 931 CBM；No.3）4 337/3 976 CBM；No.4）5 974/5 477；No.5）4 457/4 063

Service speed：13 KN on 18 MT IFO +2 MT MGO

船舶主机特征：

型号和数量：MAN 16V40/54A型柴油机，一套。

额定功率和转速：6 390千瓦，450转/分钟。

曲轴型式：整体式。

曲轴材料：合金钢。

船级检验状况：该轮的船级社检验报告及船舶各项检验证书显示，该轮于2000年6月6日完成船体和轮机的特别检验，下次检验时间为2005年5月25日；2001年3月12日入船厂做过年度修理，修理后船级社对船舶进行了全面的年度检验，各项指标均符合检验标准，船舶处于适航状态，于是签发了各项检验证书，准予正常运营。在该轮发生共同海损事故的当时，船舶所有人申请船级社对船舶进行了临时检验，检验结果显示，该轮当时没有过期的检验，也没有船级方面的不符项。船上配备了具有全球驾驶和管理经验的船长、轮机长以及其他船员，他们均具有有效的适任证书。该轮的航行经历包括亚洲、欧洲、非洲、南美洲的主要港口。

1.2 相关航次运输合同条款摘要

2001年6月19日，H与美国 ADM 大米贸易公司签订了航次租船合同，约定 G 轮从越南胡志明港运输13 000吨大米到海地。合同相关条款如下：

Performing vessel：G

Loading/discharging port：1/2 SBWA HCMC，Vietnam/1/2 SBWA 1/3 SPS Port au Prince and/or Cap Hatien，Haiti and/or SPS Caribbean Ports rotation always GEOG（intention Turbo，Colombia，Port au Prince，Cap Hatien，Haiti）.

Cargo：13 000 MT bagged rice about 52 CUFT/MT to be stowed in M/Holds. Shippers have the option of using second berth.The time for shifting between the tow berths shall count as laytime，but shifting expenses shall be for vessels account.The cargo shall not exceed what the vessel can reasonably stow and carry over and above her bunkers，apparel，stores，provisions and accommodation.The whole cargo shall be carried and stowed under deck. All cargo on board to be delivered.

General average and New Jason clause：General average shall be adjusted according to the York/Antwerp Rules 1990，but where the adjustment is made in accordance with the law and practice of the United States of America，the following clause shall apply："In the event of accident，danger，damage or disaster before or after the commencement of the voyage，resulting from any cause whatsoever，whether due to negligence or not，for which，or for the consequence of which，the carrier is not responsible，by statute，contract or otherwise，the goods，shippers， consignees, or owners of the goods shall contribute with the carrier in general average to the payment of any sacrifices, losses or expenses of a general average nature that may be made or incurred and shall pay salvage and special charges incurred in respect of the goods.If a salving ship is owned or operated by the carrier, salvage shall be paid for as fully as if the said salving ship or ships belonged to strangers. Such deposit as the carrier or his agents may deem sufficient to cover the estimated contribution of the goods and any salvage and special charges thereon shall, if required, be made by the goods, shippers, consignees or owners of the goods to the carrier before delivery".

The charterers shall procure that all Bills of Lading issued under this charterparty shall contain the same clause.

本航次装货后签发的所有提单均为"CONGENBILL"租船合同提单，提单背面条款中的共同海损条款内容如下：

General average shall be adjusted, stated and settled according to York-Antwerp Rules 1994, or any subsequent modification thereof in London unless another place is agreed in the Carter party. Cargo's contribution to General Average shall be paid to the Carrier even when such average is the result of a fault, neglect or error of the Master, Pilot or crew. The Charterers, Shippers and Consignees expressly renounce the Belgian Commercial code, Part II, art.148.

2.航行途中 G 轮主机曲轴发生断裂事故

G轮在合同约定的装货港完成大米装货开始了跨越太平洋航行，并于2001年8月19日抵达第一卸货港口哥伦比亚的Turbo港。2001年8月21日，该轮轮机长安排轮机员对主机进行例行检查。当打开主机曲拐箱时突然箱内有铜屑，轮机员们顿时感到紧张，因为这意味着主轴轴瓦可能发生了融化。进一步仔细检查，轮机员们发现主机曲轴第四道主轴轴瓦部分融化，第四道主轴颈上出现裂纹。轮机长马上明白这是一起严重的事故，主机可能已经无法继续使用了，同时也意味着该轮已经丧失了推进动力，无法继续航行了，于是轮机长立即通过海事卫星向船东报告了这一严重事故。

接到轮机长报告后，船东H也马上意识到问题的严重性，于是立即申请船级社安排验船师登轮检验。船级社验船师登轮检验后出具的检验报告显示：

（1）曲轴第四道主轴颈呈现斜向裂纹一条，长度301mm，几乎横跨整个主轴颈，深度可能达到25mm，裂纹方向与轴向呈45度。发现裂纹后，使用砂轮打磨，开槽至15mm深度后，经着色探伤，仍能清楚发现大部分深度裂纹。在上述裂纹的附近，还存在多条轴向的发纹，长度50mm～100mm不等。

（2）该第四道主轴承上、下轴瓦严重刮磨烧损，已呈现铜底。

（3）船级社意见：船级社验船师在检验报告中建议，就该主机的曲轴及第四道主轴瓦的损坏情况，曲轴已经不能再继续使用，也不宜修复，应予换新，第四道主轴承也应换新。船上剩余的去海地的9 500吨大米只能要么拖航，要么就地卸下转运。就该轮主轴裂纹发生原因，该轮船级社验船师分析认为主要原因是弯曲和扭转疲劳。

3.拖带合同——共同海损费用的产生及共同海损担保

根据当事船舶船级社验船师的意见，经过向加勒比海沿岸国家拖带服务公司的询价和比较，H最终选定了与美国佛罗里达一家海运服务公司S签订了船舶拖带合同。2001年9月17日，在经过船舶适拖检验后，G轮由S所属的E轮拖往海地的太子港。

拖船E轮于2001年9月9日离开佛罗里达，9月16日抵达Turbo港，9月17日开始拖带G轮，9月22日G轮被拖抵太子港，10月10日卸货完毕后被继续拖往Cap Haitien港，10月11日抵达卸货，拖轮返回佛罗里达。拖带服务产生拖带费用共计193 310.13美元。

按照共同海损的要求，船东H要求收货人出具共同海损担保，以保证卸货的顺利进行。Portis Corporate Insurance Marine代表收货人对1A、1B、1C号提单项下的货物（共4 950吨大米）出具共同海损担保，W. K. Webster & Co代表收货人对2号提单项下的货物（共5 013吨大米）出具共同海损担保。根据担保条款，此担保适用英国法，伦敦高等法院对所有争议拥有管辖权，双方应将所有争议不可撤销地提交英国法院（This agreement shall be governed by English Law and the High Court of Justice, London, shall have exclusive jurisdiction over any dispute arising out of this agreement, and each party shall irrevocably submit to the jurisdiction of the English court.)。上述两个担保人出具的共同海损担保原文参见附录1。

4.船东H对共同海损费用的初步理算

当事船东根据租船合同和提单背面条款的规定，对当事船舶发生的共同海损损失和分摊进行了初步理算，结果如下：

（1）拖轮拖带费用 193 310.13美元

（2）与拖带有关的费用 28 095.64美元

（3）船员的工资、伙食费 16 502.87美元

（4）额外消耗的燃料、物料−273.16美元

（5）通信费用 715.62美元

（6）咨询费用 12 489.00美元

（7）垫款手续费 4 692.21美元

（8）共同海损利息 8 943.63美元

总 计：264 475.94美元

船东H认为共同海损分摊价值，船舶的分摊价值为693 000美元，货物的分摊价值为2 739 825美元。共同海损分摊总价值，即船舶分摊价值和货物分摊价值之和为3 432 825美元。

关于共同海损分摊金额，船方分摊共同海损金额应为53 390.96美元，货方分摊共同海损金额应为211 084.98美元。

5.H与ADM的共同海损分摊辩论

H将理算的初步结果通知ADM，要求其分摊当事船舶发生的共同海损费用，租船人委托律师行W.K. Webster & Company作为代理处理此事。该律师行经过初步调查，回函拒绝承认共同海损事件的成立并拒绝分摊船东所谓的共同海损费用。律师行的回复如下：

To：ship owner

Date：29 May 2002

WITHOUT PREJUDICE

Re: MV "G" – General Average – Bs/L 1A–C & 2 dated 5–9 July 2001

We refer to your fax of 15th May in respect of this matter.

Firstly, we have always contested the issue of whether the ship was entitled to declare G.A. as we understand that this decision was taken when the vessel was safely moored alongside at Turbo. As you are no doubt aware, the nature of G.A. is that the ship and cargo must be in peril and immediate danger, which does not exist in these, circumstances. You should be in possession of exchanges with you clients which specifically refer to this, and indeed we would draw your attention to the wording of the Average Guarantee, which also incorporates this reservation.

Secondly, clause 3 of the B/L provides that any G.A. is to be adjusted in London. We note that the Shipowner has decided not to appoint an adjuster due to cost, and whilst we can understand the Shipowners position, we have no alternative but to reserve the right of our Principals in this respect. Notwithstanding this, we have not been provided with any documentary evidence of the amounts you consider would constitute G.A. expenditure or the ship's value that has been used, which will of course be required as a minimum in the event that the ship decides to maintain the claim against cargo.

Thirdly, again entirely without prejudice, we do not know how you have calculated the cargo value. As far as we are concerned, the CIF value of the cargo we represent amounts to US$ 1 300 000 and we understand the CIF value of the cargo represented by Groupe Eyssautier is US$ 1 218 725. However, these are only the CIF values and should not be interpreted as the contributory values, but nevertheless the total value is lower than the value you have used.

By copy of this e-mail to Bruno Duron, it would be appreciated if you could advise all concerned of the contributory value of the cargo you represent, i.e. the C.I.F. value less the value of damaged/short cargo.

As you may be aware, we instructed surveyors to investigate this matter. The advice we have received is, inter-alia, that:

Deflections should be taken every 250 running hours according to the engine manufacturers.

However, deflections were last taken on 14th June 2001, and prior to that on 27th October 2000, which was 1 571 and 1 755 running hours respectively.

Crank web comparators, which are used to measure the main bearing bolts for correct tightening, did not exist on board the vessel.

A tool for measuring the main bearing radial clearance was not on board.

The oil mist detector was not working properly.

In view of the foregoing, it is apparent that the vessel was unseaworthy at the commencement of the voyage, as a result of which cargo interests are entitled to decline contribution, notwithstanding the fact that we do not believe Shipowners are entitled to declare G.A. in any event.

You will of course appreciate that, by virtue of the foregoing, our principals decline to participate in this matter, and indeed will be looking to recover the advance towards towage costs, which was of course made under protest and without prejudice to the right to seek recovery, interest and costs.

We look forward to receiving any comments you may have on the content of this message.

Kind Regards

Assistant Manager

For W. K. Webster & Co

General Average & Casualty Management

接到货方律师行的上述函后，H 作出以下回复意见：

To: W. K. Webster & Co

From: ship owner

Date: 28 June, 2002

Re: MV "G" – General Average – Bs/L 1A–C & 2 dated 5–9 July 2001

Thank you for your E-mail dated 29 May 2002, which has been passed to our clients for their consideration. Please find our comments as lows: You have mentioned in your E-mail that the vessel was safely moored alongside at Turbo and the vessel was not entitled to declare G/A. However, the vessel was not safe due to the fact that the main engine had already been broken down. As to the cargo which was intended to be discharged ports other than Turbo, they were not safe since they would be in peril and immediate danger if the vessel had proceeded her voyage to destination without repair. In view of the same, the vessel declared G/A and asked tug to tow the ship as well as cargo on board to destination ports. For your information, the vessel is still under reparation, and the expenditure would be much greater if the shipowners had not taken towage measure.

As you can understand, our clients have not appointed an adjuster due to the cost and wanted to solve this claim by amicable settlement. So far as the G/A expenditure is concerned, we will provide the relevant document to you after you advise us your mailing address. However, some of the evidence may be in Chinese, translation of which would cost great amount of money. Enclosed please kindly find the quoted price report (Annex I) made by broker to certify the ship's value.

It is obvious that the cargo interests should produce the evidence of the cargo value. Since it is not available to our clients at this stage, we only use the value in a claim letter from the cargo insurer (see Annex II) as a reference. We should be grateful if you could provide us reliable evidence of the cargo value and will adjust our calculation accordingly.

We strongly object your allegation of ship's unseaworthiness on the following ground:

The requirement of checking deflection every 250 running hours is for engine newly built or right after overhaul, which is not in this claim. As you may be aware, the common practice of checking deflection is to inspect the engine on departure and arrival of each voyage, and the shipowners had done accordingly (see Annex III). The deflection figure they took on 14 June 2001 at Hong Kong where the voyage began was same with that they took on 21 August 2001 in Turbo.

While the crank web comparators was sail not on board by your surveyors, the reason is that the crew have been using dial gauge which is also a efficiently functional tool for every checking to measure the main bearing bolts for correct tightening. The record shows the elongation is 0.75mm and it is normal.

Although the tool for measuring the main bearing radial clearance was alleged not on board, the crew monitor the same by reading the crank web deflection because any change of radial clearance of wear and tear can be reflected by deflection and the deflection took by the crew was normal, hence the radial clearance is normal.

For oil mist detectors, it was in normal working condition before and at the time the voyage began. For detail, we refer you to the enclosed report from the C/E (Annex IV).

Seeing the above, we cannot agree with your position for G/A. The shipowners are entitled to declare G/A in this case, and have spent a great amount of money to save the cost and expenses from cargo interests, thus should be reimbursed. Our proposal of not appointing a G/A adjuster is for the mutual benefits of both sides, and we will be compelled to appoint an adjuster if we could not reach an amicable settlement.

We look forward to receiving your comments.

Best regards

对上述船东的回函，货方律师复函如下：

To: ship owner

From: W. K. Webster & Co

Date: 12 July 2002

WITHOUT PREJUDICE

Re: MV "G" – General Average – Bs/L 1A–C & 2 dated 5–9 July 2001

We refer to your fax of 28 June in respect of this matter.

The vessel and the cargo were not in peril and immediate danger when the owners attempted to declare General Average.

The vessel was safely moored. Whilst we can only agree with your comments that the ship and cargo would likely have been in peril and immediate danger had the vessel attempted to complete the voyage, we do not believe the vessel would have been able to leave port given the engine damage that existed.

The operative aspect of this incident is that the vessel was safely moored in port, and as the vessel was unable to complete the contractual voyage, you should have fulfilled your obligations under the Contract of Carriage and arranged for the cargo to be taken to destination at their expense. Instead, you attempted to have this matter dealt with as General Average.

Additionally, you exerted duress on cargo interests in order to get cargo interests to make a contribution to the towage costs to the cargoes destinations. Although cargo interests paid a contribution, this payment was made under reservation and indeed the G/A security that was provided incorporated the reservation to the effect that this was not a General Average matter.

We have no doubt that if you were to appoint an Adjuster to deal with this matter in accordance with the provisions of the Contract of Carriage, you would receive confirmation that we are correct in our conclusions contained in 1. above. As mentioned in our e-mail of 29 May 2002, the Bill of Lading provides that any General Average is to be adjusted in London and we have reserved the rights of our Principals in this respect.

Entirely without prejudice to the foregoing, we attach a copy of the Commercial Invoice evidencing the value of the cargo that we represent. The annexe to your fax of 28 June 2002 relates to the cargo represented by Groupe Eyssautier and we must leave it to Groupe Eyssautier to provide you with any documentation relating to the evidence of their cargo value.

You may well object to our allegation that the ship was unseaworthy at the commencement of the voyage, but the fact remains that the burden of proof rests with you to prove that you have complied with all obligations under the Contract of Carriage.

In so far as checking deflections is concerned, we wonder where you obtained the information that this is only required for new or overhauled engines. The fact remains that the engine manufacturer's instructions state that the deflections are to be taken every 250 running hours, which means throughout the life of the engine. Although deflections may well have been taken at departure and arrival on each voyage, the fact remains that this does not comply with the manufacturer's instructions, which on its own makes the vessel unseaworthy.

We note what you say with regard to the crew using a dial gauge, which would of course be in order if the engine manufacturers approved of such a tool. The fact is that the engine manufacturers do not refer anywhere to using a dial gauge or indicator, but they do require crank web comparators to be used. At the dry docking when No.4 and 5 main bearings were no readings for bolt elongation listed in the report.

Consequently, there was no way for the engine room staff to check whether the main bearing bolts were properly tightened in accordance with the engine manufacturer's advice.

We note what you say about using the correct tool and the crew monitoring crank web deflections. Taking crank web deflections does not give the actual main bearing radial clearance and if taking deflections were all that was needed, then there would be no need to ever take the measurement of the main bearing radial clearance. We understand that even if the deflections were satisfactory, the main bearing clearances could still be too large or too small.

You state that the oil mist detector was in normal working condition at the time the voyage began. When tested, the oil mist detector did not give the full deflection reading which would set off the alarm, and according to the Chief Engineer, there was no alarm that sounded to indicate problems with the main engine. The fact remains that when the oil mist detector was tested, it failed to go to the full deflection of 30 which causes the alarm to sound. It is our understanding that an overheating bearing will cause an increase in the mist density in the crankcase and consequently the alarm should sound.

Summary

It is clear that the lack of manufacturer approved tools and partially inoperative detection equipment is sufficient to render the vessel unseaworthy, apart from the fact that deflections were not taken as per the engine manufacturer's instructions. All of this is, of course, notwithstanding the fact that we are of the clear opinion that the vessel owners were not entitled to declare General Average in these circumstances.

Consequently, there is no obligation whatsoever on cargo interests to consider making any contribution to you and indeed, as mentioned in our previous e-mail, we are instructed to pursue recovery of the towage contribution paid under duress.

Best regards

Assistant Manager

For & on behalf of W K WEBSTER & CO

General Average & Casualty Management

货方进一步复函提供了一个英国法院判例，试图证明本案例中当事船舶是不适航的。

To：Ship owners

From：W K WEBSTER & CO

Date：26 July 2002

WITHOUT PREJUDICE

Re：MV "G" – General Average – Bs/L 1A–C & 2 dated 5–9 July 2001

We thank you for your fax dated 28 June（which we assume should have read 26 July）received today in response to our fax of 12 July 2002 in respect of the subject matter. Coincidentally，Lloyds Law Reports have recently published the decision on the KAMSAR VOYAGER，a copy of which we attach for your guidance. We are only sending a copy of the first part of that decision，which we believe to be relevant to the subject case，whereas the second part of the judgement dealt with the effect of the damage caused when the ship's engineers used an incorrect spare part，which is not relevant to this case.

We trust you appreciate the relevance of this decision to the GRAND ORIENT，and trust you will appreciate that whether or not Owners appoint an adjuster，and whether or not an adjustment is prepared，our Principals will continue to repudiate Owner's claim.

Best regards

6.讨论思考题

（1）共同海损与一般海损有何区别？其构成条件是什么？

（2）共同海损包括哪两个主要方面？具体内容有哪些？

（3）船舶适航和共同海损担保在共同海损案件处理中起什么作用？

（4）应如何进行共同海损分摊？

（5）本案例中H主张的共同海损是否成立？

（6）本案例中ADM的几个主张是否合理？

（7）H的拖带决定是否合理？

（8）H的理算是否合理？

7.参考文献

［1］英国1992年海上货物运输法［EB/OL］．［2025-01-10］．http：//wenku.baidu.com/view/e0443f18964bcf84b9d57b0f.html.

［2］中华人民共和国海商法［EB/OL］．［2025-01-10］．中华人民共和国海商法_相关规定_中国政府网．

［3］司玉琢．海商法［M］．5版．北京：法律出版社，2023.

［4］杨良宜，杨大明，杨大志．合约的履行、弃权与禁反言［M］．北京：法律出版社，2018.

［5］李勤昌．国际货物运输［M］．6版．大连：东北财经大学出版社，2022.

［6］李勤昌．提单的若干概念及其法律问题［J］．国际商务，2010（1）.

［7］杨良宜．合约的解释规则与运用［M］．北京：法律出版社，2020.

［8］李勤昌．论海运提单的运输合同属性［J］．世界海运，2002（5）.

8.附录

附录1　ADM提供的共同海损担保

WKW
W K Webster

AVERAGE GUARANTEE

TO: The Owners of the Vessel named below and other parties to the adventure as their interests may appear.

VESSEL: MV "GRAND ORIENT"
VOYAGE: From: Ho Chi Minh City   To: Port-Au-Prince / Cap Haitien, Haiti

In consideration of the delivery in due course of the goods specified below to the consignees thereof without collection of a deposit, we, the undersigned insurers, hereby undertake to pay to the shipowners or to the appointed Average Adjusters, on behalf of the various parties to the adventure as their interests may appear, any contribution to General Average and/or Salvage and/or Special Charges which may hereafter be ascertained to be properly due in respect of the said goods.

We further agree:-

(a)   to make prompt payment(s) on account of such contribution as may be reasonably and properly due in respect of the said goods, as soon as the same may be certified by the said Average Adjusters.

(b)   to furnish to the said Average Adjusters at their request all information which is available to us relative to the value and condition of the said goods.

For the avoidance of doubt, we do not accept there has been any General Average act or expenditure, and the obligations in this agreement are undertaken without prejudice to this contention.

In any event, our liability under this agreement shall not exceed the sum of US$75 000.00 in respect of General Average expenditure which owners have solely incurred including the costs of towage and other related expenses. US$50 000 has been paid by the receivers towards these costs and will form a credit in their favour in respect of cargo's proportion of any amounts which are allowable in General Average.

This agreement shall be governed by English Law and the High Court of Justice, London, shall have exclusive jurisdiction over any dispute arising out of this agreement, and each party shall irrevocably submit to the jurisdiction of the English Court.

Port of Loading	Port of Discharge	Bill of Lading	Quantity and Description of Goods	Insured Value	Policy Ref No. & Premium (if known)
Ho Chi Minh City, Vietna	Port-Au-Prince, Haiti	No. 2	5 013.00 metric tons (net weight) / 100 000 bags vietnamese long grain white rice	$1 430 000	

For and on behalf of Insurers:

FM Global
500 River Ridge Drive
NORWOOD MA 02062
United States of America

W K WEBSTER & CO   (As Agents)   Date: 28 September 2001

AVERAGE GUARANTEE

TO: The Owners of the Vessel named below and other parties to the adventure as their interests may appear.

VESSEL: M/V "GRAND ORIENT"
VOYAGE: From: Ho Chi Minh City To: Port-Au-Prince / Cap Haitien, Haiti

In consideration of the delivery in due course of the goods specified below to the consignees thereof without collection of a deposit, we, the undersigned insurers, hereby undertake to pay to the shipowners or to the appointed Average Adjusters, on behalf of the various parties to the adventure as their interests may appear, any contribution to General Average and/or Salvage and/or Special Charges which may hereafter be ascertained to be properly due in respect of the said goods.

We further agree:-

(a) to make prompt payment(s) on account of such contribution as may be reasonably and properly due in respect of the said goods, as soon as the same may be certified by the said Average Adjusters.

(b) to furnish to the said Average Adjusters at their request all information which is available to us relative to the value and condition of the said goods.

For the avoidance of doubt, we do not accept there has been any General Average act or expenditure, and the obligations in this agreement are undertaken without prejudice to this contention.
In any event, our liability under this agreement shall not exceed the sum of US$75 000.00 in respect of General Average expenditure which owners have solely incurred including the costs of towage and other related expenses. US$50,000 has been paid by the receivers towards these costs and will form a credit in their favour in respect of cargo's proportion of any amounts which are allowable in General Average.
This agreement shall be governed by English Law and the High Court of Justice, London, shall have exclusive jurisdiction over any dispute arising out of this agreement, and each party shall irrevocably submit to the jurisdiction of the English Court.

Port of Loading	Port of Discharge	Bill of Lading	Quantity and Description of Goods	Insured Value	Policy Ref No. & Premium (if known)
Ho Chi Minh City, Vietnam	Cap Haitien, Haiti	No. 1A	2 000.00 MT (net) / 40 000 bags vietnamese long grain white rice		
		No. 1B	2 500.00 MT (net) / 50 000 bags vietnamese long grain white rice		
		No. 1C	450.00 MT (net) / 9 000 bags vietnamese long grain white rice		

SIGNATURE OF INSURERS: .... STAMP

NAME AND ADDRESS: FORTIS CORPORATE INSURANCE (Where

DE KEYSERLEI 5 BUS 6 Required)

20 18 ANTWERP BELGIUM

....

Tel. No.: +323 222 27 23 Fax No.: +323 222 27 10

Email: .... Telex No.: ....

DATE: ....28/09/01.........

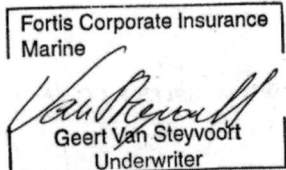

Fortis Corporate Insurance
Marine

Geert Van Steyvoort
Underwriter

附录 2　英国法院 The "Kamsar Voyager" 判例节选

[2002] Vol. 2　　　　LLOYD'S LAW REPORTS　　　　57

Q.B. (Com. Ct.)]　　　　**The "Kamsar Voyager"**　　　　PART 1

QUEEN'S BENCH DIVISION
(COMMERCIAL COURT)

July 2, 3, 4, 6; Aug. 10, 2001

———

GUINOMAR OF CONAKRY AND ANOTHER
v.
SAMSUNG FIRE & MARINE INSURANCE
CO. LTD.
(THE "KAMSAR VOYAGER")

Before His Honour Judge DEAN, Q.C.

**General average — Contribution — Unseaworthiness
— Due diligence — Vessel sustained major engine
breakdown necessitating towage — Owners claimed
general average contribution from cargo interests —
Whether owners failed to exercise due diligence to
ensure vessel seaworthy — Whether cargo interests
liable to contribute.**

The claimants' vessel *Kamsar Voyager* was a bulk
carrier of 36 526 grt and 21 783 nrt and at the material
time was trading under the Norwegian flag and classed
with DNV. She was managed by Torvald Klaveness &
Co. A/S of Norway. The main engine was built by
Mitsubishi Heavy Industries Ltd. (MHI) under licence
from the engine designers MAN.

The vessel was in the course of a voyage with a part
cargo of soybeans shipped at Reserve and Westwego,
Louisiana under five bills of lading dated July 27, 1995
and eight bills of lading dated July 30, 1995 for carriage
to Inchon in Korea. The contract of carriage evidenced
by the bills of lading included a clause paramount
incorporating the U.S. Carriage of Goods by Sea Act,
1936 with the consequence that the Hague Rules
became terms of the contract. The contract further
provided by cl. 5 that:

> General Average shall be payable according to the
> York/Antwerp Rules 1974 as amended 1990 . . . If
> the owner shall have exercised due diligence to make
> the steamer in all respects seaworthy and have her
> properly manned, equipped and supplied, it is hereby
> agreed that in case of . . . damage . . . resulting
> from . . . any latent defect in the steamer, her machin-
> ery or appurtenances or from unseaworthiness . . .
> the owners of the cargo . . . shall contribute to
> shipowner in General Average . . .

On Aug. 21, 1995 white smoke was observed leaking
from the crankcase. On Aug. 24 and 25 the oil mist
alarm sounded and the engine stopped. The ship's
engineers were unable to identify the cause of the
problem and contacted MAN who advised taking cylinder compression tests. These revealed low pressure in
cylinders Nos. 1 and 5.

On Aug. 28 cylinder No. 1 was opened up and after
the piston was withdrawn and cleaned a visual examination revealed extensive cracking extending from the
aluminium piston skirt up to the steel piston crown. The
vessel had a spare piston on board which had been

ordered by Klaveness from MAN in March, 1995 and
delivered by MAN to the vessel at Piraeus in April,
1995. The spare piston was fitted to cylinder No. 1 and
the engine gradually worked up to its full service speed
in the early hours of Aug. 29 when unusual noises were
heard from the engine followed by stoppage of the
engine and severe physical damage to No. 1 unit and
consequential damage to No. 2 unit caused by water
leakage and hydraulic shock. The vessel was immobil-
ized at sea and had to be towed to Yokohama for
repairs.

Metallurgical investigation showed that the first incident was due to propagation of a fracture by fatigue
cracking up the vertical side of the piston skirt into the
piston skirt in way of the support piston ring groove.
The original defect was due to a fault in the manu-
facture of the piston skirt and the crack had developed
over the service life of the piston.

The major damage to the engine had been caused
after the spare piston had been fitted because the
dimensions of the spare were not compatible with the
ship's main engine.

The owners proclaimed general average (G.A.) and
claimed the balance of cargo interest's proportion said
to be due under a G.A. adjustment made in London in
March, 1996.

The claim was made against the cargo insurers as
defendants under the terms of the average guarantees
given by the cargo insurers in respect of delivery of the
cargo to the consignees against customary average
bonds.

The defendants resisted the claim on the grounds that
no contribution was properly due from the cargo
interests as the G.A. expenditure was caused by the
actionable fault of the owners in failing to exercise due
diligence to ensure that *Kamsar Voyager* was seaworthy
before the beginning of the voyage in breach of the
terms of the contract of carriage contained in and
evidenced by the bills of lading.

The issues for decision were (1) whether the vessel
was unseaworthy on sailing by reason of the presence
on board of the spare pistons with dimensions that were
not compatible with the MHI version of the MAN
engine; (2) whether, the vessel being unseaworthy by
reason of the crack in No. 1 piston, the defendants were
relieved of the need to prove that this was a cause of the
G.A. expenditure by reason of cl. 5 in the bill of lading
and whether the failure of the No. 1 piston was a cause
of the G.A. expenditure; (3) whether the claimants had
established that due diligence was exercised to make
the ship seaworthy notwithstanding the presence on
board of the cracked No. 1 piston and/or the inap-
propriate spare piston.

———*Held*, by C.L.C.C. (B.L.) (Judge DEAN,
Q.C.), that (1) the Court was not satisfied that the
owners had satisfied the burden of proving that they
exercised due diligence; the risk materialized and could
have been avoided by, at the very least, adhering to the
cylinder service interval set by both MHI and Klaveness between February and early July, 1995; nothing in
the maintenance history could justify extending this
period; if the routine maintenance prescribed had been
followed the crack in the No. 1 piston would have been

found and attended to before it made itself manifest in August during the voyage (*see* p. 64, cols. 1 and 2);

(2) the experts agreed that the failure of the No. 1 piston did not cause consequential damage to the rest of the engine and that the No. 1 unit could have been isolated so that the vessel could have completed the voyage under her own power; however, there would have been no need to install the spare if the original piston had not failed at sea; although the installation of a defective spare was not reasonably foreseeable as such, if the vessel carried a spare, as a prudent shipowner would have done, its use was inevitable; accordingly the failure of the original piston was not simply an occasion giving rise to the opportunity to install the spare whose causative force had been spent; it was an operative cause that was indeed the only reason for the use of the only relevant spare part on board the vessel; it was thus causative of the installation of the spare part and the subsequent immobilization of the vessel at sea (*see* p. 64, col. 2; p. 67, col. 1);

(3) the vessel was unseaworthy by the presence on board of the unsuitable spare piston which would have damaged the engine if fitted during the voyage (*see* p. 67, col. 2);

(4) no criticism was or could have been made of the way the owners ordered the spare piston from MAN; and no criticism was made of the owners for failing to notice the difference in the height of the piston pin securing the top end of the connecting rod in the piston skirt or of the installation of the spare during the voyage (*see* p. 68, col. 1);

(5) on the evidence, if the owners bore the legal burden of proving that MAN exercised due diligence to supply the vessel with the correct spare piston they were quite unable to do so (*see* p. 69, col. 1);

(6) the submission by the defendants that the duty to exercise due diligence to make the ship seaworthy under the Hague Rules was a contractual promise by the carrier that due diligence had been exercised by any person who had been concerned in the task of making the ship seaworthy, whether that be the carrier personally, his servants, agents or independent contractors, was correct; the owners had failed to prove that MAN exercised due diligence in and about the supply of the incompatible spare piston; the owners had not satisfied the burden on them under art. III, r. 1 of the Hague Rules of proving the exercise of due diligence to make *Kamsar Voyager* seaworthy and were responsible for her unseaworthiness at the commencement of the voyage in respect of both the cracked piston in No. 1 unit and the incompatible spare piston on board which was supplied by MAN; the G.A. expenditure was caused by their actionable fault and they were unable to recover the cargoes' proportion from the defendant insurers under the average guarantees (*see* p. 69, col. 1; p. 71, col. 2).

————The *Muncaster Castle*, [1961] 1 Lloyd's Rep. 57, applied.

The following cases were referred to in the judgment:

Angliss (W.) & Co. (Australia) Pty. Ltd. v. P. & O. Steam Navigation Co., (1927) 28 Ll.L.Rep. 202; [1927] 2 K.B. 456;

Davie v. New Merton Board Mills Ltd., [1959] 2 Lloyd's Rep. 587; [1959] A.C. 604;

Evje (No. 2), The [1976] 2 Lloyd's Rep. 715;

Galoo Ltd. v. Bright Grahame Murray, (H.L.) [1994] 1 W.L.R. 1360;

Irrawaddy, The (1897) 171 U.S. 187;

Isis, The (1938) 48 Ll.L.Rep. 35;

Jason, The (1911) 225 U.S. Rep. 24;

Monarch Steamship Co. Ltd. v. A/B Karlshams Oljefabriker, (H.L.) (1948) 82 Ll.L.Rep. 137; [1949] A.C. 196;

Riverstone Meat Co. Pty. Ltd. v. Lancashire Shipping Co. Ltd. (The *Muncaster Castle*), (H.L.) [1961] 1 Lloyd's Rep. 57; [1961] A.C. 807;

Smith Hogg & Co. v. Black Sea & Baltic General Insurance Co. Ltd., (H.L.) (1940) 67 Ll.L.Rep. 253; [1940] A.C. 997.

———————

This was an action by the claimants Guinomar of Conakry and Baraka Inc. the owners of the vessel *Kamsar Voyager* claiming against the defendants Samsung Fire & Marine Insurance Co. Ltd. as insurers of the part cargo of soybeans shipped at Reserve and Westwego in Louisiana for carriage to Inchon, Korea, in respect of cargo interests' proportion said to be due under a general average adjustment, the vessel having sustained a main engine breakdown necessitating towage to Yokohama for repairs.

Mr. Stephen Males, Q.C. (instructed by Messrs. Ince & Co.) for the claimants; Mr. T. Brenton, Q.C. (instructed by Messrs. Clyde & Co.) for the defendants.

The further facts are stated in the judgment of His Honour Judge Dean, Q.C.

Judgment was reserved.

Thursday Aug. 10, 2001

———————

JUDGMENT

Judge DEAN, Q.C.: 1. In this action the owners of *Kamsar Voyager* seek to recover U.S.$135,520.91 from the insurers of a part cargo of soybeans shipped at Reserve and Westwego in Louisiana under five bills of lading dated July 27, 1995 and eight bills of lading dated July 30, 1995 for carriage to Inchon in Korea. During the voyage the vessel sustained a main engine breakdown necessitating

9.案例英文信息

A Claim for G.A.Contribution by H Shipping Company Ltd

Abstract：General average （G.A.） is both a special kind of maritime loss and a special arrangement in maritime law.Legal rules and adjustment rules in this respect are important rule of law and international customs and practice in contributing risks in marine transport. With the subject of G.A. expenditure contribution claim by H Shipping Company encountered by their ship MV G，and the introduction of the background of this claim，this case describes in details the happening of the accident of G.A.in nature，the occurrence of G.A.expenditure.Emphasis is put on the particulars of the preliminary adjustment made by H Shipping Co. Ltd of the expenditure incurred in the towing to MV G.The case reveals the pierce struggle between H Shipping Co.Ltd and ADM，an American cargo receiver，for the whether-or-not of the contribution of the G.A.expenditure.The second part of this case is the theoretical analysis and comments by the writer.

Key words：G.A.，towing expense，G.A.bond，seaworthiness of ship

案例使用说明

一、教学目的与用途

　　本案例适用于国际货物买卖合同和国际货物运输合同中关于共同海损问题的教学，通过案例讨论，使学生掌握共同海损的概念、共同海损的构成条件、共同海损的计算方法与分摊方法等知识，以便学生在未来的实际工作中正确运用相关准则和方法，合理地计算和分摊共同海损牺牲和费用问题。

　　本案例适用于"国际贸易实务"、"国际货物运输"和"国际物流"课程中关于共同海损知识点的教学。案例的编写目的是，通过案例中描述的争议焦点讨论，引导学生领会有关共同海损的法律规定和国际惯例，培养学生处理共同海损问题的实践能力。通过阅读、分析和讨论本案例资料，引导学生思考和掌握下列具体问题：一是共同海损与一般海损的本质区别；二是共同海损的法定构成条件；三是共同海损费用的理算；四是承运人共同海损索赔的前提条件。

本案例的概念难度、分析难度和陈述难度均适中，适用对象包括国际贸易专业、国际物流专业和国际商务专业的本科生、研究生和国际商务专业学位研究生。对于缺乏专业基础理论知识的本科生，可以根据教学大纲，有选择地引导阅读案例相关材料，重点熟悉共同海损的概念，掌握共同海损的构成条件和承运人索赔的前提条件；对于缺乏实践经验的研究生，可以引导其将所掌握的理论知识运用于本案例每一个具体问题的分析，对案例中争论的几个焦点问题，作出自己的是非判断，锻炼其处理实际问题的能力。

本案例规划的理论教学知识点包括：

（1）共同海损的概念和特点；

（2）共同海损的法定构成条件；

（3）相关国际惯例关于共同海损费用的理算规则；

（4）各国海商法关于共同海损的法律规定。

本案例规划的能力训练教学内容包括：

（1）判定一项海损是否为共同海损的能力；

（2）共同海损担保出具的组织能力；

（3）共同海损证据的收集能力；

（4）共同海损的初步理算能力；

（5）应对承运人共同海损索赔的能力。

二、分析思路

本案例争议的核心问题是 G 轮的主机曲轴断裂是否构成共同海损事件，以及 H 的理算是否合理和 G 轮是否适航。本案例的教学知识点是共同海损的概念、构成条件和理算原则。因此，建议案例讨论按照下列思路展开：

第一，引导学生讨论有关共同海损的一般性法律问题。具体分析：共同海损的概念是什么？与一般海损有何区别？共同海损的构成条件有哪些？共同海损包括哪些主要事件或费用？共同海损牺牲或费用应当如何分摊？共同海损担保的意义是什么？共同海损理算规则的主要内容是什么？

第二，讨论 G 轮的共同海损是否成立。涉及的具体问题有：G 轮主机事故及其后果是什么？事故原因是什么？事故威胁船舶和货物的共同安全吗？拖带安排是 H 的主观有意安排吗？以拖带替代转运合理吗？拖带取得良好效果了吗？

第三，讨论 H 的理算是否合理。涉及的具体问题有：H 的理算合理吗？船舶的分摊价值合理吗？货物的分摊价值合理吗？

第四，讨论 G 轮是否适航问题。涉及的具体问题有：轮机员对主机曲轴间隙的例行检测时间间隔符合主机保养手册每 250 小时检测一次的要求吗？轮机员以千分尺代替曲轴间隙检测专业工具可能导致该次事故吗？烟雾报警器失灵了吗？ADM 提供的英国 Voyger 判例适用于本案吗？

上述问题讨论完后，引导学生讨论两个延伸问题：一是共同海损的索赔时效有何规定？二是 H 可以就没有收回的 ADM 应当分摊的共同海损费用向保险公司索赔吗？

三、理论依据及分析

1.共同海损的含义与性质

共同海损（general average）有两层意思。作为海上损失，它是指在同一海上航程中，当船舶、货物和其他利益遭遇到共同危险时，为了共同安全，船方有意地、合理地采取避险措施而人为造成的特殊牺牲或支付的特殊费用。作为一种法律制度，它是指确定共同海损行为、共同海损牺牲和费用以及共同海损分摊的原则。

一般情况下，国际保险界将海上损失分为全部损失和部分损失。而部分损失又分为单独海损（particular average）和共同海损（general average）。由于自然灾害、意外事故造成的船舶或货物损坏，属于单独海损。但为摆脱自然灾害、意外事故对船货造成的共同威胁，船长有意采取的合理避险措施，造成的船舶或货物损失或产生的特殊费用就属于共同海损。共同海损在海上风险保险制度中是一种特殊的风险，经过上千年的发展过程，逐渐形成了一套不同于一般海上风险的特殊法律制度。

本案例中，承运人 H 之所以要求货方 ADM 公司提供共同海损担保并在对共同海损费用初步理算后要求 ADM 公司分摊该项费用，其依据的就是国际上通行的，也是航次租船合同和提单中约定的共同海损分摊制度。在该项制度下，即使共同海损事故中发生的费用不是 ADM 公司造成的，它也应当分摊该项费用。

2.共同海损事件的构成条件

共同海损与单独海损经常相伴发生。在遇到共同危险时，或在实施共同海损措施时，常常存在单独海损。因此，必须确立一定的原则加以区分，防止将单独海损当作共同海损处理。一项海损事件只有符合下列条件时才构成共同海损。

（1）危及船货共同安全的危险必须是真实存在的。主观臆断的危险不是真实的危险，船长主观臆断存在危险而作出的牺牲和产生的费用不得算作共同海损。

（2）采取的措施必须是有意的与合理的。所谓有意的措施（intentional act），是指船长在主观上明知采取该种措施会导致船舶或货物的进一步损失，但为了避免船货的共同危险，而不得不采取的行为。所谓合理的措施（reasonable act），是指本着以最小的牺牲换取船货安全的原则而采取的措施。一项措施是否合理，没有绝对的标准，应综合考虑周围的客观条件、方案的可行性和客观效果。

（3）作出的牺牲和支付的费用必须是特殊的。在非正常情况下，因船长在法定义务或合同义务之外采取措施所造成的损失和支付的费用，称为特殊牺牲和特殊费用（extraordinary sacrifice and expenditure），此种牺牲和费用应列入共同海损。

在本案例中，H 为了说明自己的共同海损索赔是合理的，从上述 3 个方面阐明了 G 轮的拖带费用以及其他相关费用符合上述 3 个条件，因而构成共同海损费用。

3.共同海损的范畴

根据国际上的共同海损理算规则，共同海损可划分为共同海损牺牲和共同海损费用两种基本类型。

共同海损牺牲（sacrifice of general average）是指由共同海损措施所直接造成的船舶、货物或其他财产在形态上的灭失或损害。抛弃货物（jettison of cargo）及抛弃货物所引起的财产的进一步损失，扑灭船上火灾（extinguishing fire on shipboard）所造成的损失，割弃残损物（cutting away wreck）所造成的损失，有意搁浅所致的损害（damage done by voluntary stranding），机器和锅炉的损害（damage to engines and boilers），作为燃料而使用的货物、船用材料和物料（cargo，ship's material and stores used for fuel）损失，在卸货等过程中造成的损害（damage to cargo in discharging，etc.）等应列入共同海损。

共同海损费用（general average expenditure）是指为采取共同海损措施而支付的额外费用，主要有下列几种：①救助报酬（salvage remuneration）。②搁浅船舶减载费用以及因此遭受的损坏（expense in lightening a ship when ashore，and consequent damage）。③避难港费用（expense in port of refuge）。当船舶因意外事故、牺牲或其他特殊情况，为了共同安全而进入避难港口（包括驶回原来的装货港）发生的费用，应列入共同海损。避难港费用包括：进入避难港的费用与驶离避难港的费用（如果该避难港不是原定的挂靠港口）；从出事地点驶入避难港直至驶回原出事地点期间的航程延长费用；为共同安全需要，或为安全完成航程而对船舶进行修理时所发生的货物、燃料或物料的倒载、卸下、存储（包括保险）和重装费用。④驶往和停留在避难港等地支付给船员的工资、伙食费及其他开支（如驶往、停留和驶离避难港期间所发生的燃料费、物料费、港口费）。⑤修理费用（expense in repairs）。⑥替代费用（substituted expenses）。替代费用是为了节约或取代原应列入共同海损的费用而支出的费用。例如，为了节省船舶在避难港的费用，支付给修理工人的加班费；为节省船舶进入避难港修理等费用而采用拖带所产生的拖带费用。⑦垫款手续费和保险费（provision of funds，commission and the cost of insuring）。⑧共同海损利息（interest on losses in general average）。共同海损措施造成的牺牲和支付的费用一般要经过很长的时间才能分摊回来。对这些费用的利息应计算为共同海损。《1994年约克-安特卫普规则》规定，应按年息7%计算。⑨理算费用（adjustment fee）。共同海损因涉及的项目特别复杂，通常都由专门的理算机构进行理算，为此支付的费用应列入共同海损。

本案例中，G轮在此次共同海损事故中并没有发生共同海损牺牲，但为了船货的共同安全，安排了拖轮将G轮和货物一起拖到目的港。本来，拖带费用不是共同海损制度中列明的项目，但拖带费用替代了为了船货的共同安全所应当进行的临时性修理的费用，根据理算规则，该项替代费用可以列入共同海损费用。H的这项安排和费用计算是符合共同海损理算规则的。

4.船舶适航与共同海损的关系

多数共同海损是由于出租人的过失引起的。出租人过失可分为可免责的过失和不可免责的过失，二者导致的共同海损法律后果完全不同。

可免责的过失是指承运人虽有过失，但依据法律或海上运输合同的规定，承运人可以免除赔偿责任的这类过失。在《海牙规则》规定的承运人17项免责事项中，与共同海损最相关的是船长、船员在驾驶船舶和管理船舶过程中的过失免责。因船长、船员在驾驶船舶方面的过失导致的共同海损，出租人可以要求货方参加分摊。

不可免责的过失是指法律或运输合同规定的免责范围以外的过失，例如未提供适航的船舶、运输中未尽快派遣船舶、不合理绕航等。由于上述承运人过失导致的共同海损，其他利益方无须参加共同海损分摊。

根据上述法律，本案例中，货方ADM认为G轮的曲轴断裂是船舶不适航导致的，根据上述法律，H无权向他主张共同海损分摊。ADM的律师为了说明这一点，还转送给H一个英国的判例（见附录2）。但是，认真阅读该判例可发现，这项判决中的事件与G轮发生的事件有着本质上的不同，因此，不具有参照性。实践中，当发生船东的共同海损索赔时，货方首先应采取的对策就是要尽快查验当事船舶是否存在不适航问题，这是避免共同海损分摊的唯一办法。

5.共同海损理算规则及本案的共同海损费用理算

（1）共同海损理算规则

共同海损理算规则是由民间组织协商制定的实务性章程，其中规定了共同海损行为的成立条件、共同海损损失和费用的范围以及分摊共同海损的标准，因其成为国际惯例而被广泛接受。目前，国际上普遍接受和使用的共同海损理算规则是《1994年约克-安特卫普规则》。中国国际贸易促进委员会也制定了《北京理算规则》。

（2）共同海损的分摊方法

共同海损理算是指由有一定资格的专业机构或人员，按照理算规则，对共同海损的损失和费用、各受益方的分摊价值及各方应分摊的共同海损数额进行审核、计算工作。计算分摊的办法：

各方应分摊金额=各方分摊价值×分摊比率

各方的分摊价值应为获救财产抵达第一港口的当地价值。

分摊比率 =共同海损损失总额÷分摊价值总额 ×100%

（3）对本案例中H的共同海损理算的评价

第一，本案例中H放弃修理而采用拖带的方法是正确的。因为，如采用修理方式，由于Turbo港不具备修理条件，必须采用拖带方式将G轮拖带至具有修理能力的港口。经过船东查询，合理的修理港口为委内瑞拉卡贝略港（Port Cabello），拖带的航程为 740 海里。鉴于修理必须卸下部分货物并予以仓储，经过合理计算，最少要卸下 2 140 吨货物。2001 年 9 月 5 日，船东向哥伦比亚 Turbo 港询问捣载费用，并得知 Turbo 港不具备仓储条件。因此采用拖轮全程拖带的方式替代在 Turbo 港的修理是合理的。如采用修理方式必将产生如下费用：

一是捣载费用。由于修理必须卸下 2 140 吨货物并使用驳船，根据 Turbo 港的报价，捣载费用为 18 美元/吨，即装卸共需要 77 040 美元（2 140 吨×18 美元/吨×2），同时该费用不包括货物在驳船上的仓储费用。

二是拖带费用。G 轮必须拖带至委内瑞拉卡贝略港修理。拖带的航程为 740 海里，与 Turbo 港至太子港的距离（793 海里）基本相当，参照拖轮 E 轮的费用结算单，预计拖带费用为 90 000 美元。返程的距离约为 1 400 海里，拖带时间为 5.83 天（1 400 海里÷10 节/小时÷24 小时/天）至 6.48 天（1 400 海里÷9 节/小时÷24 小时/天），取中间值为 6.16 天，拖带费用为 27 104 美元（6.16 天×4 400 美元/天），燃油费用为 10 730.72 美元（268 美元/吨×6.5 吨/天×6.16 天）；往返的拖带费总计为 127 834.72 美元。

三是与拖带有关的费用。如上文所述，西英保赔协会要求追加保费 10 000 美元，以及安排适拖检验产生检验费 11 428.57 美元。

四是避难港费用。进出修理港的费用及代理费用等约为 14 200 美元。

五是延长航程所产生的船员工资，燃料、物料费用。预计的修理时间为 30 天（实际的修理时间远远长于 1 个月），延长航程所产生的船员工资，燃料、物料费用约为 34 000 美元。

上述费用共计 274 503.29 美元（尚未包括仓储费用），均应列为共同海损。

如果采取拖航方式，相同项目下产生的共同海损费用为：拖带费用 193 310.13 美元，与拖带有关的费用 28 095.64 美元，延长航程产生的船员工资、伙食费 16 502.87 美元，共计 237 908.64 美元。

因此，考虑到未计算的仓储费，与采用修理方式的费用相比，采用拖带方式完成航程是节省的、合理的，同时考虑船载货物的保质期问题，采用拖带替代修理的方式所需时间最短，因此符合共同海损的条件。

第二，本案的共同海损费用计算也是正确的。本案例中船东的共同海损费用计算及分摊符合合同约定的《1994 年约克–安特卫普规则》。具体地说，拖轮拖带费用193 310.13美元有拖带合同和费用结算单佐证，是真实的；与拖带有关的费用28 095.64美元均有客观材料佐证；航程时间延长期间支付给船员的工资、伙食费16 502.87美元是根据船舶拖带的实际航行时间和船东与船员的雇佣合同的工资标准计算的；额外消耗的燃料、物料费用为−273.16美元，由于拖带，当事船舶节省了主机燃油消耗，应当从共同海损费用中扣除，而采取共同海损行为消耗的柴油费用应当计入，此项计算是根据当事船舶的实际消耗水平和燃油的市场价格计算的，因此也是合理的；咨询费用（律师费用）12 489美元由船东聘请的咨询公司账单佐证；垫款手续费4 692.21美元是根据《1994年约克−安特卫普规则》第20条"按共同海损费用2%计算的手续费，应计入共同海损"的规定计算的。本案例中，扣除船员工资、物料费、燃油费及收款人垫款，船东作为承运人和收货人的垫款数额总计：共同海损费用−船员工资、物料费、燃油费=193 310.13+28 095.64+715.62+12 489 =234 610.39（美元）。因此，垫款手续费=234 610.39×2%=4 692.21（美元）；共同海损利息8 943.63美元是根据《1994年约克−安特卫普规则》第21条"对于共同海损费用、牺牲和应受补偿项目，应给予利率7%的利息，计算至共同海损理算书编就之日止"的规定计算的。本案利息自共同海损发生之日起计算，暂按半年计算，列入共同海损，其金额为：

共同海损费用×7%÷2=255 532.31×7%÷2=8 943.63（美元）

以上各项总计264 475.94美元。

第三，本案例中船东的共同海损分摊计算是合理的。船舶共同海损分摊价值693 000美元是根据当时国际二手船舶买卖市场的询价确定的。货物共同海损分摊价值2 739 825美元是按照《1994年约克−安特卫普规则》第17条"……货物应以卸货时的价值为基础，此项价值应根据送交收货人的商业发票确定……"的规定计算的。共同海损分摊总价值，即船舶分摊价值和货物分摊价值之和应为3 432 825美元。

船方分摊共同海损金额为：

共同海损费用÷共同海损分摊总价值×船舶分摊价值=264 475.94÷3 432 825×693 000
=53 390.96（美元）

货方分摊共同海损金额为：

共同海损费用÷共同海损分摊总价值×货物分摊价值=264 475.94÷3 432 825×2 739 825
=211 084.98（美元）

四、关键要点

阅读本案例并正确回答讨论思考题，需要学生把握以下要点：

（1）国际货物买卖合同和国际货物运输合同的履行均须掌握共同海损基础知识。共同海损的性质不同于一般损失，是一种特殊的法律制度中规定的特殊损失，该损失的赔偿有一套独立的规则。

（2）把握共同海损的构成条件是正确处理共同海损的重要前提。

（3）船东要求货方参加共同海损分摊的前提条件是船东首先保证当事船舶是适航的，否则货方可以拒绝分摊。船舶是否适航应当以《海牙-维斯比规则》及相关法律规定作为标准，严格依据事实来判断。这常常是船方和货方争论最激烈的问题。

（4）把握共同海损的计算和分摊标准是处理共同海损问题的最基本内容。

五、课堂教学计划建议

本案例可以作为专门的案例讨论课来进行。如下是按照时间进度提供的课堂计划建议，仅供参考。

对于本案例教学，建议在给出本案例前，教师用50分钟的课堂时间预先讲授相关知识，并在相关知识讲授完毕后，立即给出本案例素材和讨论思考题，然后根据思考题的数量将全班学生分成若干组，每一组分配一个问题，要求各组在课后阅读案例材料，根据所学知识对分配的问题作出分析性答案，并将主要分析依据和结论做成PPT。然后准备100分钟全班同学听取汇报和教师评论。课中计划：

简要的课堂前言，明确主题：2～5分钟

小组发言：每组10～15分钟，控制在80分钟内

引导全班进一步讨论并进行归纳总结：15～20分钟

第七章

国际仲裁

Z进出口公司关于交货期违约的国际仲裁

摘要：商务国际仲裁与诉讼相比具有多项好处，因此，掌握国际商务仲裁规则和仲裁技能对于从事国际商事的人们来说具有重要意义。本案例正文以Z进出口公司就卖方交货期违约而在伦敦发起仲裁为主线，在介绍了案件发生的背景和基本事实的基础上，细致地描述了Z进出口公司的仲裁请求及其理由、被请求人C国际贸易公司的针锋相对的答辩及其理由、Z进出口公司对C国际贸易公司的各项答辩的抗辩及其理由，以及Z进出口公司在仲裁中冗长的有理有据的最后陈词，刻画了Z进出口公司与C国际贸易公司在近3年的仲裁期间的激烈交锋场景。案例的使用说明部分对案例正文描述的主要情节进行了理论分析和评价，并附上GAFTA仲裁庭对本案的仲裁裁决。

关键词：商务仲裁　交货期　倒签提单　时效

1. 本案例描述和分析的关于交货期违约的国际仲裁是一个真实的事件，案例编者当年也在一定程度上卷入了这场仲裁之战。尽管事件发生在20世纪末，但鉴于事发至今的相关法律规则没有发生实质性变化，因此案例对国际商务仲裁问题教学仍具有使用价值。为了锻炼案例读者的实战能力，案例正文基于当年英文往来文件用英语编写。由于企业保密的要求，在本案例中对有关当事方做了必要的掩饰性处理。
2. 本案例只供教学之用，并无意明示地或暗示地褒奖或贬低案例中涉及的公司的相关行为。

案例正文

This case describes and analyses an arbitration for loss arising from late delivery on the Seller side under a contract of sale of soybean meal.In 1998, Z Imp.& Exp.Co (hereafter referred to as Z) as Buyer submitted a claim to the tribunal of The Grain and Feed Trade Association (abbreviated as GAFTA) against C International Trading Pte Ltd (hereafter referred to as C) for late delivery under a contract of sale of soybean meal, the later concealed the fact of late delivery of the goods by ante-dating the relevant bills of lading.The two parties were struggling uncompromisingly in the tribunal for almost three years for whether the goods were late delivered and whether the submission was beyond the time bar according to the rules of GAFTA 125.

1.THE BACKGROUND

1.1　For better understanding the true reason of Z's submission, let's getting to know the relevant background firstly.In 1997, due to the shortage on the supply side, the price of soybean meal in China market was getting higher and higher.Merchants are always sensitive to the market.Having noticed the market situation, some capable trading company rushed to foreign market to secure soybean meal.

1.2　Z was a large agricultural product trading company with feed trading as a main line and with extensive business channels worldwide. The intelligent and capable business personnel in this company sensitively noticed the silent market situation changing.In a short time they had ordered several tens of thousands tons soybean meal through different business channels, including the 11 000 tons Indian yellow soybean meal from C.An initial estimation showed that Z should have a profit of several tens of million RMB yuan if all the ordered soybean meal were sold up later.

1.3　Ranking in the top four in the world, the mother company of C was a large transnational company with business scope covering almost all agricultural products and with numerous subsidiary companies in all over the world, C was one of them.On November 6th that year, C concluded a transaction with Z in GAFTA 100 contract form and GAFTA 125 rules for arbitration for 11 000 tons with 10% more or less Indian soybean meal yellow flakes type.In fact, the subject goods was from P Trading Pte Ltd in India (hereafter referred to as P), a subsidiary company of C's mother company, thus P was the genuine shipper of the goods. In January 1998, C concluded a voyage charterparty with H Shipping Company (hereafter referred to as H) for the carriage of the subject goods with their MV D as the carrying Vessel.

1.4   Several months later, as the soybean meal shipments purchased from abroad by several trading companies reached China one after the other, the market price of soybean meal began to drop down.Till MV D reached Nantong Port on March 5th, 1998, not only Z's preliminary estimated profit disappeared, but also a net loss of 5.2 million RMB yuan appeared due to the continuous price dropping according to their claimed amount against H in the later stage.Z therefore applied to the court to arrest MV D, demanding the shipowner to compensate their market loss by reason of ante-dating the relevant Bills of Lading.Due to a mortgage to the loan providing bank on that vessel, Z failed to get what they wanted fully.Therefore, they turned to fight C for compensation by submitting claim to GAFTA tribunal in London by reason of nonperformance of Seller's contractual duty to deliver the goods in time.

1.5   Z entrusted L, a worldwide famous law office to handle the case.The later spent lengthy time to collect enough evidences and on June 12th, 1998 sent an arbitration notice to C according to the arbitration clause in the sale contract and GAFTA rules.On July 24th in the same year, L, on behalf of Z designated their arbitrator and noticed the same to C.According to their submission to the tribunal, Z demanded a market price loss of US Dollar 736 988 from C by reason of C ante-dating Bills of Lading to conceal their late delivery of goods and quality defect.

1.6   For defending, C submitted plenty of evidences to demonstrate that firstly, the completing date of loading for MV D at port Visakhapatnam was February 15th instead of February 16th.Secondly, the inspection certificate issued at loading port showed clearly that the quality of the goods at the time of loading was in conformity with that set out in the sale contract, and most importantly, the arbitration notice and the arbitrator designation notice by the claimant to the respondent was beyond the time limit set forth in the GAFTA 125 2: 2 (c) rules.

Therefore, the respondent demanded the tribunal to refuse the claimant's submission.

1.7   The tribunal organized two hearing, and for issue of time bar, fact of ante-dating Bills of Lading and market loss etc.the two parties submitted and exchanged lengthy written request, defence, reply, rejoinder and final submission, details of which and basic facts are as follows.

2.THE FACTS

2.1   By a contract dated 6th November 1997, Sellers sold to Buyers 11 000 tonnes 10% more or less Indian Soya Bean Meal Extraction CIFFO from one Indian port to one China main port at a price of US$278.50 per tonne.

2.2   The key terms as far as concerns the matter in dispute are:

Quantity: 11 000MT Plus/Minus 10%.

Price: US$278.50 per metric ton CIFFO from one Indian port to one
              China main port.

Payment: By 100% irrevocable Letter of Credit at sight.

Shipment: 15 January – 15 February, 1998.

Shipping

Documents: Sellers' Commercial Invoice.

              Clean On-board C/P B/L Marked freight prepaid.

              Certificate of Origin certified by any Chamber of Commerce and
              Industry.

              Certificate of Weight issued by Geo-Chem Laboratories (P) Ltd.

              Certificate of Quality issued by Geo-Chem (P) Ltd.

              Phytosanitary Certificate issued by Authority under Ministry of
              Agriculture of the Government of India.

              Other Terms and

Conditions: as per GAFTA 100 when not in conflict with above.

Arbitration: as per GAFTA 125.

2.3   On 8th December 1997, Buyers opened a Letter of Credit in an amount of

US$3 063 500 (Three million Sixty Three Thousand Five Hundred United States Dollars) in line with the terms of the contract, to which four amendments were subsequently issued. Although the applicants for the fourth amendment were not the Buyers themselves but one of their subsidiaries, the parties agreed that this had no effect on Buyers' rights and duties under the contract.

2.4   Sellers chartered the vessel "D" for the carriage of the contract goods and she loaded at Visakhapatnam, India and appropriated 10 479 tonnes to the contract on 18th February 1998. Shipping documents were presented via the Bank of China to Buyers, who authorised their payment on 3rd March 1998. Non-negotiable copies of the shipping documents had already been sent to Buyers on 21st February. Both original and copy Bill of Lading, Certificates of Origin, Weight and Fumigation Certificates bore the date of 15th February 1998 as the date of completion of loading, inspection and fumigation respectively.

2.5   The vessel arrived at the port of Nantong on 5th March 1998 where she discharged her cargo, completing on 17th March 1998.

2.6   On 23rd March 1998, Buyers, being dissatisfied with the quality and condition of the cargo at discharge, faxed Sellers summoning them to Nantong to take samples of the allegedly damaged cargo, failing which they threatened to sell the whole cargo at a greatly reduced price and hold Sellers responsible therefor. In the same fax, Buyers referred to "their lodged claim" against Sellers which they hoped "to be settled through amicable way, if not, we'll claim arbitration against this matter according to the arbitration clause in the contract".

2.7   On 12th June 1998, Buyers' Beijing lawyers faxed Sellers advising that they had reviewed the documents in connection with the "D" shipment and had come to the conclusion that the Bills of Lading had been back-dated, as a consequence of which their client (Buyers) had lost US$1 500 000, which they would be entitled to claim against Sellers. Amongst the documents cited by Buyers' Beijing lawyers as having been reviewed by them were "GAFTA 100 and 125". And in the penultimate paragraph of their fax, Buyers' Beijing lawyers stated as follows: "We refer to our client's fax dated 23rd March 1998 with attention to Mr. Andrew O. Lau, now we are confirming again that our client has the intention to refer this dispute to arbitration as per GAFTA 125".

2.8　On 24th July 1998 Buyers, having put the matter in the hands of English lawyers, appointed Mr. R. Rookes as their arbitrator in respect of their claim under the contract. Mr. K. E. Hairs was subsequently appointed by Sellers and Mr. J. S. Smid was appointed by GAFTA as third arbitrator and Chairman of the Tribunal.

2.9　There followed the divers exchanges and interlocutory applications referred to in 1 above and the generation by the parties' lawyers of a considerable number of submissions, counter-submissions and witness statements leading to the preliminary meeting in London on 23rd March 1999 at which Buyers' representatives, in the presence of Sellers' representatives, presented the Tribunal with certain original documents (essentially the original carbon copies of the daily loading sheets of the Ships' agents at Visakhapatnam for the "DONG FA" obtained by Buyers from the Owners of the vessel).

3.CLAIMANT BUYERS' SUBMISSIONS

3.1　Buyers argue that the Bills of Lading presented for payment under the contract are false bills in that they were dated 15th February 1998 when, in fact, they should have been dated 16th February 1998. In support of this argument, they point to the evidence of the Log Book (and more particularly the entries at p. 19 detailing the loading carried out on 16th February 1998) and which, together with the berthing programme at the load port clearly showed that the vessel was still loading at the berth EQ-3 on 16th February 1998 i.e. outside the contractual shipment period and contrary to what was stated in the bills and other documents.

3.2　In presenting such false documents Sellers were clearly in breach of the obligation under the contract to present documents which accurately described the goods (including their date of shipment), and it avails Sellers not to argue that they were not aware of the ante-dating at the time the documents were presented.

3.3　It follows that Buyers are entitled to compensation for this breach in the form of damages based on the difference between the contract and the market price at the time they were accepted, i. e. 3rd March 1998, when they would have been rejected if the Bill of Lading had been accurately dated.

3.4   In consequence, Buyers claim damages under this head calculated as follows:

a)	the contract price US$278.5 per m.t. (C&F Nantong) equivalent to RMB2 311.55 per m.t. (exchange rate: US$1 = RMB8.30)	RMB 2 311.55 per m.t.
	Plus customs duty （5%）	RMB 116.00 per m.t.
	Plus other expenses including customs clearance, quality inspection, package and delivery	RMB 150.00 per m.t.
	Total	RMB 2 577.50 per m.t.
	This is sometimes called "free on small boat or truck" for the purpose of domestic sales in China	
b)	the market price （the contract price between two domestic Chinese companies for Indian yellow soyabean meal extraction as at 4th March 1998—see pages 38-40） free on small boat or truck	RMB 2 000.00 per m.t.
Difference between （adjusted） contract price and market price		RMB 2 577.50 per m.t.
Less		RMB 2 000.00 per m.t
Total		RMB 577.50 per m.t.
Which at US$1 to RMB8.30=US$68.00 per m.t.		
US$68.00 per m.t.× 10 479.00 m.t.=		Total US$712 572.00

3.5   Buyers argue that while the contractual description of the goods was "Indian Soyabean Meal Extraction （Toasted Soyabean Meal, Yellow Flakes type）", the goods inspected on arrival by the Jiangsu Import and Export Commodity Bureau were found to include a high percentage of brown cargo not corresponding to the contractual description. For this further breach of contract, Buyers reserves their right to damages for their losses.

3.6   Buyers also argue that not only the Bill of Lading but also the Certificate of Quality was fraudulent.In support of this contention, they point to the wording of the certificate stating that samples were drawn between 16th January and 15th February when manifestly loading did not finish until 16th February. It follows from this that they are not bound by the figures in this （fraudulent） Certificate of Quality and are thus entitled to rely on the sampling and analysis carried out at discharge. For this further breach of contract, Buyers reserved their right to claim damages and/or further quality allowances.

4.RESPONDENT SELLERS' DEFENCE SUBMISSION

4.1   Sellers argue that Buyers are really putting forward two separate claims. The first is in respect of the alleged consequences of the alleged （but denied） issuance of an ante-dated Bill of Lading （ "the Bill of Lading claim" ）. The second is for alleged deficiencies in respect of the quality of the cargo （ "the Quality claim" ）. Sellers contend that Buyers' claims are time-barred by virtue of their failure to comply with the terms of Rule2 of GAFTA125 which were incorporated into the contract.

4.2   As to the Bill of Lading claim, pursuant to Rule 2: 2 （a） （iii） of GAFTA 125, Buyers were required to give notice that they were claiming arbitration not later than 90 consecutive days after the last day of the contractual delivery period （i. e. Within 90 days of 15th February 1998） and should have appointed their arbitrator within 7 consecutive days from the last day for claiming arbitration. Accordingly Buyers should have claimed arbitration by 17th May 1998 （being 90 days from 15th February） and should have appointed their arbitrator by 24th May 1998.

4.3   As to the Quality Claim, pursuant to Rule 2: 4 （a） of GAFTA 125, Buyers should have claimed arbitration not later than 28 consecutive days after the date of final completion of discharge of the ship at the port of destination and should have appointed their arbitrator within 7 consecutive days thereafter. Discharge operations in china were completed on 17th March 1998. Accordingly, the last date for appointing an arbitrator in respect of the Quality Claim was 22nd April 1998.

4.4   In the event, Buyers apparently did not appoint their arbitrator until 24th July （that is the day on which notice of the appointment of their arbitrator was given to Sellers). Sellers accordingly invoke Rule 2: 7 of GAFTA 125 and invite the Tribunal to treat the entirety of Buyers' claim as waived and absolutely barred.

4.5   Without prejudice to their primary contention that Buyers ' claim are already Waived and time - barred, Sellers deny that the Bill of Lading issued in respect of the cargo was ante - dated and that loading continued into 16th February 1998.It is Sellers' case that loading was completed at 23: 15 hours on 15th February 1998. Sellers will rel upon the following matters, documents and statements to support their contention in this regard:

(1) Sellers were fully aware of their contractual obligation to load the cargo within 15th February 1998 and made sure that their agents at the loadport supervised loading so as to ensure compliance with the obligation.

(2) At 10: 30am, Singapore time (which was 8: 00 am, Indian time) on 16th February Sellers received a fax from Bothra Shipping Services (Bothra), who were acting as both shipowners' and Sellers' loadport agents.The fax stated that about 11 000 tonnes of cargo had been loaded as of 15th February and that the cargo was in the process of being trimmed .It is clear from the fax and from the statements of Mr. Reddy, the Bothra executive responsible for the loading of the vessel, and Mr.P. Dhanarj, the shift supervisor of the loadport at that time, that loading was not in progress at that time. Bothra's fax did say, however, that more cargo would be loaded after trimming if space was found to be available.

(3) Sellers responded to Bothra by fax instructing them that no further cargo was to be loaded.That fax was sent at 14: 00 hours Singapore time and received in India at 11: 30 hours local time. The loadport agent, Mr. Reddy, immediately contacted the shift supervisor at the ship and informed him that no future cargo to be loaded.It is clear from the evidence of Mr.Reddy and the shift supervisors for the 22: 00—04: 30 shift on 16th February, respectively Mr. A. V. Karunakar and Mr. P. Dhanaraj that no cargo had been loaded on 16th February prior to receipt of Sellers' fax.

(4) Bothra wrote "your instructions notes" on the fax from Sellers and faxed it back to them at 11: 43hours, within 15 minutes of receipt.It is fair to assume from this exchange alone that no cargo was loaded on 16th February.This is confirmed by

the statements of Mr.Reddy and the shift supervisors.

(5) Bothra sent a fax in the early hours of 17th February to Sellers confirming that the vessel had uncompleted loading at 23：15 hours on 15th February and confirming that a total of 10 479 tonnes of cargo had been loaded.

(6) Bothra maintained daily loading reports which were signed by them and by the ship's officers.It is clear from those reports that loading was completed at 23：15 hours on 15th February.

(7) The Mate's Receipts completed and signed /stamped by the Master and Chief Officer acknowledged that the cargo was shipped on 15th February.

(8) The loadport Statement of Facts which was signed by Bothra and the ship's Officers confirmed that loading had been completed at 23：15hours on the 15th February.

(9) The Certificate of Completion signed and stamped by the Master confirmed that loading was completed by 23：15 hours of 15th February.

(10) The Visakhapatnam Chamber of Commerce and Industry issued a Certificate of Origin in respect of the cargo.That certificate was dated 15th February.

(11) Independent cargo surveyors, Geo - Chem Laboratories (P) Limited ("Geo-Chem"), issued a Certificate of Weight on 16th February confirming that 10 479 tonnes of cargo had been loaded.The certificates was expressly in the basis of inspections carried out by Geo-Chem between 9th and 15th February.Geo-Chem also issued a Certificate of Quality on 16th February which in turn was based upon inspections carried out between 16th January and 15th February.

(12) Official forms completed by Bothra as Sellers' agents in relation to Exchange Control Regulations confirmed that the cargo had been shipped on 15th February.

4.6　In short, the contemporaneous loadport documentation consistently confirms that loading was completed on 15th February. If, contrary to the contemporaneous documentary evidence and the and the statements of those directly involved in loading the vessel, loading actually continued into 16th February as has been alleged by Buyers, then this would involve a fraudulent conspiracy involving at the very least of the following parties：

（1）The ship's Officers;

（2）The loadport agents Bothra;

（3）The independent surveyors, Geo-Chem; and

（4）The local Chamber of Commerce.

It is submitted that this is a highly unlikely scenario.

4.7　To support their case, Buyers seek to rely exclusively on two classes of documents:

（1）Photocopies of what purport to be extracts from the vessel's log book.

It is to be noted, however, that these documents are entirely unauthenticated and Buyers do not say how they came into existence or how they came to be their possession. The authenticity of these copy document is denied. If, which is not admitted, the alleged extracts were provided by the ship, Sellers will say that the extracts are false.

Alternatively, if, which is denied, the log books are genuine there is a simple and reasonable way of reconciling to a large extent the apparently conflicting contemporaneous loadport documents and the entries in the alleged log. Aspects of the loading operations （i.e. trimming /conduct of draft survey） took place on 16th February; this is clear from the documents referred to above. It is therefore submitted that the reference on page 19 of the log book to cargo "work" and "loading " should be taken as references to these operations rather than the actual physical placing on board of an unspecified quantity of cargo. This is clearly consistent with the fact that the alleged extracts from the log book make no reference to any particular quantity of cargo having been loaded on 16th February.

（2）The Berthing Schedule

Buyers rely on this to prove that the vessel was still at the berth on 16th February. This is not in contention—the vessel was at the berth and did not leave until 17th February. Buyers rightly do not rely upon the Berthing Programme to prove that the vessel was loading cargo on 16th February because the Programme is evidence of no such thing, accordingly, the Berthing Schedule does not advance Buyers' case in any respect.

4.8　It has been alleged by the owners of the vessel that the loadport agents put pressure upon the Master to issue a back-dated Mate's Receipt in relation to a portion of the cargo. The allegation is denied and is manifestly false. Sellers postulate that the allegation came about in the following way. It is understood that Buyers arrested the ship in China for security for a cargo claim in the sum of RMB 12 000 000 (equivalent to about US $1.4m). The shipowners were unable to provide security. It is therefore postulated that the shipowners and Buyers colluded so as to manufacture a claim against Sellers, in this way the owners procured the release of their vessel without the production of security and Buyers were provided with an apparent claim against a more solvent target. In the light of the contemporaneous loadport documents. The statements, the underlying fallacy of the suggestion that No. 9 Mate's Receipt was backdated, the manifest falsehood of the alleged extracts and the absence of any protest or suggestion that the Master had been coerced into signing a back-dated Mate's Receipt until the vessel was arrested one month after loading, it is suggested that this is a far more plausible explanation than the extensive web of deceit that would have been required at the loadport in the falsification of all contemporaneous documentation.

4.9　In summary, there is a large amount of contemporaneous loadport documentation and statement evidence which fully supports Sellers' contention that the cargo loading ceased on 15th February. There is only one document, the alleged extract from the logbook, the authenticity of which is denied, which is potentially in Buyers' favour. The document is inherently implausible for the reasons given by Mr. Reddy (see 4: 5). Even if the document is genuine, it may, on a fair and reasonably unstrained interpretation, to read consistently with Sellers' position that no loading took place on 16th February.

4.10　In order to find for Buyers, the Tribunal will have to accept authenticity of the vessel's logbook and find that all of the loadport documentation was forged pursuant to a fraudulent conspiracy involving at least four separate entities. It is respectfully submitted that far clear evidence than photocopies of alleged extracts from an un-authenticated logbook should be adduced before allegations of fraudulent conspiracy can be made out.

4.11　In the premises, Buyers' claim as set out in their Claim Submissions is denied.

4.12 If, contrary to the above submissions, it is held a quantity of cargo was loaded on 16th February, Sellers will say as follows:

(1) They were/are unaware of this and had absolutely no knowledge of or part in the production of an ante-dated Bill of Lading;

(2) As of 23: 59 on 15th February, sufficient cargo had already been loaded to satisfy the minimum shipment quantity under the contract with Buyers, that is, the vessel had loaded in excess of 9 900 tonnes (i.e.11 000 less 10%);

(3) The shipowners say that the vessel loaded 194 tonnes on 16th February. This represents 1.85% of the total cargo loaded. Put another way, on the shipowners' figures, some 98.15% of the total loaded cargo or 10 285 tonnes had already been loaded by the contractual cut-off point of midnight on 15th February. The cargo loaded by midnight on 15th February therefore exceeded the contractual minimum quantity by 385 tonnes;

(4) Sellers will say that as of midnight on 15th February they had complied with their contractual obligation to load a contractual cargo;

(5) If the vessel loaded a quantity of further cargo on 16th February in the order of the owners' figures, such cargo was de minimis and should not be taken into account in assessing Sellers' liability to Buyers;

(6) Alternatively, Buyers should be awarded damages only in respect of that portion of cargo which was loaded on 16th February on the basis that a valid Bill of Lading could have been issued in respect of the cargo that a valid Bill of Lading could have been issued in respect of the cargo that has been loaded by midnight on 15th February, since a valid bill could have been issued in respect of that portion of cargo, no right of rejection would have arisen and, accordingly, the tender of an ante-dated Bill of Lading would not have deprived Buyers of a right to reject that portion of the cargo, in which case only nominal damages lie (see Procter &Gamble v.Becher (1988) 2 Lloyd's Rep 21 (CA);

(7) To award Buyers damages in the magnitude claimed (i.e. US$712 500) would be manifestly unjust in circumstances where sufficient cargo had been loaded in time to satisfy the contract but a tiny portion of cargo was placed on board on the

day after the expiry of the shipment period without Sellers' knowledge and contrary to their express instructions, particularly as Sellers dad in any event a contractual right to extend the shipment period pursuant to clause 9 of GAFTA 100;

(8) To award substantial damages to Buyers would give them a windfall recovery in a case with little or no merit (see the comments of Mr.Justice Donaldson in The Kastellon (1978) 2 Lloyd's Rep 203 at page 207, and the comment of the authors of Benjamin's Sale of Goods (4th Ed) at paragraph 19-173). Such a recovery would be totally out of proportion to Sellers' alleged breach, which if proved, occurred through absolutely no fault on their part.

(9) In any event, the quantum of Buyers' claim is denied and they are put to strict proof thereof

4.13 Sellers reject Buyers' claim in respect of alleged quality deficiencies. Buyers have provided no evidence of any quality deficiencies and it is intolerable that six months after discharge they should purport to assert an unsubstantiated, unparticularised and unqualified quality claim. It is respectfully submitted that the alleged quality claim should be struck out.

4.14 Sellers moreover, deny that Buyers have any right, or entitlement to reserve a right to claim damages in respect of the alleged quality deficiencies or the alleged discoloration of part of the cargo.

5.CLAIMANT BUYERS' REPLY SUBMISSIONS

5.1 Sellers reject all three of Sellers' arguments set forth in the Defence Submissions.Thus they reject the first argument based largely on the statement of Mr. Reddy of Ship's agents, Bothra, at the load port and on the documents issued by Bothra at load to the effect that loading was completed at 23: 15 hours on 15th February 1998. They reject the second that the cargo, if any, loaded on 16th February was so little as to be de minimis and thus not such as to give the buyer a right to claim damages for breach.And they reject the third to the effect that the claim was time-barred and was not of such a nature as to justify the exercise of discretion by the arbitrators.

5.2   In rejecting the first argument, Buyers place reliance on a number of new documents put in with their Reply Submissions and at the same time argue that the statement of Mr. Reddy of Bothra and the documents issued by or under Mr. Reddy's authority at load, put in as part of Sellers' evidence, were simply untrue.

5.3   As regard the new documents put in with their Reply Submissions, Buyers highlight the original loading reports issued by Bothra at load and which Buyers obtained from the owners after Sellers had put in their documents purporting to be the complete set of Loading Reports. In particular, they place reliance on a document withheld by Sellers from their set of Loading Reports submitted in this reference. This document is, they say, the genuine, original and true Loading Report dated 15th February 1998 and the similarly dated document put in by Sellers is, they say, a forgery designed to mislead the Tribunal.

5.4   This document, contrary to what is stated in the version put in by Sellers, shows that as of 06: 00 hours on 16th February only 10 159 tonnes had been loaded. It further shows that during the third shift, from 22: 40 hours on 15th February to 04: 30 hours on 16th February, the vessel loaded 480 tonnes, but most importantly it is expressly recorded that loading of Hold No.1 was completed at 05: 30 hours on 16th February 1998. Buyers claim that this is the true and original Loading Report for the last day of loading and that loading was not completed on 15th February but on 16th February. Further, while the exact time loading was completed figures nowhere in the various loading reports, the fact that the (genuine) Loading Report dated 15th February 1998 shows a total quantity on board of 10 159 tonnes and the undisputed final quantity shipped was 10 426 tonnes indicates that after completing Hold No.1 at the end of the third shift at 05: 30 hours on 16th February, a further quantity of some 267 tonnes was loaded later on 16th February.

5.5   In further support of their argument that their Loading Report dated 15th February is the genuine report, they referred the Tribunal to the report dated 15th February put in by Sellers and seek to explain why it is a forgery. They refer in this connection to a fax sent by Mr. Reddy to Cargill, Singapore at 08: 00 hours Vizag time on 15th February 1998. This message falsely states that the vessel had already loaded about 11 000 tonnes and that the vessel might load more cargo after trimming before sailing （ETD that evening）. Why Mr. Reddy should make such a false statement regarding the quantity loaded may only be conjectured at, as may be quite unnecessary underlining in the （false） loading report reading "V/L loading cargo completed at 23: 15 on15.2.98". However, the fact that Cargill answered Mr. Reddy's fax with a very firm order not to load any more cargo, as Cargill needed a bill dated 15th February may explain why the original and genuine loading report dated 15th February had to be suppressed and replaced by Sellers' version so emphatically attesting to the completion of loading at 23: 15 hours on 15th February.

5.6 Buyers rejected Sellers' further arguments that they were unaware of and, therefore, not responsible for the acts of their agents, on the grounds that a principal was always responsible for the acts of his agents where those acts fell within the functions for which the agent had been appointed （as here, those of organising the loading of the vessel）. As for Sellers' argument that the quantity involved was only 194 tonnes and therefore the de minimis rule precluded Buyers from obtaining damages.Buyers argued that the quantity concerned even if only 194 tonnes, which was dented, would not fall within the de minimis rule, as such a role only applied to trifling quantities of cargo （0.1% not 1.85% or, more probably, 3% ~ 4%） and was quite inapplicable here, where the question at issue was of time not of quantity.

5.7 As for the argument that a falsely dated Bill of Lading does not give rise to a right of rejection simply because some of the cargo had been loaded in time, this is a novel argument entirely unsupported by either commercial practice or the law.Thus, it has been accepted from time immemorial that a Bill of Lading can only be issued after all the cargo covered by that bill has been shipped and that bill must then be dated on the day the last part of the cargo has been shipped on board.

5.8 Sellers' reference to the Procter & Gamble case in support of their argument that only nominal damages would be appropriate is misplaced since the case concerned a cargo which, unlike the cargo in the present case had all been shipped within the contractual period of shipment.Similarly their invocation of the "Kastellon" case helps them not at all, as in that case the judge held that full damages should be payable and what he said regarding the circumstances in which he considered the awarding of only nominal damages would be more equitable is only an obiter dictum and, therefore, not binding on this Tribunal. Likewise what is put forward by the authors of Benjamin in much the same vein is not the law as it is but the law as those academic writers would wish to see it. It follows therefore that both the law and long established commercial practice require that full and not only nominal damages should be awarded.

5.9 As regards Sellers' arguments that the claim was time-barred and that no discretion to extend should be executed by the Tribunal, Buyers concede that the claim was prima facie time-barred under Rule 2: 3 (a) of GAFTA 125, but considered that there were overwhelming arguments in favour of the Tribunal granting an extension of time and allowing the claim to proceed.

5.10 In favour of their request to extend and allow the claim Buyers pointed to the fact that they had properly given notice of their intention to claim arbitration on 12th June 1998 via their Beijing lawyers thereby leaving Sellers in no doubt as to the imminent initiation of GAFTA arbitration proceedings against them. However, as the matter was at the time in the hands of Beijing lawyers unacquainted with GAFTA arbitration procedures those same lawyers, like their clients, failed to realise that they should have appointed an arbitrator for their clients latest by 24th June 1998.

5.11 It was only after Buyers had appointed London solicitors that the problem was discovered. Not surprisingly, their first act for their clients was immediately to appoint Mr. R. Rookes on 24th July 1998.

5.12 Buyers argue that discretion should be granted for the following reasons:

(1) their only offence was that they did not know they had to nominate their arbitrator within the 9 day time-limit;

(2) it is a claim where there is a very strong case that a Bill of Lading has been ante-dated.

(3) there can be no prejudice to Sellers since notice of intention to arbitrate was given in time and the notification of the appointment of Mr. Rookes was only thirty days late.

5.13 Finally Buyers add to their reply a recalculation of their damages in respect of their principal head of claim and a number of further points not by way of response to Sellers' defence as such but as a follow-on from their earlier submissions claiming that they had the right to reserve their rights in respect of their possible claims for discoloration and damaged cargo.

5.14　Thus damages in respect of their principal claim in relation to the misdating of the Bill of Lading are recalculated from the earlier figure of US$712 572 to the recalculated figure of US$736 988.32 as follows:

a)	the contract price: US $278.5 per m. t. (C&F Nantong) equivalent to RMB2 311.55 per m.t. (exchange rate: US$1 = RMB8.30)	RMB 2 311.55 per m.t.
	Plus customs duty (5%)	RMB 114.09 per m.t.
	Plus other expenses including customs clearance, quality inspection, package and delivery	RMB 158.10 per m.t.
	Total	RMB 2 583.74 per m.t.
	This is sometimes called "free on small boat or truck" for the purpose of domestic sales in China	
b)	the market price (the contract price between two domestic Chinese companies for Indian yellow soyabean meal extraction as at 4th March 1998—see pages 38–40) free on small boat or truck	RMB 2 000.00 per m.t.
	Difference between (adjusted) contract price and market price	RMB 2 583.74 per m.t.
	Less	RMB 2 000.00 per m.t
	Total	RMB 583.74 per m.t.
	Which at US$1 to RMB8.30=US$70.33 per m.t.	
	US$70.33 per m.t.× 10 479.00 m.t.=	Total US$736 988.07

5.15　Further, Buyers ask that their other claims in respect of discoloration and damaged cargo be left aside for a subsequent award once the final position with regard to the action between receivers and owners in China is known, but that their principal claim to damages (recalculated as above) should be the subject of an

Interim Final Award.

6.RESPONDENT SELLERS' REJOINDER

6.1   Sellers argue that there are two discrete claims, a Quality claim and a Bill of Lading claim to which different GAFTA Arbitration Rules and time-limits apply.

6.2   Their claims to discoloration and damaged cargo are "Quality" claims and subject to the special regime of GAFTA 125 covering such disputes.Rule 2: 1 (c) required service of a notice stating an intention to refer the quality dispute to arbitration within 21 days of completion of final discharge.This Buyers failed to do at any time, since their Chinese lawyers' fax of 12th June was restricted to the Bill of Lading dispute.Further, under Rule 3: 2 (a) Buyers had 9 days from the last day for giving notice of their intention to refer the matter to arbitration to notify the appointment of an arbitrator.This they equally failed to do since the last day forgiving notice was 16th April and they only nominated Mr.R.Rookes on 24th July.

6.3   Accordingly, unless discretion is exercised, Buyers' Quality claims are irrevocably barred and waived on two counts, failure to give notice of intention to arbitrate, and failure to give timely notice of their appointment of an arbitrator.

6.4   On the Bill of Lading claim Sellers concede that Buyers were in time under Rule 2: 3 (c), when, on 12th June, they gave notice of their intention to arbitrate. But having given notice of their intention to arbitrate on 12th June they should have followed this notice with a further notice notifying the appointment of their arbitrator, at latest, on 21st June.Having only given notice on 24th July, this claim is equally irrevocably barred and waived unless the Tribunal exercises its discretion to extend.

6.5   Sellers argue that no discretion to extend should be exercised in the circumstances of the present case.First, they say that the current judicial climate, following the passing of the 1996 Arbitration Act is distinctly unfavourable to interfering in commercial men's bargains including agreed time-limits for initiating arbitration proceedings.The Act itself, moreover, specifically limits the scope for the court's intervention in arbitration proceedings and the circumstances in which the court may grant extensions of time for the commencement of arbitration proceedings. While not arguing that the stricter criteria for extension contained in S.12 of the Act are formally binding on the Tribunal, the Tribunal should nonetheless take account of these new criteria and the less permissive judicial approach to the grant of extensions.

6.6　As to the merits of the Quality Claim.Sellers point to the fact that buyers have thus far entirely failed to adduce any evidence in support.However, it appears that Buyers have successfully pursued this claim against Owners before the Chinese courts and it is only the risk of a successful appeal by owners against the judgment at first instance which motivates Buyers to attempt to preserve a possibility of proceeding with this highly speculative and totally unsubstantiated claim before this Tribunal.

6.7　As it would be quite contrary to the spirit and practice of GAFTA arbitration to allow such an unspecified potential claim to be held in abeyance for an indeterminate period to time, the Tribunal is respectfully asked to strike it out.

6.8　As to the merits of the Bill of Lading claim, Sellers consider that it is entirely technical in nature and wholly disproportionate to any blame or fault that may be levelled against Sellers.In this connection Sellers argue that even if （which they deny） any loading was carried out on 16th February, they had no control over the loading; they were unaware of any such loading: they did not themselves falsely date the Bill of Lading; if any loading took place on 16th February it was of such a small amount （1.2% of the total cargo） as to be de minimis; as of midnight on 15th February, Sellers had already loaded enough to be within the minimum contractual tolerance of 9 900 tonnes, so there was no reason for the loadport agents to load more on the 16th February; and finally, Sellers could have called for an extension.In these circumstances, it would be manifestly unfair to give a windfall profit of US $740 000 to Buyers in respect of the tiny parcel allegedly loaded on 16th February.

6.9　Sellers accordingly argue that in the absence of any culpable conduct on their part the Tribunal should not exercise its discretion to allow the claim and should bear in mind the comments of Donaldson J. and the learned authors of Benjamin （vid.4.12.VIII supra） articulating, as they do, both judicial and academic unease at awarding substantial damages in cases of this kind where Sellers were not involved in any way in issuing ante-dated bills.

6.10   Further on the question of the possible grant of discretion. Sellers would point to the contemporaneous correspondence whereby Sellers consistently rejected any responsibility and to Buyers' Chinese lawyers' fax of 12th June 1998 wherein they stated that they had reviewed all documents in relation to the dispute "particularly the GAFTA 100 and 125". It is clear from this that Buyers' Chinese lawyers were perfectly cognisant of the GAFTA Rules. Accordingly the plea of ignorance on their part and of their Chinese lawyers should not be accepted.

6.11   On the question of the alleged ante-dating of the Bill of Lading, Sellers repeat much of what they had said before, pointing to the actual documents issued at load and a Supplementary Statement of Mr. Virat Reddy of Bothra Shipping, annexed to the Rejoinder, all of which attest to loading having been completed at 23: 15 hours on 15th February. They argue that the statement of the Master to the contrary is not to be relied upon as not only is it full of inaccuracies but also because either the Master acquiesced in the issuance of a falsely dated bill (which they deny) or his last statement of the effect that the vessel loaded on 16th February constitutes false testimony. Either way his evidence is tainted and rather than rely on such a man's evidence to come to a finding of fraudulent conspiracy, the Tribunal should take into account the weight of evidence in favour of the completion of loading at 23: 15 hours on 15th February.

7. CLAIMANT BUYERS' FINAL SUBMISSIONS

7.1   Buyers entirely reject Sellers' arguments to the effect that they were not responsible for the acts of their agents or for what various Indian shippers may or may not have done. Sellers, as principals, were responsible for what their agents did provided what was done was done within the scope of their tasks and responsibilities. Here what the agents did was clearly within their scope as agents appointed to supervise loading. As for the pre-sellers, in a string, a seller is responsible for the actions of his pre-sellers so it is no defence to argue that what was done was done by the pre-sellers.

7.2　As to the renewed arguments of Sellers in their Rejoinder, supported by the Supplementary Statement of Mr. Reddy of Bothra, to the effect that the loading report submitted by them in evidence accurately states that loading was completed on 15th February at 23: 15 hours, they consider it necessary to compare the two versions of the report of 15th February in some detail against the information supplied by Mr. Reddy in his earlier statement in order to show that the version of the report relied on by Sellers is a document falsified by Bothra and the explanation given by Mr. Reddy in his Supplementary Statement is not true.

7.3　Thus the system operated by Bothra for checking the quantity of cargo loaded, as explained by Mr. Reddy in his earlier statement and by Mr. Karunkar (also of Bothra) is essentially as follows:

(1) Loading is carried out in three shifts, for each of which a loading report is prepared dated on the day the first shift starts but running into the early hours of the second day. The shift are: 06: 30—14: 30 "morning"; 14: 30—22: 00 "afternoon" and 22: 00—06: 00 the next day "overnight".

(2) For each of the three shifts. Bothra have a supervisor present who collects the Tally Sheets in respect of the number of slings loading into each hold, as well as keeping a "slip" of all material events occurring during each shift.

(3) The shift supervisor of the "morning shift" collects Tally sheets and slips of the previous three shifts and after checking with the Chief Officer on the total quantity loading during the previous 24 hours (06: 00—06: 00), calculates the quantity of cargo loading into each hold.

(4) He then fills in the daily (more accurately "24 hours") loading report, signs it and gets it countersigned by the Chief Officer. That these reports are both precise and accurate is attested to Mr. Reddy in his first statement where he states "the daily loading sheets are quite specific about the actual quantity loaded hatch by hatch" and "The quantities recorded as loaded in the daily loading sheets are far more accurate and reliable than those in the Port Berthing Schedule".

What actually happened on 15th February 1998 was the following:

Mr. Dharanaj was the overnight supervisor. He prepared the daily loading sheet dated 15th February based on information given for the three previous shifts. For the third and last "Overnight' shift from 22:30 hours on 15th February until 06:00 hours on 16th February, he recorded that the three gangs " came on board at 22:30 hours. Work commenced at 22:40 hours. Work stopped for labour shift break. NB No.1 Cargo Loading Completed at 05:30 hours on 16th February 1998.

7.4   The document completed by Mr. Dharanaj was countersigned by the Chief Officer and signed in the left‐hand corner by the supervisor. That this was Mr. Dharanaj is clear from his rather distinctive signature which appears on five of the previous loading sheets as well as twice on his statement enters with the Defence Submissions.

7.5   That this document is the true and accurate loading report for the three shifts from 06:00 on 15th February to 06:00 on 16th February should be beyond dispute but a detailed comparison of the two versions of the loading report for 15th February 1999 will serve to dispel all possible doubt.

7.6   The truth of the matter is that Bothra falsified the second loading report for 15th February and Mr. Reddy's explanation, contained in his Supplementary Statement, for the existence of two loading reports both dated 15th February 1999 simply does not stand up to scrutiny. Mr. Reddy says that the original report for 15th February stating that loading went on into 16th February during the third (overnight) shift had to be replaced by the second report containing "the more accurate and up to date information" because it did not correspond with the draft survey and final figures for what was loaded based on the results of independent surveyors.

7.7   If we are to accept Mr. Reddy's explanation, we must also accept that the supervisor compiling the original report for 15th February simply imagined that a third shift had been worked and also imagined the details of the loading. Thus according to the original report for 15th February, 197 tonnes were loaded during the first shift; 259 tonnes during the second and 480 tonnes during the third. Further the supervisor compiling the original report for 15th February not only gave figures showing that 100 nets and 480 tonnes had been loaded during the third shift but also recorded that three gangs had started working at 22:40 hours and had stopped at 04:30 hours. Again he stated that loading of No.1 hold was completed at 05:30

hours on 16th February. It is submitted that it is simply not credible that the supervisor compiling the original report for 15th February would invent all this detail for the third shift but, given Sellers' strict orders that no goods should be loaded on 16th February, the second report falsified to show that no goods were loaded during the third shift 16th February becomes entirely understandable, albeit inexcusable.

7.8   On the question of exercise of discretion, Buyers first reject Sellers' argument that the claims in respect of discoloration and damaged cargo are "Quality disputes" for the purposes of GAFTA 125.They are claims for breach of description and for this reason and to the extent that they are based on the allegation that the Quality Certificate was fraudulent are governed by Rule 2: 3 (a).

7.9   Buyers deny Sellers' argument that Buyers' claim to arbitration only covered the Bill of Lading claim.As early as 23rd March 1998, Buyers referred to their claim to damaged cargo, which obviously covers discoloration and its consequences.Further, when Buyers' Chinese lawyers gave notice of their intention to arbitrate on 12th June 1998, they cited this message and confirmed that Buyers intended to submit this dispute to GAFTA arbitration.Thus their message of 12th June covered all claims and not only the Bill of Lading dispute.

7.10   Buyers admit that no evidence had been put forward in support of these claims but consider that there is nothing unusual in a Tribunal issuing an interim award in respect of the main claim and leaving the other in abeyance.

7.11   Buyers take the view that all claims are on the same footing, with notice of arbitration having been given in time and that their only failure has been to have appointed Mr. R. Rookes 30 days late. Under the circumstances Sellers' arguments against the exercise of discretion are out of proportion.

7.12   On the respective merits of the Quality claim and the Bill of Lading claim, Buyers consider that the arguments adduced by Sellers In the Rejoinder, e.g. that Sellers are not responsible for the acts of their agents or that the quantity loaded on board was de minimis or that it was all the fault of the pre - sellers have already been refuted and that, in consequence, their claims are both valid and significant.

7.13   With regard to Sellers' argument in their Rejoinder that Buyers' Beijing lawyers understood GAFTA 125 and that, in consequence, the argument of ignorance of the time-limits should not avail Buyers, the response is clearly that Beijing lawyers did not understand GAFTA 125, for had they understood it they would have nominated an arbitrator in time.

7.14 Accordingly, Buyers ask the Tribunal to exercise discretion to extend for three principal reasons already advanced in their Reply submissions:

(1) Buyers only offence was that they did not know about the need to name their arbitrator within the 9 day limit.

(2) This claim was a Claim where there is, again to put it at its lowest, a very strong case that a Bill of Lading has been ante-dated.

(3) This case is a case where there can be no conceivable prejudice to Sellers since notice of intention to arbitrate was given in time and the notification of Mr. Rookes' name was only 30 days late.

7.15 In conclusion, Buyers ask the Tribunal to issue an Interim Final Award:

(1) Exercising its discretion on to allow all claims to proceed;

(2) Finding and holding that the Bill of Lading was ante-dated and should properly have been dated 16th February 1998;

(3) Awarding that Sellers should pay the costs of the Interim Final Award;

(4) Awarding that Sellers should pay Buyers' legal costs, to be taxed if not agreed;

(5) Directing that Sellers should serve their submissions on the quantum of Buyers' claim within 5 days of the publication of the Interim Final Award.

8.QUESTIONS FOR DISCUSSION

(1) What's the differentcharactors between arbitration and lawsuit?

(2) What's the function of an arbitration agreement?

(3) What's the general process of a commercial arbitration?

(4) What's the main charactors of GAFTAarbitration rule?

(5) How to write an arbitration application?

(6) How to response the defender's defence in the rejoinder?

9.参考文献

［1］ UK Arbitration Act 1996 ［EB/OL］. ［2008-04-16］. http：//www.bjac. org.cn/news/view.asp？id=1082.

［2］英国 1992 年海上货物运输法［EB/OL］. ［2025-01-10］. http：// wenku.baidu.com/view/e0443f18964bcf84b9d57b0f.html.

［3］杨良宜，莫世杰，杨大明. 仲裁法：从 1996 年英国仲裁法到国际商务仲裁［M］. 北京：法律出版社，2006.

［4］杨良宜，莫世杰，杨大明. 仲裁法：从开庭审理到裁决书的作出与执行［M］. 北京：法律出版社，2010.

［5］李勤昌. 海运提单持有人索赔权问题研究［J］. 黑龙江对外经贸，2005（5）.

［6］. 韩立新，袁绍春，尹伟民. 海事诉讼与仲裁［M］. 2版. 大连：大连海事大学出版社，2016.

［7］邓杰. 伦敦海事仲裁制度研究［M］. 北京：法律出版社，2002.

［8］中国海事仲裁委员会网站：http：//www.cmac-sh.org/

［9］GAFTA ARBITRATION GUIDE：http：//www.gafta.com/arbitration

［10］ GAFTA ARBITRATION RULES NO. 125.： http：//www. gafta. com/ arbitration

10.附录

附录 1　GAFTA ARBITRATION GUIDE

<u>What is Gafta Arbitration?</u>

Arbitration is a process for the resolution of disputes which avoids the cost and complexities of legal action through the law courts. The parties to a dispute refer the matter to one or more persons （the arbitrators）, who adjudicate the matter and whose decision （the Award） is binding on the parties.

Gafta arbitrations are conducted under English Law. The provisions of the Arbitration Act 1996, and of any amendment or re-enactment to the Act, apply to every arbitration and appeal.

Gafta's internationally respected arbitration service is the foundation of the Gafta standard form contracts.

All Gafta contracts include an Arbitration clause, which incorporates the Gafta Arbitration Rules Form No.125 into the contract.

For simple dispute resolution, where the problem is not complicated or does not involve large sums of money, the parties may agree to use Gafta Simple Dispute Arbitration Rules Form No.126 instead of Form No.125.

For Charter Party contracts, the Gafta Charter Party No. 1 incorporates the Maritime Arbitration Rules Form No.127.

Gafta Arbitration Rules are designed with the trade in commodities in mind.

In general, whenever the two parties to a contract or the charter party cannot mutually resolve their dispute, rather than going to the courts, the matter will be resolved by arbitration. Where an arbitration award is not accepted by one of the parties, an Appeal may be lodged and an Appeal hearing will make a final, binding decision.

Benefits of Gafta Arbitration

Arbitration has several benefits:

First and foremost it is totally private and confidential. Arbitration hearings are held in private and the proceedings, decisions and awards are confidential to the two parties involved.

Arbitration is inexpensive, and can be a rapid solution to an expensive problem. Arbitration can be cheaper than having the problem resolved by a court of law. It can also be faster than litigation. By avoiding unnecessarily lengthy arguments, and by managing the case in an efficient way, arbitration can save the parties both time and expense.

Arbitration is impartial and conducted by Gafta Qualified Arbitrators, who are Members of Gafta in the Arbitration category. All arbitrators are required to meet a high standard of professionalism. They must have an in-depth understanding of the complications and problems facing the trade, attend training courses and comply with the standards and criteria laid down in the Gafta Continuing Professional

Development Programme.Gafta's Dispute Resolution Service: A Guide 3

The arbitration process is less formal than court procedures and parties can be assisted with the presentation of their submissions or represented at any hearing by experienced Gafta Members.From time to time, there are difficult, complex legal aspects to a case and the parties may then choose to rely on lawyers to advise them, and if they mutually agree, to have legal representation at any oral hearing.

<u>The Arbitration Process</u>

At its simplest, the arbitration process is as follows:

The Claimant serves notice on the Respondent stating his intention to refer a dispute to arbitration;

The dispute shall be heard by a tribunal of three arbitrators (one appointed by each party, the third appointed by Gafta), or if both parties agree, by a sole arbitrator (appointed by Gafta);

The Claimant draws up submissions detailing the claim, and serves them to both the Respondent and Gafta.

The Claimant deposits with Gafta a sum specified by Gafta on account of the costs, fees and expenses of the arbitration;

The Respondent draws up counterclaim submissions, which are sent to both the Claimant and Gafta.

The tribunal may not require an oral hearing, however, the parties may request an oral hearing.

The arbitration process may involve additional submissions after the initial claim and counterclaims.

The decision of the tribunal shall be made and issued in writing as an Award.

Either party may appeal against an Award.

If appeal is made, an Appeal tribunal will be set up, the decision of which is final and binding on both parties.There is no right of appeal following an Appeal hearing.

There are clear time limitations set out in the Arbitration Rules Form No.125 within which a claim for arbitration can be made, arbitrators appointed, submissions made, and an appeal against an award made.

More details about the process of appointing an arbitrator and completing documentary submissions are available on the Arbitration section of the Gafta website.

How does Gafta Arbitration work?

When there is a dispute the party with a claim (claimant) advises the other party (respondent) that they intend to refer the dispute for settlement by arbitration.

The claimant then prepares a statement of the details of his case, together with all supporting documents.In reply, the respondent prepares his statement, and with supporting evidence, sends copies both to Gafta and the claimant.

The claimant then has a final opportunity to comment and provide further evidence on any new points raised in the respondents' statement. Gafta's Dispute Resolution Service: A Guide 4

In order for the arbitration to progress, the claim, the appointment of arbitrators and the submission of documents must be made in accordance with deadlines that are a part of the Gafta rules.

Gafta has two levels or a two-tier arbitration service - level one (also known as "first tier") is arbitration and level two is the appeal.

First Tier Arbitration

At the first level arbitration, the parties can agree to the appointment of either a sole arbitrator or a tribunal of three arbitrators.A list of Qualified Arbitrators may be obtained from Gafta.Each party has the right to appoint one arbitrator of the three arbitrators, with the third being appointed by Gafta.

Gafta's goal is to have an arbitration decision ("the award") within six months of the date of the first submissions. Arbitrations are mainly dealt with by reading the documents submitted and without the need for the parties or their representatives to attend an oral hearing. The arbitrators will decide on the issues being disputed and their decision will be made in writing.Upon payment of the costs, fees and expenses their award will be published to both parties.

The Appeal (Second Tier Arbitration)

Both parties have the right to appeal against the first level award.

A board of Qualified Arbitrators appointed by Gafta will hear the appeal. There will be three appeal board members if the first award was by a sole arbitrator or five board members in the case of an appeal against an award by three arbitrators.

The appeal is traditionally more formal and there is usually a hearing at which the parties are represented by experienced commercial people.

How are awards enforced?

Most of Gafta's awards of arbitration are complied with. However, if a party refuses to settle the final award, the Council of Gafta may choose to inform all of its members worldwide that the party has failed to comply with the award.

Awards can also be enforced under the New York Convention or the Geneva Convention, both of which concern international arbitration matters.

At present there are over 145 signatory countries to the New York Convention. This means that in general, arbitration awards rendered in one country will be enforced in another signatory country through their legal system.

Simple Dispute Arbitration

Gafta Simple Dispute Arbitration Rules No.126 was introduced as an alternative service for matters that may not involve large sums of money or complex arguments and problems.Gafta's Dispute Resolution Service: A Guide 5

If the buyers and sellers wish to resort to these rules they complete an agreement form provided by Gafta that instead of having an arbitration provided by form No.125, they agree to refer their dispute for settlement under the Simple Dispute Rules.

Gafta Arbitration Rules No.126 are dealt with speedily.Gafta will appoint a sole arbitrator, and the parties will be notified of the fees in advance.There is no appeal against the arbitrator's decision, which should be provided within a couple of months from the time the matter is referred to Gafta.

附录2 EXCERPT FROM GAFTA 125

2.PROCEDURE AND TIME LIMITS FOR CLAIMING ARBITRATION

The claimant shall serve on the respondent a notice stating his intention to refer a dispute to arbitration within the following time limits. (The appointment of arbitrators shall be in accordance with Rule 3).

2.1 Disputes as to Quality and/or Condition

(a) In respect of disputes arising out of the "Rye Terms" clause not later than the 10th consecutive day after the date of completion of final discharge. (See Rule 6).

(b) In respect of claims arising out of certificates of analysis in respect of which allowances are not fixed by the terms of the contract, not later than the 21st consecutive day after the date on which the claimant receives the final certificate of analysis.

(c) In respect of all other quality and/or condition disputes, not later than the 21st consecutive day after the date of completion of final discharge, or delivery, or the unstuffing of the container (s), as the case may be.

2.2   Other Disputes

In respect of all other disputes relating to the sale of goods:

(a) arising out of CIF, CIFFO, C & F and similar shipment contract terms, not later than one year after the expiry of the contract period of shipment, including extension if any, or (ii) the date of completion of final discharge of the ship at port of destination, whichever period shall last expire,

(b) arising out of FOB terms, not later than one year after (i) the date of the last bill of lading or (ii) the expiry of the contract period of delivery, including extension if any, whichever period shall first expire,

(c) on any other terms, not later than one year after the last day of the contractual delivery, collection or arrival period, as the case may be.

(d) Irrespective of the time limits in (a), (b) and (c) above, in the event of non-payment of amounts payable, not later than 60 consecutive days from the notice that a dispute has arisen as provided for in the Payment Clause of the contract.

2.3   No award by the tribunal shall be questioned or set aside on appeal or otherwise on the ground that the claim was not made within the time limits stipulated in this Rule if the respondent to the claim did not raise the matter in their submissions, so as to enable the tribunal to consider whether or not to exercise the discretion vested in it by Rule 21.

附录3　GAFTA仲裁庭对本案的裁决节选

𝕬𝔴𝔞𝔯𝔡 𝔬𝔣 𝔄𝔯𝔟𝔦𝔱𝔯𝔞𝔱𝔦𝔬𝔫

Gafta

G . A . F . T . A .
07 FEB 2000

The Grain and Feed Trade Association

Gafta House 6 Chapel Count，Chapal Place

Rivington Street，　London ECZA 3OQ

United Kingdom

OFFICIAL FORM　NO.12466

We，the undersigned，having been appointed to arbitrate in a dispute that has arisen between

CLAIMANT：Z.IMP.AND EXP CORP.Beijing，china，（BUYERS）

and

RESPONDENT： C. INTERNATIONAL TRADING PTE. LTD，Singapore，（SELLERS）

in respect of a contract dated 6th November 1997 for the sale of about 11 000 tonnes 10% more or less Indian Yellow Soyabean Meal Extraction （Toasted Soyabean Meal，Yellow Flakes Type） at a price of US$278.50 per tonne.Cost and freight Free Out from one Indian port to one China main port，shipment 15th January 1998—15th February 1998 basis GAFTA 100 where not in conflict with other terms of the contact and with arbitration as per GAFTA 125， DO HEREBY FIND AND AWARD as follows：

1.BACKGROUND TO THIS AWARD

1.1　This reference raises serious allegations of documentary falsification. Not

—it must be underlined— by the parties to this reference, but by those responsible for issuing certain of the documents called for under terms of the contract.Further, the respondents have raised the argument of prescription as an in limine defence to the claim.

1.2   For these reasons, the tribunal, upon divers applications of the parties, allowed a number of extensions to the original timetable to allow the parties to obtain evidence in India and China on the important matter of the veracity of the documents submitted under the contract: by its Order of 5th March 1999, advised the parties that it would first hear arguments and submissions on prescription, possible exercise of discretion and liability for the purposes of issuing an award, preliminary or final, in respect of these matters, leaving the question of quantum to be argued at a later stage if its preliminary determination was in Claimants' favour, and lastly, upon application by the Claimants, agreed to allow the Claimants to submit to the visual scrutiny of the Tribunal certain original documents relating to their claim at a meeting held at GAFTA on 23rd April 1999, at which representatives of both parties and of the Tribunal were present.

8. DISCUSSION AND FINDINGS

(A) Time-bar and possible exercise of discretion to admit prima facie time-barred claims.

8.1   Buyers' claims are of two kinds: a principal claim based on Sellers'alleged breach in presenting falsified documents and in respect of which Buyers have adduced a great deal of evidence and a very detailed calculation of their damages (the Bill of Lading Claim) and a secondary claim based on alleged deficiencies in the cargo ascertained at discharge (the Cargo claim) in respect of which Buyers, on the own admission, have adduced no evidence whatsoever.To these various claims Sellers primary defence is that they are time-barred and that the Tribunal should so rule dismissing these claims and not exercise its discretion to admit. Buyers, unsurprisingly, argue in favour of the exercise of discretion to admit, having conceded that their appointment of an arbitrator was out of time under the GAFTA 125 (Arbitration Rules) in respect of both the Bill of Lading and the Cargo claim. The Tribunal, accordingly, will address and determine these issues of prescription in limine.

8.2　　The salient facts are largely undisputed. Thus the "D" completed her discharge at Nantong on 17th March 1998. On 23rd March 1998, Buyers notified Sellers to send a representative to Nantong to carry out a joint sampling and sealing operation in respect of a perceived problem of cargo damage, threatening to claim arbitration if the problem could not be resolved amicably. On 12th June 1998, Buyers' Beijing lawyers advised Sellers that having reviewed the documents in relation to the "D" shipment, including the Shipping documents, Sales contract, the "Berthing Programme" for 15th—17th February 1998. Extracts from the Log Book, GAFTA 100 and GAFTA 125, they had come to the conclusion that Sellers had presented an ante‑dated Bill of lading and that in so doing they had caused Buyers losses amounting to US$1 500 000 for which they were legally responsible. In the same message, Buyers' lawyers, referring to Buyers' fax of 23rd March 1998, stated "now we are confirming again that our client had the intention to refer this dispute to arbitration as per GAFTA 125". On 24th July Buyers' London solicitors appointed Mr. Roger Rookes as Buyers' arbitrator in respect of their claims under the contract.

8.3　　Buyers admit that their appointment of Mr. Rookes on 24th July 1998 was 30 days out of time in respect of both claims but that notice of intention to claim arbitration was correctly given in time under the Rules by their Beijing lawyers on 12th June 1998. In consequence, they ask the Tribunal to admit these late claims for the various reasons set out in their submissions pursuant to its unfettered discretion under the Rules. Sellers deny that notice of arbitration was ever given in respect of the Cargo claims and that in respect of these claims the appointment of Mr. Rookes was not only 30 days' late. On the contrary they argue that the appointment of Mr. Rookes was over three months late as the claims in question were Quality disputes falling under the shorter time limits of GAFTA 125 covering such disputes. Buyers rejected both these arguments on the grounds that the disputes concerned falsified documents including the Quality Certificates and that Buyers Beijing lawyers' fax of 12th June 1998 in notifying an intention to claim arbitration specifically referred to the damage claim articulated in Buyers' earlier message of 23rd March 1998.

8.4   Taking into consideration the facts, the provisions of GAFTA 125 and the arguments of the parties as summarised above and as set out in full in their submissions, we hereby find and hold as follows:

(i) Buyers failed to appoint an arbitrator within the time-limits prescribed by GAFTA 125.In consequence, prima facie, all their claims are barred and waived.

(ii) Buyers' Claim in respect of the cargo at discharge (the Cargo claim), in relation to which Buyers themselves in their fax of 23rd March used the words "damaged cargo", falls within the provisions of GAFTA 125 on Quality disputes setting short time-limits for the notification of an intention to arbitrate and for appointing an arbitrator.Accordingly, under the provisions of 2 (1) (c) of GAFTA 125, they should have notified their intention to arbitrate within 21 days of the completion of final discharge on17th March, i.e.at latest on 7th April.This they failed to do.They should also have appointed their arbitrator within 9 days of giving notice of their intention to arbitrate or of the last day for giving such notice, i.e.latest on16th April.This they also failed to do, only appointing their arbitrator in respect of this (Cargo claim) over three months later, on 24th July 1998.

(iii) As regards the bill of lading claim, valid and timely notice of an intention to claim arbitration was given by Buyers' Chinese lawyers on 12th June 1998 but the appointment of Mr.Rookes as arbitrator on 24th July, was 30 days out of time under Rule 2: 3 (c) GAFTA 125 governing this claim.

8.5   In approaching the question of the possible exercise of discretion, the Tribunal is mindful of the fact that the circumstances in which Buyers missed the time-limits set by GAFTA 125 differ substantially from one claim to the other.Thus whereas the delay in respect of the nomination of an arbitrator in respect of the Bill of Lading claim was only 30days, the delay in respect of the Cargo claim was over three months.Again whereas the Bill of Lading claim is for a considerable sum of money based upon a serious accusation of documentary fraud and has been argued extensively by Buyers supported by a great deal of evidence, the Cargo claim has only been argued in outline and, as is candidly admitted by Buyers, is a possible claim in future for which no evidence at all has been forthcoming.

8.6   In all these circumstances and as ours is an unfettered discretion, not circumscribed by the narrower grounds on which the courts may give leave to appeal under the provisions of the 1996 Arbitration Act, we find and hold that the Cargo claim is irrevocably barred and waived but we exercice our discretion to admit, and we do hereby admit the Bill of Lading claim.

(B) The Bill of Lading Claim

8.7   While, pursuant to our Order dated 5th March 1999, we are not concerned in this award with the question of quantum but only that of liability, it may be noted that Buyers are claiming some US$ 736 988.32 in respect of Sellers' alleged breach in obtaining payment of the contract price against the presentation of falsified documents and more particularly of a Bill of Lading dated 15th February 1998. When in reality, loading had continued into 16th February 1998 and the bill should have been dated 16th February 1998 thereby rendering it and the other shipping documents rejectable. The importance of one extra day when that extra day follows the last day of the contract period of shipment and when the market has or is falling is a factor to which merchants and traders are highly sensitive. And it is this point, namely, whether the Bill of Lading dated 15th February presented and against which payment was made was a false document which should have been dated one day later, on 16th February, that we must decide before being able to pronounce upon the liability or otherwise of Sellers to Buyers in this arbitration.

8.8   A great deal of evidence and many witness statements (many of them contradictory) have been produced on both sides in this arbitration. On the one hand, you have the full set of documents presented under the contract, all perfectly consistent with each other, issued at load and clearly pointing to the vessel having completed loading on 15th February. These documents are supported by witness statements of the personnel of Bothra who arranged and checked the loading of the vessel. On the other hand you have the Ships' Log and the Masters' statements to the effect that loading continued into 16th February. There are discrepancies and contradictions in the various statements with the consequence that if we were to have to determine the issue on the totality of the aforementioned evidence, we would be obliged to find that Buyers had failed to meet the relatively high standard of proof required to support what is, in effect, an allegation of documentary falsification.

8.9   However, there is the further evidence of the original loading reports obtained by Buyers from the owners of the "D." and submitted to the examination of the Tribunal at the special meeting arranged for this purpose in London on 23rd April 1999. This evidence essentially consists of a report for 15th February absent from Sellers' set of loading reports put in to support their submissions that loading was completed on 15th February 1998 at 23: 15 hours. This report differs from the report for 15th February put in by Sellers in a number of important respects. Thus Sellers' report shows that no work was carried out on the third shift (22: 00 hours on 15th February to 06: 00 hours on 16th February) and that the vessel completed loading at 23: 15 hours on 15th February with a total of 10 479 tonnes on board basis independent surveyors' figures. Per contra, Buyers' report for 15th February shows that a total of 100 nets equalling 480 tonnes had been loaded in hatches I, IV, and V during the third shift and that cargo loading had been completed with the completion of hatch No 1 at 05: 30 hours on 16th February 1998, resulting in a total quantity on board as of that time of 10 159 tonnes.

8.10   Sellers, through the Supplementary Statement of Mr. Reddy of their agents Bothra, accept that Buyers' report for 15th February was produced by them in the morning of 16th February, i.e. It was not a forgery. However, they argue that it was discarded and superseded by Sellers' report, as this report contained the more accurate and up to date information based on the draft survey and final figure. Thus Sellers' report stating that loading was completed at 23: 15 hours on 15th February 1998 is the accurate report.

8.11   The parallel existence of two authentic reports produced by the same company and even written in the same hand on the same day, but stating quite different facts, presents something of a problem. Where, as here, the differences between the two reports may be decisive for the purposes of determining liability and the possible award of very substantial damages, the problem becomes acute. Put bluntly, which report of the two reports both prepared by Bothra are we to believe and what credibility do we attach to the explanations of Mr. Reddy in favour of the truth and accuracy of the report relied upon by Sellers?

8.12   Having carefully examined both versions of the report for 15th February in the light of the very extensive arguments addressed to us by both sides and comparing these reports with the other reports issued during the course of loading, having considered at length Mr.Reddy's explanation for the existence of two authentic reports of which only the report relied upon by Sellers is said to contain the accurate time and date of completion of loading, having considered Buyers' argument against the veracity of Mr. Reddy's explanation and having taken into account all the surrounding circumstances, including the importance under the contract of completing loading within the contract period of shipment, we do hereby find that loading was only completed on 16th February 1998 and that, in consequence, the Bill of Lading dated 15th February was a misdated document and that it and the other similarly tainted documents could have been rejected by Buyers at the time of presentation had the truth then been known.

8.13 Having determined that the Bill of Lading and other documents for payment by Sellers were mis-dated and mis-dated in the important respect that they attested to loading having been completed within the contract period of shipment ending of 15th February 1998 when the truth of the matter was that loading was not completed until the following day, we find and hold that Sellers are in default both in having presented false documents for payment and in having failed to ship the goods within the contract period of shipment. we make no findings as to the date of this default, as this important question has not been addressed in the parties' submissions. Moreover, as it falls more properly within the ambit of our final award on damages, we leave it over to be argued by the parties in the second phase of this arbitration.

8.14 In so finding, the Tribunal categorically rejects the various arguments raised by Sellers in their submissions seeking to avoid liability in the event the Tribunal should find, as it has, that falsified documents were presented and that shipment was effected uncontractually outside the contract period of shipment. These arguments, which have been strenuously opposed by Buyers in the Reply submissions, may be qualified as:

(i) the "don't know, and not responsible for agents' act" argument;

(ii) the "de minimis" argument.

(iii) the "no right of rejection if most of the cargo loaded within the contract period" argument.

8.15 Regarding (i) above, while the Tribunal accepts that Sellers were not aware that their agents had back-dated the Bill of Lading and that an argument might be made that such an act presumably constitutes an act outside the terms of the agents' mandate from Sellers, this does nothing to relieve Sellers from their contractual obligation to present true documents and to ship within the contract period of shipment.

8.16 Regarding (ii) above, while the quantity shipped out of time may only have been a small quantity in relation to the total shipped within the contract period of shipment, it was a significant quantity of several hundred tonnes and as such not de minimis within the meaning of that phrase in law. Moreover, the real default of Sellers was not so much related to quantity as to time and it is well established in both law and the practice of merchants that shipment periods, especially where, as here, the contract actually provides for extension subject to the proper exercise of this option and payment, are fixed and definite in line with the general principle that in commercial contracts time is of the essence.

8.17 Regarding (iii) above, this entirely novel argument has no basis in either the law or the practice of merchants. Further, while it might conceivably be raised in connection with a defence to a claim that goods had been shipped out of time, it can afford no defence whatsoever to a case such as the present where Sellers are, in addition, found to have breached their obligation to present true documents and are found, albeit unwittingly, to have obtained payment under false pretences.

8.18 A further argument raised by Sellers in defence to Buyers' claim was that the "Kastellon" and "Procter and Gamble" cases, together with certain passages in Benjamin, supported their view that where a Bill of Lading is incorrectly dated but the bulk of the cargo has been loaded by date on the Bill of Lading, it would be unfair to award more than nominal damages to Buyers. The Tribunal prefers not to express any views on the merits of this argument as it would appear more properly to call for examination within the context of an award on quantum and as such not to fall within the scope of this Award.

9. IN ALL THESE CIRCUMSTANCES AND FOR ALL THESE REASONS THE
TRIBUNAL AWARDS AS FOLLOWS:

9.1　This Award is its Preliminary Final Award dealing exclusively with the issues of time - bar, exercise of discretion to extend and liability; the issue of quantum being left over to be dealt with in a Final Award.

9.2　Buyers' claim in respect of cargo damage or quality deficiencies (the Cargo claim) is irrevocably time barred and waived and accordingly FAILS.

9.3　Buyers' claim in respect of the Bill of Lading and other allegedly falsified documents (the Bill of Lading claim) while prima facie out of time under the GAFTA Arbitration Rules is admitted pursuant to the exercise of our absolute discretion to admit such claims and SUCCEEDS on the issue of liability.

9.4　Sellers' to pay 80% and Buyers' to pay 20% of the costs of this Preliminary Final Award including the Association's fees and the arbitrators' fees and expenses set out overleaf.

9.5　Sellers' to pay 80% of Buyers' legal costs and Buyers' to pay 20% of Sellers' legal costs of this Preliminary Final Award with costs to be taxed if not agreed.

9.6　Sellers to serve their submissions on the quantum of Buyers' claim within 15 days of the date this Award of any Appeal therefrom becomes final.

And the Fees and Expenses of this Arbitration as under:

Association Fees	1 841.00
Discount for Members	0.00
Expenses	540.00
Arbitrators' Fees	5 000.00
	VAT 0.00
	£7 381.00　　(DATED)

are to be paid by Sellers £5 604.80 and Buyers £1 776.20.

In the event of an Appeal being lodged against this Award, Appeal fee for Members and Non-Members shall be: £2 000.00

GAFTA's VAT Identification No：G3 243 8967 24

Seller's VAT Identification No：not applicable

Buyer's VAT Identification No：not applicable

11.案例英文信息

An Arbitration Lodged by Z Imp.& Exp.Co.for Late Delivery

Abstract：Arbitration has advantage over lawsuit，therefore to master relevant rules and skill is necessary for people in the field of commerce.Following the subject of arbitration for late delivery lodged by Z Imp.& Exp.Co.，this case firstly introduces the background and facts of the claim lodging，then describes in detail the request and reasons in the submission by the claimant，the defence submission by the respondent，the reply submission by the claimant，the respondent's rejoinder and the final submission by the claimant.The case depicts the vivid scenarios of the claim struggling between the claimant and the respondent in nearly three years.The second part of the case gives the theoretical analysis and comments to each story.Award by GAFTA tribunal is attached at the end of this case.

Key words：commercial arbitration，delivery period，ante-dated B/L，time bar

案例使用说明

一、教学目的与用途

本案例适用于"国际贸易实务"、"国际货物运输"和"国际物流"课程中关于商务仲裁知识点的教学。案例编写的目的是，通过案例中描述的各争议焦点的讨论，引导学生领会商务仲裁的相关法律规定和掌握商务仲裁技能，培养学生处理商务仲裁问题的实践能力。通过阅读、分析和讨论本案例资料，帮助学生思考和掌握下列5个具体问题：一是商务仲裁协议的法律意义；二是商务仲裁规则；三是商务仲裁的程序；四是商务仲裁的技巧。

本案例的概念难度、分析难度和陈述难度均适中，适用对象包括学习国际贸易专业、国际物流专业和国际商务专业的本科生、研究生和国际商务专业学位研究生。对于缺乏专业基础理论知识的本科生，可以根据教学大纲，有选择地引导阅读案例相关材料，重点分析商务仲裁的基本法律依据和基本程序；对于缺乏实践经验的研究生，可以引导其将所掌握的理论知识运用于本案例每一个具体问题的分析，对案例中争论的几个焦点问题，作出自己的是非判断，锻炼其处理实际问题的能力。

本案例规划的理论教学知识点包括：

（1）商务仲裁协议的法律意义；

（2）商务仲裁的法律依据；

（3）商务仲裁的法定程序；

（4）商务仲裁裁决的执行。

本案例规划的能力训练教学内容包括：

（1）商务仲裁的正确组织；

（2）仲裁协议的草拟；

（3）索赔证据的搜集；

（4）商务仲裁申请如何操作；

（5）仲裁员如何指定；

（6）仲裁申请书如何草拟；

（7）如何把握仲裁时效；

（8）如何反驳答辩人的抗辩；

（9）仲裁裁决如何执行。

二、分析思路

第一，引导学生讨论商务仲裁的一般性思路。可以让同学们从日常生活中"找个人评评理"的经历中，或从曾经参与过的商务仲裁经验中，结合从教科书中所学的相关知识，总结商务仲裁的一般性程序：签订仲裁协议、确定索赔性质、确定损失金额、搜集索赔证据、发出仲裁通知、指定仲裁员、准备和提交仲裁申请。随后，将同学们总结的这一仲裁一般性程序引导到本案的讨论中，并结合本案例事实和课前发给大家的讨论思考题，具体讨论每一具体环节涉及的理论知识和需要解决的具体问题。

第二，从签订仲裁协议的角度，引导学生讨论下列问题：仲裁和诉讼相比有什么特点？厘清这一问题有助于同学们理解和掌握如何在商务工作中确定纠纷的解决方式。何时签订仲裁协议？厘清这一问题有助于同学们理解即使在纠纷产生之前没有签订仲裁协议，也可以在纠纷产生之后补充签订，甚至在合同有诉讼条款的情况下，通过事后签订仲裁协议改变合同中的争议解决方式，从而使争议解决简单化。

第三，从仲裁协议内容角度，引导学生讨论下列问题：（1）如何选择仲裁机构？讨论这一问题的意义在于它不但涉及仲裁地点的确定，还涉及法律适用和仲裁程序规则；（2）如何确定仲裁类型？讨论这一问题的意义在于它涉及仲裁的难易程度、所需时间的长短和仲裁费用多少；（3）准确掌握仲裁程序与规则的意义是什么？讨论这一问题的重要意义在于它是选择仲裁机构的重要参考，更是仲裁进行的行动指南，还涉及仲裁的时效；（4）如何保证仲裁裁决的执行？讨论这一问题的意义在于让同学们掌握仲裁裁决在国内或国际得以执行的方法。

第四，从实体争议的角度，引导学生讨论倒签提单反映了什么实质性问题？本案例中发货人为什么倒签提单？很短的倒签时间可以改变倒签提单的性质吗？本案例中发货人倒签提单导致了什么法律后果？通过讨论这些问题，可以引导学生深入本案例的情境，汇集相关知识，掌握上述问题的判定准则。

三、理论依据及分析

1.商业仲裁的特点

仲裁也是俗话所说的打官司的一种，是指争议双方通过协议，自愿地将争议交由作为第三方的仲裁员来公断的做法。仲裁之所以受到法律保护，又受到商界欢迎，主要是因为它具有以下几个特点：

一是公正性。仲裁法要求仲裁员的仲裁必须公正。尽管仲裁员由争议双方各自选定，但他们不同于诉讼中的辩护律师，后者的职责是不管被代理人是否有错，都要努力去证明他无过错，目的是打赢官司，哪怕暗地里采用不公正的手段。但仲裁不是这样，法律要求仲裁员要做到公平公正，判案时要处于公正第三人的位置上判定是非，而与谁指定无关。

仲裁员必须依据法律规定或是参照先例进行裁决。仲裁在程序上基本按照法院的做法，实施对抗制，即由双方各自陈述理由，出具证据，仲裁员在双方提供的证据基础上进行裁决。仲裁员必须依据证据法有关规定采信相关的证据，而且双方的证据都公开给对方，不得有所保留。所以，仲裁从公正性、程序及证据的合法性上都与诉讼相似，保证了仲裁的公正。

二是国际性。1958年，联合国组织制定了《承认及执行外国仲裁裁决公约》（Convention on the Recognition and Enforcement of Foreign Arbitral Awards），简称《1958年纽约公约》。截至2023年5月全球已有172个国家在公约上签字，承认该公约的效力。首先，这个公约的制定稳定了法律管辖权。按照公约规定，有仲裁协议的纠纷只能由仲裁解决，如果一方当事人起诉到法院，法院不得受理。在这一制度下，即使法院通过扣船取得了管辖权，如果争议双方订有仲裁协议，法院也应当让当事人先去仲裁，法院按照仲裁裁决对被扣船舶进行处理，从而避免了管辖权混乱。其次，该公约使得仲裁结果在世界范围有了可执行性。仲裁的目的不仅是要得到一个谁是谁非的结果，更重要的是要保证仲裁结果可以执行。该公约的根本目的就是让一个国家的仲裁结果在其他国家也被承认并执行，否则，一国的仲裁裁决在另一国将变成废纸。在这个问题上，法院的判决是不能与之相比的。

三是秘密性。仲裁的进行及结果是不公开的（美国除外），这对商人的信誉及商业秘密的保护都是十分重要的。因此，英国的LMLN（Lloyd's Maritime Law Newsletter）也只对少数典型的案件进行报道。

四是非正式性。同诉讼相比，仲裁尽管也有相应的程序，但宽松很多。诉讼通常要请律师，在法院正式开庭，双方进行激烈的辩论，甚至使用简单的"是"与"不是"去回答复杂的问题，诱使证人作出有利的证词。仲裁的情况则大不相同，大部分案件事实是通过传递文件的方式来完成的，当事人双方无须开庭见面，仲裁员完全是依据双方呈递的材料审理案件。当然，仲裁员根据案件的复杂程度也可以组织开庭，但气氛相当缓和，开庭与否也可由仲裁员决定。

五是快速、经济。尽管仲裁法及各仲裁庭规定了相应的程序，例如，《中国海事仲裁委员会仲裁规则规定》，被申请人应自收到仲裁通知后15日内选定或委托仲裁委员会主任指定一名仲裁员，30日内提交答辩书，有正当理由的，可申请延期开庭审理。由于仲裁员拥有对仲裁程序的自由决定权，使得仲裁比诉讼要快得多。而且，提交仲裁本身有时就可以将争议解决。例如，对于一些怀着侥幸心理的债务人，一见对方真的提交了仲裁，自知理亏，干脆提早清偿债务了事；有的在中途披露文件的过程中自知败诉已成定局，便可能及早和解了事，只有少数是硬着头皮打到底的。

仲裁的快速、非正式性节省了大量的法律费用。首先，仲裁不必委托律师，提供证据、递交答辩书是公司内部的法律部，甚至是懂得法律及相关业务知识的业务员就可以胜任的事情，从而节省了大笔的律师费；其次，由于仲裁程序比较简单，特别是在小额仲裁的情况下，仲裁费用也比诉讼费用少得多。

六是专业性。仲裁员大多都是业内的专家，具有丰富的专业知识和法律知识，而且当事人还可以自己选定仲裁员，这就保证了案件审理的权威性和公正性。难怪英国只有在仲裁中涉及法律原则争议时才允许上诉，对于技术问题，法院尊重仲裁员的裁决。

本案例中的Z与C熟知仲裁的上述特点，在签订买卖合同之时就约定，如果未来在合同的执行过程中产生争议，双方将按照GAFTA 125仲裁规则在GAFTA仲裁庭进行仲裁。双方的这一安排是明智的，后来的仲裁提交机构也是正确的。

2.仲裁协议与程序

法院诉讼是不需要任何协议的，但仲裁却不同。如果当事双方欲将争议提交仲裁，必须对此达成协议。仲裁协议可以是口头的，也可以是书面的；可以事先达成，也可以在争议发生后达成。仲裁协议一经达成，争议的任何一方都不得再就该争议进行诉讼，法院也不得接受这种诉讼。为防止债务人事后采取不同意仲裁的技术手段拖延案件，最好的办法是事先签订仲裁协议，即在合同中规定仲裁条款。仲裁协议应广泛、全面，以免事后被判无效或难于执行。一般情况下，仲裁协议应包括以下几项基本内容：

一是仲裁地点。它是仲裁协议的一项重要内容。在没有相反规定的情况下，选择了仲裁地，就等于选定了仲裁适用的程序法和审理案件适用的实体法。因此，仲裁地的不同，适用的法律就不同。当然，合同双方可以在合同法律管辖条款中规定合同的实体法，而仲裁地选在另一个国家，这种做法不利于仲裁的顺利进行。

二是仲裁类型。仲裁有两种类型：一种是随意仲裁；另一种是机构仲裁。随意仲裁是指一种非正规的仲裁，在争议发生后，双方自愿找一个比较权威的人裁决，双方自愿服从裁决结果。在海事争议中，有许多这类仲裁。它程序非常简单，也非常经济，常由一个人独立仲裁。伦敦海事仲裁员协会（LMAA）的仲裁就是随意仲裁。

国际上正规的仲裁是由仲裁机构进行的。一些商业团体成立一个仲裁机构，制定仲裁程序，对提交的案件依规定的程序进行仲裁。如国际商会设在巴黎的国际仲裁院、中国国际贸易促进委员会下的中国国际经济贸易仲裁委员会及中国海事仲裁委员会、英国的仲裁庭和谷物与饲料贸易协会（GAFTA）仲裁庭、瑞典的斯德哥尔摩商会仲裁庭等。正规的仲裁应在仲裁协议中指定仲裁机构，否则可能被认定为随意仲裁。

三是仲裁程序与规则。每个仲裁机构都制定了自己的仲裁程序和规则。一般情况下，如无相反规定，指定了仲裁机构，也就意味着适用该机构的仲裁程序和规则。

四是仲裁裁决效力。国际上普遍规定仲裁裁决是终局（final）的，对双方均有约束力。裁决作出后，双方必须依照执行，败诉方不执行的，胜诉方可申请法院强制执行。败诉方在另一国家的，如果是《1958年纽约公约》的签字国，可以申请该国法院协助执行。

英国法律制度允许仲裁中的败诉方在不服裁决时，到法院上诉，但法院对此有较严格的限制，主要是当仲裁员适用法律不当时，并且这一不当适用导致一方受到严重不公正裁判，才允许该案上诉。这也是劳氏法律报告中存在许多仲裁上诉案的原因。这种做法的好处是，它给人们确立了审案指南，毕竟仲裁裁决只能做参考而不能作为法律先例。

本案例中的买卖合同仲裁条款指定的是GAFTA仲裁庭，适用的是GAFTA 125规则，它对仲裁程序和仲裁时效的规定明显不同于一般的仲裁规则，应特别予以注意。

3.GAFTA仲裁规则的主要特点

GAFTA仲裁规则除了具有一般仲裁庭的仲裁规则所具有的普遍特点外，还具有其独有的特点，主要涉及仲裁请求的时效问题。与一般仲裁规则不同，GAFTA仲裁规则根据请求的性质为不同性质的仲裁请求送达规定了严格、苛刻的时间限制。这一时间限制实际上被作为仲裁的时效，错过了时效，答辩人可以请求仲裁庭拒绝申请人的仲裁申请，这就如同法院拒绝立案一样，其结果是申请人丧失了提出仲裁申请的权利。

GAFTA 125仲裁规则规定的仲裁申请送达更强调送达答辩人。它规定了申请人的仲裁申请和仲裁员的指定向答辩人通知的最迟时间，而一般的仲裁规则没有这类时间规定，只是要求仲裁机构在接到仲裁申请之后应当通知答辩人。GAFTA 125规则根据请求的性质规定的通知时间从几天到一年不等，因此，当争议发生后，申请人必须在规则规定的时间内将仲裁通知送达被申请人。GAFTA 125的具体仲裁时效请参见其仲裁规则。

4.国际商务仲裁的操作

一要及时发出仲裁通知和指定仲裁员。如同诉讼时效一样，任何仲裁规则都有仲裁时效的规定。诉讼时效截止时间以正式向法院提交起诉书为准，而仲裁时效的截止时间通常以向争议的另一方发出仲裁通知和根据仲裁规则指定仲裁员为准。不同的仲裁庭的仲裁规则对不同诉求规定了不同的仲裁时效，有的短到数日，有的可达一年以上。仲裁申请人应当准确把握相关的仲裁时效，在发生争议后，根据争议的性质，在仲裁时效内向争议的对方发出仲裁通知，在规定的时间内指定仲裁员并告知争议的对方。错过仲裁时效，答辩方就有权申请仲裁庭拒绝仲裁申请。本案例中双方争议的焦点便是Z是否在GAFTA 125规则规定的时效内向C发出了仲裁通知并在规定的时间内指定了仲裁员。对此，Z明显存在疏忽。如果不是英国仲裁法有相关规定，单凭仲裁规则，Z的申请会被仲裁庭彻底拒绝。

二要准备仲裁申请书。发出仲裁通知书和指定仲裁员后，申请人应当在仲裁规则规定的时间内，向仲裁庭提交正式的仲裁申请书。申请书就如同诉讼中的起诉书一样，写明申请人与被申请人的名称和地址、所依据的仲裁协议、案情和争议的要点、申请人的请求和所依据的事实证据，并一并提交证明文件。

三要对答辩方的答辩作出抗辩。根据仲裁规则，被申请人在接到申请人的通知后，应当在规定的时间内作出答辩书并提供证明文件。这些答辩书和证明文件会转给申请人。申请人在接到后，应仔细阅读，并在规定的时间内对被申请人的答辩作出抗辩并提供证明文件。

对于复杂的案件，仲裁庭还会组织双方开庭聆听答辩，以便仲裁庭澄清各项事实，根据需要，开庭聆听可能会进行多次。对此，双方都应做好充分准备。

四要准备最后陈述。在经过答辩和抗辩、开庭聆听后，仲裁庭认为所有事实都已澄清，各方再没有新的诉求后，会让申请人作出最后书面陈述。此时，申请人应当将案件及整个审理过程中对方所做的各种答辩和反请求作出梳理，并依据事实证明文件作出最后诉求陈述及依据，等候仲裁庭作出裁决。

本案例中，除了申请人在上述第一项上出现了疏忽从而导致后来的激烈争议外，在其他三个方面的操作都是充分、翔实和正确的，值得参考。

四、关键要点

阅读本案例并正确回答讨论思考题，需要学生把握以下要点：

（1）与诉讼相比，仲裁具有很多优点，合同中应当约定仲裁条款。

（2）仲裁需要订立协议，选定仲裁庭、仲裁程序和规则。

（3）国际谷物和饲料贸易一般都选用GAFTA的格式合同，约定根据GAFTA 125仲裁规则进行仲裁。但该规则与一般的仲裁规则差异较大，应当熟练掌握其特点。

（4）合同履行发生争议需要提交仲裁时，应当根据仲裁规则在规定的时间内完成各项程序性工作，备足证据提出仲裁申请。胜负的关键是证据是否充分。

五、课堂教学计划建议

本案例可以作为专门的案例讨论课来进行。如下是按照时间进度提供的课堂计划建议，仅供参考。

对于本案例教学，建议在给出本案例前，教师用30分钟的课堂时间预先讲授相关知识，之后立即给出本案例素材和讨论思考题，然后根据思考题的数量将全班学生分成若干组，每一组分配一个问题，要求各组在课后阅读案例材料，根据所学知识对分配的问题作出分析性答案，并将主要分析依据和结论做成PPT。然后准备100分钟全班同学听取汇报和教师评论。课中计划：

简要的课堂前言，明确主题：2～5分钟

小组发言：每组10～15分钟，控制在80分钟内

引导全班进一步讨论并进行归纳总结：15～20分钟

第八章

滞期索赔

A贸易公司的滞期费赔付纠纷

摘要：本案例正文以A贸易公司的滞期费赔付纠纷为主题，描述了A贸易公司与H海运公司、A贸易公司与其货物的卖方和买方较为复杂的滞期费计算纠纷的全过程。通过对纠纷细节的描述，展示了装卸时间和滞期费计算中涉及的买卖合同和海上运输合同的相关约定、装卸时间事实记录的原始材料、各相关方滞期费计算的不同结果和滞期费纠纷的性质等主要内容。案例的使用说明部分提供了滞期费计算的大陆法和普通法原则，分析了当事人在滞期费计算中存在的问题，提供了正确处理这类纠纷的方法。

关键词：装卸时间　滞期费条款　WWWW　NOR

1.本案例描述的滞期费赔付纠纷是一个真实的事件，案例编者是当年的主要参与者，为提高案例阅读的新鲜感，将事件的发生时间改为2014年。鉴于事发至今的相关法律规则没有实质性变化，因此本案例对装卸时间和滞期费问题的教学仍具有很强的使用价值。由于企业保密的要求，在本案例中对有关当事人做了必要的掩饰性处理。

2.本案例只供教学之用，并无意明示地或暗示地褒奖或贬低案例中涉及的公司的相关行为。

案例正文

以下描述的是一场运输合同下和买卖合同下滞期费的纠纷。2014年，A贸易公司与H海运公司，以及A贸易公司与其卖方和买方，在化肥于越南胡志明港卸货后，就本航次下的滞期费发生争议，A贸易公司就滞期费和速遣费的义务、金额多少与相关各方进行了多场争辩。

1.背景

1.1 A贸易公司的化肥买卖合同

在国际货物买卖中，比较高明的做法之一就是做中间贸易，也称三角贸易。在这种贸易中，中间贸易公司依靠对某类货物的进出口市场的灵通信息，通过签订背对背买卖合同谋取利益。新加坡的A贸易公司（以下简称A）便是常年从事中间贸易的公司之一。该公司事实上是美国人出资在新加坡注册的，将公司注册在新加坡并在那里从事经营，对于他们捕捉亚洲市场信息非常便利。多年来，他们利用新加坡得天独厚的地理位置和丰富的市场信息，在东南亚成功地完成了大量交易，获利颇丰。

2014年9月初，A得知越南Y公司（以下简称Y）欲进口尿素，便在大量出口尿素的中国市场寻找供应商。经过若干天的多个渠道询价，最终与中国南通C公司（以下简称C）以FOB条件达成了购买合同。合同主要条款为：中国产尿素，10 000公吨允许5%数量增减，50公斤塑料编织袋装，包装袋上标记约定的运输标志。装运期为2014年10月，装运港口为中国南通港，卸货港为胡志明市，贸易条件为FOBS，结算方式为可转让信用证。

在与C商定购货合同的同时，A与Y同步商定销售合同，并在已经商定的采购合同基础上签订了供货合同。A是一个做中间贸易的老手，知道如何通过两个合同条款的背对背来规避风险。因此，与Y贸易公司的销售合同主要条款，如货物描述、货物数量、货物包装、交货期、装卸港口、结算方式等，与采购合同完全一致，但贸易条件改为CFR，这意味着A要负责租船，以便A在商定租船合同时有机会要求船舶出租人同意以提单副本和保函换取交换提单，从而保护商业秘密，货物单价各不相同。

1.2 A与H海运公司的租船合同

A的CEO是一个美国人，具有一般美国商人的乐观、豪放性格。采购合同与销售合同的签订，意味着A又可以凭丰富的经验和掌握的信息狠赚一笔。于是在两个背对背合同签订的当晚，公司CEO在五星级的莱弗士酒店餐厅设宴慰劳下属。席间，大家频频举杯，感谢CEO的厚爱，也庆祝尿素买卖合同的顺利签订。但CEO毕竟是个头脑清醒的掌舵人，在大家的欢声笑语中，也没有忘记叮嘱下属及早洽谈租船合同。

第二天，A物流部便开始着手在租船市场上寻找合适的船舶。经过4天的比较和讨价还价，最终与H海运公司（以下简称H）达成了10 000公吨尿素的运输合同。合同约定，装卸时间起算以GENCON 1994年版本规定为准，船舶抵达装卸港锚地后即可递交货物装卸准备就绪通知书（Notice of Readiness, NOR，简称准备就绪通知书），WWWW（不论进港与否，不论靠泊与否，不论完成清关与否，不论通过检疫与否），从等泊地点到泊位的航行时间不计为装卸时间，其他与本案相关的租船合同条款如下：

Quote

16. The vessel is to load a minimum/maximum of 10 000 net metric tons Urea in bags, estimated stowage about 58~60 cubic feet per metric ton, without guarantee. All cargo is to be stowed in places easily accessible to the ship's loader. Charterers privilege to ship two percent empty/spare bags/clips free of freight, which charterers may or may not show in the Bill (s) of Loading.

The owners have the option to combine with steel products at Xingang, rotation at owner's option. The owners are to warrant the steel cargo to be stowed in separate holds and rot to have any contact with this Bagged Urea cargo. The owners warrant that the maximum port stay at Xingang for loading the steel cargo is 3 days. Any longer stay than 3 days at Xingang, then the owners agree to give the charterers a freight discount of US$1.00 (ONE USDOLLAR) per net metric ton.

Cargoes are to be discharged simultaneously in all hatches. However, the owners shall endeavor to give priority to discharging the Urea first, if so required.

17. Cargo to be loaded free in and stowed and to be effected by Stevedores appointed and paid by the Shippers (by Shippers' means and for their own account free of expense and risk to the vessel), at the average rate of 2 500 (TWO

THOUSAND FIVE HUNDRED) net metric tons per weather working day of 24 consecutive hours, Sundays and Holiday included. Stevedores' damages to ship, if any, to be settled directly between Owners and Stevedores, but Charterers to render their utmost assistance to Owners for recovering these damages.

18. Before commencement of loading, vessel's holds to be clean, dry and absolutely free from rust and residue of any previous cargoes, to an independence surveyor's satisfaction.

19. Cargo to be discharged free of expense and risk to the vessel by receiver's stevedores, at the average rate of 1 000 (ONE THOUSAND) net metric tons per weather working day of 24 consecutive hours, 12: 00 hours Saturday or day before a Holiday to 08: 00 hours next Monday or next regular working day, not to count, even if used. Stevedores' damages to ship, if any, to be settled directly between Owners' and Stevedores, but Charterers to render their utmost assistance to Owners for recovering these damages.

20. Vessel to be equipped with pontoon type hatch covers, which owners warrant to be tight, strong and absolutely waterproof and in good working order for the protection of the cargo. Vessel's gear to be in good working order at all times and capable of serving all holds/hatches simultaneously, and Charterers privilege to use same for loading and discharging. Time lost by reason of vessel's gear breakdown is not to count pro-rata. Vessel to supply free of charge, during any time day/night, Fridays/Sundays and Holidays included, light, steam/power for ship's gear if required. Vessel's equipment shall comply with the regulations of the countries in which vessel will be employed and Owners are to ensure that the vessel is at all times in possession of valid and up-to-date certificates of efficiency to comply with such regulations.

If Stevedores, Longshoremen or other workmen are not permitted to work due to failure of the Master and/or Owners Agents to comply with the aforementioned regulations of efficiency, any time lost is not to count pro-rata.

In the event cargo is discharged by shore or floating cranes, vessels discharging gear and equipment to be stowed out of the way and not to interfere with the timely and efficient operation of shore/floating equipment.

Charterers have privilege to place bulldozers in holds to facilitate discharge using vessel's gear to place/remove same in/form vessel, always subject to vessel's tank top strength and gear capacity.

21. No cargo to be stowed in deeptanks or poorly accessible places. Any extra expenses, time, damage or breakage incurred by reason of loading, stowing and/or discharging cargo from poorly accessible places to be for Owners' account, and Owners to undertake to stow the cargo only in compartments suitable for the safe stowage, carriage in transit and delivery of all underdeck of fertilizer in bags, Owners confirm all areas where the cargo will be stowed are easily accessible places to the ship loader. Should any cargo be loaded in such excepted places as aforementioned, any time or laytime lost and any additional expenses incurred in loading and/or discharging this cargo, to be for vessel's account.

22. Overtime and other extra expenses connected with same, to be paid by the party who orders it. If overtime ordered by Port Authorities, same to be for Charterers'/ Shippers'/Receivers' account. If overtime ordered by Port Authorities, same to be for Charterers'/Shippers'/Receivers' account. In any case, Officers' and Crew's overtime is always for Owner account.

23. Both at loading and discharging ports, vessel to perform opening and closing of hatches in order to prevent damage to the cargo. Vessel to present for loading with hatches open and ready to receive cargo. First opening and last closing of hatches to be for Owner's account and all subsequent opening/closing of hatches to be for charterer's account. Opening and closing to be done by ship's crew if allowed by Port Authorities, otherwise opening and closing to be for Charterer's account. Vessel to ensure that all hatches are immediately closed in the event of rain and when loading/ discharging is completed or stopped at each respective hatch.

24. Demurrage at the loading and the discharging ports to be paid at the rate of US$2 500.00 (TWO THOUSAND FIVE HUNDRED US DOLLARS) per day and pro-rata. Owners to pay despatch money at half the demurrage rate on laytime saved at the discharge port. Demurrage/despatch to be settled between Owners and Charterers.

25. The Statement of Facts issued at the loadport is to be signed by the Master,

Vessel Agent, and Suppliers representatives, and the Master is to airmail a copy, if possible, to Charterers at the address of …In case suppliers refuse or can not sign the Statement of Facts, then Master's and Agents' signature are sufficient, in which case Master to note same on the Statement of Facts.

26.The Owners or Master to give notice of estimated time of arrival to all parties listed below upon Charterers confirmation of clean fixture.Thereafter, Owners/Master to give 7/5/3 days, then 48+24 hours definite notice of estimated time of arrival to the Agents at both loading port and discharging port and the Charterers.

Unquote

2.装卸港口的事实记录

2.1　L轮在装货港的装货时间事实记录

2014年10月5日，H根据与A签订的航次租船合同向本公司所属的L轮下达了航次指令，指示该轮开往南通港装运10 000公吨尿素运往胡志明市。10月20日，L轮抵达长江口锚地并向当地港务监督部门报告了船舶动态。因为南通港暂无空闲泊位，根据长江船舶航行安全的相关规定，港务监督官员指令该轮在长江口锚地待命。L轮船长在长江口锚地下锚后，通过海事卫星向南通港的船舶代理公司发出了船舶装卸准备就绪通知书（NOR）。NOR原文如下：

NOTICE OF READINESS

This is to advise you that the above named vessel arrived at CHANG JIANG KOU at 1210 hrs on OCT, 20th, 2014, and she is in all respects ready and fit to load her cargo of PRILLED UREA IN BAGS at this port.

Master of MV "L"

N/R tendered at 1210 hrs.On OCT 20th, 2014

N/R accepted as per relevant Charter-Party

10月23日上午，L轮代理通知船长做好进港装货准备，引航员下午将引领船舶进港。当日下午15：35时引航员登轮引领船舶进港，17：20时，船舶靠上南通港2号泊位。24日，海关、边防、卫生检疫等部门的官员登轮进行联合检验，10：00时，L轮通过联检。与此同时，货舱检验人对货舱的适货性进行检验，但船舶没能通过检验。船舶出租人获知此消息后，指示船长组织船员对货舱进行清扫。船长接到指令后，一方面组织船员清扫货舱，一方面向公司汇报称，船舶在开往南通港的航行途中，已经组织船员对货舱进行了彻底的清扫，货舱事实上不存在不适货问题，怀疑是发货人为了掩盖没有备妥货物的事实而采取的一种不当的技术性手段，提醒船东注意核查。该轮当日14：00时通过货舱检验并立即开始装货，到10月29日22：50时，全部货物装船完毕。随后，L轮起航开往胡志明市。L轮在南通港的装卸时间事实记录如下所示。

L轮在南通港的装卸时间事实记录

LAYTIME STATEMENT OF FACTS

船名：MV "L"   装卸货种类及吨：10 032 METRIC TONS OF PRILLED UREA IN BAGS

| DATE | DAY OF WEEK | TIME | | DESCRIPTION |
		FROM	TO	
OCT 20TH	MON		12：10	VSL ARVD CJK ANCHORAGE，NOR TENDERED
		12：10	24：00	WAITING FOR FREE PRATIQUE AND CUSTOM CLEARANCE
21ST	TUE	00：00	24：00	--DO--
22ND	WED	00：00	24：00	--DO--
23RD	THU	00：00	15：35	--DO--
		15：35	17：20	HEAVED UP ANCHOR AND PROCEEDED TO BERTH AND BERTHED ALONGSIDE WHARF NO.2
		17：20	24：00	WAITING FOR JOINT SURVEY
24TH	FRI	00：00	10：00	ENTRY JOINT SURVEY AND PASSED
		10：00	14：00	HOLDS FITNESS SURVEY FAILED CREW CLEANING HOLDS
		14：00	24：00	HOLDS FITNESS SURVEY PASSED AT 1400 HRS N LOADING COMMENCED
25TH	SAT	00：00	24：00	LOADING CONTINUED
26TH	SUN	00：00	08：30	LOADING CONTINUED
		08：30	09：00	LOADING SUSPENDED DUE TO FOG
		09：00	24：00	LOADING RESUMED AND CONTINUED
27TH	MON	00：00	04：30	LOADING CONTINUED
		04：30	07：00	LOADING SUSPENDED DUE TO FOG
		07：00	12：00	LOADING RESUMED AND CONTINUED
		12：00	12：30	LOADING SUSPENDED DUE TO SHIFTING FORWARD 20M
		12：30	24：00	LOADING RESUMED AND CONTINUED
28TH	TUE	00：00	08：30	LOADING CONTINUED
		08：30	19：30	LOADING SUSPENDED DUE TO RAIN
		19：30	24：00	LOADING RESUMED AND CONTINUED
29TH	WED	00：00	22：50	LOADING CONTINUED AND COMPLETED

2.2 L轮在胡志明市的装卸时间事实记录

经过约10天的航行，L轮于2014年11月8日21：30时抵达越南胡志明港，次日通过船舶各种检验手续，于10：30时靠泊卸货，但由于船舶同时还装有部分钢材需要卸下，卸货速度也较慢，加上坏天气和其他因素的影响，船舶在该港停留了14天才完成全部货物的卸载工作。船舶装卸准备就绪通知书如下：

NOTICE OF READINESS

TO：D.COMPANY OF AGRICULTURAL MATERIALS

TO：C.INTERNATIONAL PTE LTD

Dear Sirs，

This is to notify you that the above vessel has arrived at pilot station of HO CHI MINH CITY PORT，VIETNAM at 21：30 hours local time on the date of 08 November，2014，and she is ready in all respects to commence discharging 10 032.00 MTS（B/L No.10LV01A：3 009.60 GROSS MT；B/L No.10LV01B 2 006.40 GROSS MT；B/L No.10LV01C：5 016.00 GROSS MT）cargo PRILLED UREA IN BAGS in accordance with the terms and conditions of the Charter Party.

This Notice of Readiness tendered at：2 130 LT，08 November，2014.

Very truly yours

Master of MV. "L"

卸货港的装卸时间事实记录如下：

PAGE：1/6

LAYTIME STATEMENT OF FACTS

VESSEL："L" .PORT：HOCHIMINH CITY.CARGO：10.032GMT/200.000 BAGS PRILLED UREAIN BAGS & 2 652.2498 MT STEEL PRODUCT.

B/L QUANTITY：B/L NO，10LV01A：3 009.6 GMT，B/L NO.10LV01B 2006.4 GMT，B/L NO.10LV01C：5 016GMT.S/O NO.YHFY-1：745 BUNDLES/1 249.997MT STEEL BAR And 814 BUNDLES/1，402.2524MT WIRE ROD.

ARRIVING AT 21: 30 ON 08/11/2014

DATE	WEEK'S DAY	TIME		RECORDS
		FROM	TO	
08/11	SAT		21: 30	Arrived At Vung Tau Pilot Station, NOR tendered
		21: 30	24: 00	Awaiting daylight
09/11	SUN	00: 00	04: 20	Awaiting daylight
		04: 20	04: 50	Inward clearance Free pratique granted
		04: 50	10: 30	P.O.B, to K15B-Ben Nghc, HCMC N berthed
		10: 30	19: 00	Awaiting discharging cargo
				-19: 00LT: Commenced discharging urea cargo
		19: 00	23: 00	Discharging urea cargo H1, H5
				H2, H3, H4: waiting for disch steel cargo
		23: 00	24: 00	Break time
10/11	MON	00: 00	01: 00	Break time
		01: 00	01: 50	Discharging urea cargo H1, H5
				H2, H3, H4: waiting for disch steel cargo
		01: 50	03: 15	Discharging urea cargo H1
				H5: No work due to ship's derrick trouble
				H2, H3, H4: waiting for disch steel cargo
		03: 15	05: 00	Discharging urea cargo H1, H5
				H2, H3, H4: waiting for disch steel cargo
		05: 00	07: 00	Break time
		07: 00	11: 00	Discharging urea cargo H1, H5
				H2, H3, H4: waiting for disch steel cargo
		11: 00	12: 30	Break time
		12: 30	14: 30	Discharging urea cargo H1, H5
				H2, H3, H4: waiting for disch steel cargo

PAGE：2/6

DATE	WEEK'S DAY	TIME		RECORDS
		FROM	TO	
		14：30	17：00	Discharging urea H1，H5/Steel cargo H2，H3，H4
		17：00	18：30	Break time
		18：30	23：00	Discharging urea H1，H5/Steel cargo H2，H3，H4
		23：00	24：00	Break time
11/11	TUE	00：00	01：00	Break time
		01：00	04：30	Discharging urea H1，H5/Steel cargo H2，H3，H4
		04：30	07：00	Break time
		07：00	11：00	Discharging urea H1，H5/Steel cargo H2，H3，H4
		11：00	12：30	Break time
		12：30	17：00	Discharging urea H1，H5/Steel cargo H2，H3，H4
		17：00	18：30	Break time
		18：30	23：00	Discharging urea H1，H5/Steel cargo H2，H3，H4
		23：00	24：00	Break time
12/11	WED	00：00	01：00	Break time
		01：00	05：00	Discharging urea H1，H5/Steel cargo H2，H3，H4
		05：00	07：00	Break time
		07：00	11：00	Discharging urea H1，H5/Steel cargo H2，H3，H4
		11：00	12：30	Break time
		12：30	17：00	Discharging urea H1，H5/Steel cargo H2，H3，H4
			17：00	Completed discharging steel in tween deck H3
		17：00	18：30	Break time
		18：30	22：00	Discharging urea H1，H3，H5/Steel cargo H2，H4
			22：00	Completed discharging urea H1
		22：00	23：00	Discharging urea H3，H5/Steel cargo H2，H4
		23：00	24：00	Break time
13/11	THU	00：00	01：00	Break time
		01：00	05：00	Discharging urea H3，H5/Steel cargo H2，H4
		05：00	07：00	Break time

PAGE: 3/6

DATE	WEEK'S DAY	TIME		RECORDS
		FROM	TO	
14/11	FRI	07：00	11：00	Discharging urea H3, H5/Steel cargo H2, H4
		11：00	12：30	Break time
		12：30	17：00	Discharging urea H3, H5/Steel cargo H2, H4
		17：00	19：00	Break time
		19：00	23：00	Discharging steel cargo H2, H4 H3, H5: No work due to awaiting survey alleged dirty bagging
		23：00	24：00	Break time
		00：00	01：00	Break time
		01：00	03：20	Discharging steel cargo H2, H4, 03：20LT: Completed discharging steel cargo in tween deck H2, H3, H5: No work due to awaiting survey alleged dirty bagging
		03：20	05：00	Discharging steel cargo H4 −H2, H3, H5: No work due to awaiting survey alleged dirty bagging
		05：00	07：00	Break time
		07：00	11：00	Discharging steel cargo H4 11：00LT: Completed disch steel in tween deck H4 H2, H3, H5: No work due to awaiting survey alleged dirty bagging
		11：00	12：30	Break time
		12：30	14：00	No work due to awaiting survey alleged dirty bagging
		14：00	16：00	Discharging urea H2, H3, H4, H5
		16：00	19：30	No work due to rain and bad weather
		19：30	23：30	Discharging urea H2, H3, H4, H5
		23：30	24：00	No work due to rain and bad weather
15/11	SAT	00：00	07：00	No work due to rain and bad weather
		07：00	11：00	Discharging urea H2, H3, H4, H5
		11：00	12：30	Break time
		12：30	17：00	Discharging urea H2, H3, H4, H5
		17：00	19：00	Break time
		19：00	20：00	No work due to rain and bad weather
		20：00	23：00	Discharging ureaH2, H3, H4, H5
		23：00	24：00	Break time

PAGE：4/6

DATE	WEEK'S DAY	TIME FROM	TO	RECORDS
16/11	SUN	00：00	01：00	Break time
		01：00	05：00	Discharging urea H2，H3，H4，H5
		05：00	07：00	Break time
		07：00	08：00	Discharging urea H3
				H2，H4，H5：No work due to no gangs
		08：00	09：00	No work due to no trucks
		09：00	10：00	Discharging urea H5
				H2，H4，H5：No work due to no gangs
				10：00LT：Completed discharging urea of
				B/L No.10L V01A& E/L No.10l v01B
		10：00	13：20	awaiting shifting to K1 Terminal at the request of Charterer
			13：20	P.O.B and vessel shifted to K1 Terminal，HCMC

PAGE：5/6

DATE	WEEK'S DAY	TIME FROM	TO	RECORDS
16/11	SUN		15：30	Vessel berthed At K1 Terminal
		15：30	19：00	Awaiting discharging
		19：00	23：00	Discharging urea H2，H3，H4，H5
		23：00	24：00	Break time
17/11	MON	00：00	07：00	No work due to no gangs
		07：00	11：00	Discharging urea H2，H3，H4，H5
		11：00	13：00	Break time
		13：00	17：00	Discharging urea H2，H3，H4，H5
		17：00	19：00	Break time
		19：00	21：00	Discharging urea H3，H4
				H2，H5：No work due to no gangs
		21：00	23：00	Discharging urea H2，H3，H4

续表

DATE	WEEK'S DAY	TIME		RECORDS
		FROM	TO	
18/11	TUE			H5：No work due to no gangs
		23：00	24：00	Break time
		00：00	01：00	Break time
		01：00	04：30	Discharging urea H2, H3, H4
				H5：No work due to no gangs
		04：30	07：00	Break time
		07：00	11：00	Discharging urea H2, H3, H4, H5
		11：00	13：00	Break time
		13：00	16：30	Discharging urea H2, H3, H4, H5
		16：30	19：00	Break time
		19：00	24：00	Discharging urea H3, H4
				H2, H5：No work due to no gangs
19/11	WED	00：00	01：30	Discharging urea H3, H4
				H2, H5：No work due to no gangs
		01：30	07：00	No work due to no gangs
		07：00	11：00	Discharging urea H2, H3, H4, H5
		11：00	13：00	Break time
		13：00	15：00	Discharging urea H2, H3, H4, H5
				15：00 LT：Completed discharging cargo H3

PAGE：6/6

DATE	WEEK'S DAY	TIME		RECORDS
		FROM	TO	
		15：00	17：00	Discharging urea H2, H4, H5
		17：00	19：00	Break time
		19：00	20：00	No work due to bad weather
		20：00	23：00	Discharging urea H2, H4, H5
		23：00	24：00	Discharging urea H2, H4
				H5：No work due to stevedore rough handling

DATE	WEEK'S DAY	TIME		RECORDS
		FROM	TO	
20/11	THU	00：00	01：30	Discharging urea H2，H4
				01：30LT：Completed discharging cargo H4
				H5：No work due to stevedore rough handling
		01：30	02：00	Discharging urea H2
				H5：No work due to stevedore rough handling
		02：00	05：00	No work due to no gangs
		05：00	14：00	No work due to rain & bad weather
		14：00	17：00	Discharging urea H2，H5
		17：00	19：00	Break time
		19：00	23：00	Discharging urea H2，H5
				23：00LT：Completed discharging cargo H2
		23：00	24：00	Break time
21/11	FRI	00：00	01：00	Break time
		01：00	05：00	Discharging urea H5
		05：00	07：00	Break time
		07：00	09：30	Discharging urea H5
				09：30LT：Completed discharging cargo H5
		09：30	15：30	Awaiting suitable Current
			15：30	P.O.B & vessel sailed to Malaysia

3.装卸两港的滞期费/速遣费计算争议

3.1 南通港的滞期费计算争议

根据租船合同的相关规定，A 和 H 各自对装货港口的滞期费进行了计算，但二者的计算结果并不一致。根据 H 的结算，A 应向 H 支付 9 629.50 美元的滞期费，而 A 计算的应付滞期费只有 4 031.25 美元，两者相差了 5 598.25 美元。H 认为 A 不诚实守信，甚至觉得自己的尊严受到了冒犯，因此决定向 A 讨个说法。但是，双方为此多次致函磋商，却始终无法达成一致。船东最后声称，如果 A 不在规定的时间内支付船东主张的滞期费，将就此案诉诸法院。双方的装货港滞期费计算结果如下：

OWNER'S LAYTIME CALCULATION

MV "L"　　　　　　　　　　　　LDGPORT：NANTONG

NOR TENDERED：12：10 20TH OCD　　LDG RATE：2 500MT/DAY

DEMURRAGE RATE：USD2 500/DAY　　LDG COMPLTD：2 250 29TH

DATE	WEEKDAY	FROM	TO	TIME USED			REMARKS
				DAYS	HOURS	MUNITE	
21ST	TUE	06：00	24：00		18.00		
22TH	WED	00：00	24：00	1.00			
23TH	THU	00：00	15：35		15.00	35.00	
		17：20	24：00		6.00	40.00	
24TH	FRI	00：00	10：00		10.00		
		14：00	24：00		10.00		
25TH	SAT	00：00	24：00	1.00			
26TH	SUN	00：00	08：30		8.00	30.00	
		09：00	24：00		15.00		
27TH	MON	00：00	04：30		4.00	30.00	
		07：00	12：00		5.00		
		12：00	24：00		12.00		
28TH	TUE	00：00	08：30		8.00	30.00	
		19：30	24：00		4.00	30.00	
29TH	WED	00：00	22：50		22.00	50.00	
	TOTAL TIME USED：			2.00	137.00	225.00	

7.8646 DAYS

TIME ALLOWED：4.0128 DAYS

DEMURRGE：3.8518 DAYS × USD2 500 = USD9 629.50

CHARTERER'S LAYTIME CALCULATION

MV "L"   C/P date 10/11/14

Loading port:	NANTONG	
Demurrage rate:	USD/day	2 500.00
Despatch rate:	USD/day	1 250.00
Cargo quantity:	MT	10 032.00
Loading rote:	MT/day	2 500.00

Vessel arrived:	Mon	10/20/14	12：10
NOR tendered:	Mon	10/20/14	12：10
Left anchorage:	Thu	10/23/14	15：35
Berthed:	Thu	10/23/14	17：20
Loading commenced:	Fri	10/24/14	14：00
Loading completer:	Wed	10/29/14	22：50
Laytime commenced:	Thu	10/23/14	17：20
Laytime completed:	Wed	10/29/14	22：50

Day	Date	From HRS	To HRS	Rate %	Used HRS	D	Total H M	Remarks
Thu	10/23/14	17：20	24：00	100.00	06：40	0	06：40	
Fri	10/24/14	00：00	24：00	100.00	24：00	1	06：40	
Sat	10/25/14	00：00	24：00	100.00	24：00	2	06：40	
Sun	10/26/14	00：00	08：30	100.00	08：30	2	15：10	
		08：30	09：00	0.00	00：00	2	15：10	NTC-Bad Weather
		09：00	24：00	100.00	15：00	3	06：10	
Mon	10/27/14	00：00	04：30	100.00	04：30	3	10：40	
		04：30	07：00	0.00	00：00	3	10：40	NTC-Bad Weather
		07：00	12：00	100.00	05：00	3	15：40	
		12：00	12：30	0.00	00：00	3	15：40	Shifting Berth
		12：30	21：08	100.00	08：38	4	00：18	
		21：08	24：00	100.00	02：52	4	03：10	
Tue	10/28/14	00：00	08：30	100.00	08：30	4	11：40	
		08：30	19：30	0.00	00：00	4	11：40	NTC-Bad Weather
		19：30	24：00	100.00	04：30	4	16：10	
Wed	10/29/14	00：00	22：50	100.00	22：50	5	15：00	Loading completed

Time allowed		4 d	00：18	(4.01250 days)
Time used		5 d	15：00	(5.62500 days)
Time lost		1 d	14：42	(1.61250 days)

Demurrage due:　　　　　　　USD4 031.25

3.2 胡志明港的速遣费计算争议

根据租船合同的相关规定，H 和 A 对卸货港的装卸时间也各自进行了计算，但 A 计算的速遣费比船东计算的多出了 3 565.13 美元。双方的计算结果如下：

OWNERS' LAYTIME CALCULATION

MV "L" DISPORT：HCMC

NOR TENDERED：21：30 8TH NOV DISCHG RATE：1 000MT/DAY

DESPATCHRATE：USD 1 250/DAY DISCHG COMPLTD：09：30 21ST

DATE	WEEKDAY	FROM	TO	TIME USED			REMARKS
				DAYS	HOURS	MUNITE	
9TH	SUN	06：00	24：00		7	12	BSS 2/5 HOLD
10TH	MON	00：00	01：50		0.4	20	DO
		01：50	03：15		0.2	5	BSS 1/5 HOLD
		03：15	24：00		8	18	BSS 2/5 HOLD
11TH	TUE	00：00	24：00		9	36	DO
12TH	WED	00：00	17：00		6	48	DO
		17：00	24：00		4	12	BSS 3/5 HOLD
13TH	THU	00：00	24：00		14	24	DO
14TH	FRI	00：00	03：20		1.8	12	DO
		03：20	11：00		5.6	32	BSS 4/5 HOLD
		11：00	16：00		5		BSS 5 HOLDS
		19：30	23：30		4		DO
15TH	SAT	07：00	19：00		12		DO
		20：00	24：00		4		DO
16TH	SUN	00：00	24：00	1			DO
17TH	MON	00：00	24：00	1			DO
18TH	TUE	00：00	24：00	1			DO
19TH	WED	00：00	19：00		19		DO
		20：00	24：00		4		DO
20TH	THU	00：00	05：00		5		DO
		14：00	24：00		10		DO
21ST	FRI	00：00	09：30		9	30	DO
TOTAL TIME USED：				3	128	249	
TOTAL TIMED USED IN DAYS：		8.5063 DAYS					
TOTAL TIME ALLOWED：		10.0320 DAYS					
DESPATCH MONEY：		1.5257 DAYS × USD1 250 = USD1 907.13					

CHARTERERS' LAYTIME CALCULATION

MV "L"   DISPORT: HCMC

NOR TENDERED: 21: 30 8TH NOV   DISCHG RATE: 1 000MT/DAY

DESPATCHRATE: USD 1 250/DAY   DISCHG COMPLTD: 09: 30 21ST

DATE	WEEKDAY	FROM	TO	DAYS	HOURS	MUNITE	REMARKS
9TH	SUN	19: 00	24: 00		2		BSS 2/5 HOLD
10TH	MON	00: 00	01: 50		0.4	20	DO
		01: 50	03: 15		0.2	5	BSS 1/5 HOLD
		03: 15	24: 00		8	18	BSS 2/5 HOLD
11TH	TUE	00: 00	24: 00		9	36	
12TH	WED	08: 00	18: 30		4	12	DO
		18: 30	24: 00		3	18	BSS 3/5 HOLD
13TH	THU	00: 00	19: 00		11.4		DO
14TH	FRI	14: 00	16: 00		2		BSS 5 HOLDS
		19: 30	23: 30		4		DO
15TH	SAT	07: 00	19: 00		12		DO
		20: 00	24: 00		4		DO
16TH	SUN	00: 00	10: 00		10		DO
		19: 00	24: 00		5		DO
17TH	MON	00: 00	24: 00	1			DO
18TH	TUE	00: 00	24: 00	1			DO
19TH	WED	00: 00	19: 00		19		DO
		20: 00	24: 00		4		DO
20TH	THU	00: 00	05: 00		5		DO
		14: 00	24: 00		10		DO
21ST	FRI	00: 00	09: 30		9	30	DO
TOTAL TIME USED:				2	122	139	=7.1799 DAYS
TOTAL TIME ALLOWED:				10.0320 DAYS			
DESPATCH MONEY:			2.8521 DAYS × USD1 250=USD3 565.13				

4.A 与卖方和买方就装卸时间产生了争议

在与 A 就本案例中滞期费问题多次协商未果的情况下，H 派出代表赴新加坡与 A 进行当面交涉。经过两天多的反复协商，考虑双方的长期合作，船东最终作出让步，接受 A 按照船东计算金额的 80% 支付滞期费。A 的 CEO 当场开具了美元支票，支付了这笔滞期费。

然而，事后 A 在梳理整个案件后发现，本案例中的大量滞期费产生在南通港装货期间。根据买卖合同，卖方 C 负有及时装载货物的义务，但 C 在船舶抵达长江口锚地后没有及时安排船舶靠泊，也没有及时备妥全部货物，从而导致船舶滞期。A 认为 C 应当对这笔滞期费承担责任，于是致函 C，要求补偿 A 的滞期费损失。

C 收到 A 索赔函后回复辩称，双方货物买卖合同约定的是 FOB 贸易条件，而根据 INCOTERMS 2010 解释通则的规定，卖方的义务是在船舶靠泊后，及时地将约定的货物装到买方指定的船上，而事实上卖方已经履行了该项义务。FOB 术语解释中并没有关于卖方要承担滞期费的规定，双方的买卖合同对此也没有约定，故无法接受 A 的主张。A 则在随后的函中辩称，虽然 INCOTERMS 2010 解释通则中没有关于卖方承担装货港滞期费义务的规定，双方买卖合同也没有对此作出明确约定，但根据英国普通法中的默示义务原则，C 应当对装货港产生的滞期费负责。理由是，C 有义务在船舶抵达装货港后保证有泊位可以靠泊，但事实上船舶在长江口锚地等泊近 3 天。船舶靠泊后，C 安排的装货速度又很慢，延长了船舶在港的时间。C 不接受 A 的辩解，于是双方就此陷入了纠纷。

对于卸货港的卸货速度问题，A 也致函买方 Y，要求 Y 对其在卸货过程中没有完全履行义务所导致的那部分时间损失进行赔偿。观察卸货港的装卸时间事实记录可以发现，在卸货过程中，有部分货舱中断卸货，原因有：收货人声称有货损而陷入现场纠纷、没有足够的码头工人、收货人要求船舶移泊。A 认为，这部分时间损失均为 Y 没有履行法律上默示的及时收受货物义务造成的，因此，应当对这部分时间损失承担赔偿责任。Y 则声称，卸货时发现有的货物外包装污损，需要与船东协商解决，对此造成的时间损失应当由船东负责；码头没有足够的装卸工人是胡志明港的通常现象，收货人无法控制；移泊是因为码头公司的安排，自己也无法控制。因此，对这些事件导致的时间损失 Y 没有赔偿义务。再者，Y 与 A 的买卖合同中没有对卸货时间问题作出任何明确的约定，因此 A 的主张没有任何依据。双方就此各说各的理，互不相让。

5.讨论思考题

（1）掌握滞期费计算原则和方法对于买卖合同和运输合同的履行有何意义？

（2）如何妥善地约定装卸时间？

（3）应如何界定船舶的抵达？

（4）应如何界定船舶的准备就绪？

（5）应如何审核准备就绪通知书是否妥善地递交？

（6）怎样计算滞期费？

（7）买卖合同下的非租船方对滞期费有何义务？

6.参考文献

［1］杨良宜. 装卸时间与滞期费［M］. 大连：大连海事大学出版社，2006.

［2］TIBERG.The Law of Demurrage［M］. fourth edition.London：Sweet & Maxwell，1996.

［3］李勤昌. 国际货物运输［M］. 6版. 大连：东北财经大学出版社，2022.

［4］龚育华. 航次租约下滞期费相关法律问题研究［D］. 上海：上海海事大学，2003.

［5］朱民强. 浅议英国 The Happy Day 一案［EB/OL］.［2011-01-11］. http：//haishang.lawtime.cn/hslw/2011071120675.html.

7.参考判例

7.1　关于船舶抵达港口的英国判例

The "Johanna Oldendorff"［1973］2，Lloyd's Rep 285（H.L.）

本案确定了以下原则，即在港口租约的情形下，如租约未作特别约定，船舶要到港口范围内，且处于承租人的有效控制下才可被视为到达了约定地点，否则就不是已到达船舶。需说明的是，该标准强调船舶"要达到港口范围内"，即使是港口或者港口当局让船舶在港口范围外等待，该船舶仍然未到达约定地点。

案情概要

船东 E.L.Oldendorff & Co.G.M.B.H 和 Tradax Export S.A. 订立了一个航次租船合同，约定将 Johanna Oldendorff 出租给 Tradax 公司，租约是"港口租约"，船东和承租人其后关于装卸时间的起算产生了争议。

涉案租约约定的卸货港口是 Liverpool/Birkenhead，当船舶到达卸货港口时，港口没有泊位，于是港口当局命令船舶在 Mersey Bar 等待，该地点距离码头区域大约 17 公里，但是仍位于港口的行政管辖范围（Administrative limits）内。案件的争议点是 Johanna Oldendorff 轮在 Mersey Bar 等待靠泊时递交的 NOR 是否有效，即在当时其是否已经到达了租约约定的地点，即是一艘已到达船舶。船舶在锚地等待了长达半个多月，如果在 Mersey Bar 等待时不是一艘已到达船舶，意味着装卸时间要在 1 月 22 日才开始起算，而如果在到达 Mersey Bar 时是一艘已到达船舶，装卸时间在 1 月 6 日就可开始起算。

仲裁员支持了船东的主张，裁决船东可以主张 7 800 英镑的滞期费，而上诉法院却认为应当在 1 月 22 日才可开始起算装卸时间，案件后来到了上议院（House of Lords）。

判决：

在该案中，上议院批评了 1961 年的先例 The Aello［1961］A.C.135 确立的船舶抵达"商业区域（Commercial Area）"才是一艘已到达船舶的原则。

在本案例中，Lord Reid 发表了以下重要观点：

Before a ship can be said to have arrived at a port she must, if she cannot proceed immediately to a berth, have reached a position within the port where she is at the immediate and effective disposition of the charterer. If she is at a place where waiting ships usually lie, she will be in such a position unless in some extraordinary circumstances proof of which would lie in the charterer...

If the ship is waiting at some other place in the port then it will be for the owner to prove that she is as fully at the disposition of the charterer as she would have been if in the vicinity of the berth for loading or discharge.

Lord Reid 的上述观点后来被称为"Reid Test",即 Reid 标准,这是确立船舶是否为已到达船舶的基本标准。

最终,由于 Mersey Bar 处于利物浦港的行政管辖范围内,且其是通常的待泊地点,上议院判定船舶在 Mersey Bar 时就是已到达船舶,即自 1 月 6 日起就可起算装卸时间。

7.2 关于准备就绪通知书是否生效的英国判例

本案是关于装卸时间起算的重要案例。The Mexico 1 案确立了以下原则:在租约无特别约定的情形下,已递交的无效 NOR 并不会在满足递交 NOR 条件后自动生效,如船东未递交新的 NOR,装卸时间通常无法开始起算。

我们知道,普通法默示规定船东需在第一装货港递交 NOR,此外,租约通常还会约定船东需在每一装卸地点递交 NOR,否则装卸时间不能开始起算。进一步地,英国法下,除非租约另有约定,在未满足船舶到达指定地点、船舶未准备就绪及未满足租约约定的其他条件(如有)的情形下递交的 NOR 是无效的。

在 The Mexico 1 案中,船东在船舶未做好卸货准备时递交了一个 NOR,而在船舶做好卸货准备后,船东并未递交新的 NOR。船东和承租人的争议是船舶自做好卸货准备时开始起算装卸时间,还是自开始卸货才开始起算装卸时间。

案情

就涉案航次,船东和几个承租人签订了租约,即一个航次运输几个承租人的货物。其中和案件有关的主要为 1984 年 7 月 27 日签订的运输 5 000 吨袋装玉米的租约。船舶于 1985 年 1 月 20 日抵达卸货港,船长于 1 月 21 日递交了 NOR。但是,此时玉米上压载着其他租约下的货物,船东实际无法卸载玉米,也即船舶实际上并未做好玉米租约下的卸货准备。

1985 年 2 月 6 日,终于可以卸玉米了,也即船舶已经准备就绪,此时如船东递交新的 NOR,该 NOR 会是有效的 NOR。不过,船东在 2 月 6 日之后未递交任何 NOR,涉案货物实际于 2 月 19 日才开始卸载。

争议

案件所涉的争议之一是就玉米所涉租约,装卸时间自 2 月 6 日起算还是 2 月 19 日起算。船东认为,1 月 21 日递交的 NOR 虽未生效,但该 NOR 在船舶已实际准备就绪时变为了有效的 NOR,承租人或其代理知道或有途径知道船舶准备就绪的事实，装卸时间可以从2月6日船舶准备就绪时开始起算。承租人则认为船东递交的NOR始终是无效的。最终，承租人的律师让步认为装卸时间最晚也应从货物实际卸货即2月19日开始起算，法官判决同意此观点。

7.3 关于船舶是否抵达和是否准备就绪的若干判例

判例1："THE DELAN SPIRIT"（1971）

"DELAN SPIRIT"轮航次租给一苏联公司，被指派到黑海的TUAPSE港装运原油。合同中订有装卸率和滞期费率，船长在工作时间递交准备就绪通知书后可以起算装卸时间。1964年2月19日01：00时，船抵达TUAPSE港锚地，08：00时，船长递交了准备就绪通知书。由于该港4个泊位均有船舶作业，该轮直到2月24日才被安排靠泊，并在靠泊时办理并通过检疫。事后，船东根据合同按船长递交准备就绪通知书时起算装卸时间，向承租人索赔4 365英镑滞期损失。承租人不服，申请仲裁。双方对仲裁结果不满，上诉至上诉院。在上诉院，DONALDSON法官及JORDAN法官认为：①该轮为抵达船舶；②租船人违反合同，未能及时安排船舶停靠；③没有办理检疫不妨碍该轮为"抵达船舶"；④装卸时间从递交准备就绪通知书时起算。最后，法庭判定承租人向船东支付滞期费。邓宁法官总结说，尽管船舶未办理检疫，如果它持有卫生合格证书和船员健康证书，就不必担心该轮会耽误装卸货物，船长就有权发出准备就绪通知书，并且开始起算装卸时间。

判例2："THE TRES FLORES"（1973）

"TRES FLORES"轮航次出租，去保加利亚的瓦尔纳港装运散装玉米。合同订有装卸率和滞期费率，并要求船舶在发出准备就绪通知书时必须保证货舱干净、干燥、无异味，在各方面适合装载玉米达到承租人或发货人满意。备妥通知可以用电报发出，不论船舶进港与否，靠泊与否，通过检疫与否，均可起算装卸时间。

1970年11月22日（星期日）05：00时，该轮抵达瓦尔纳港锚地，船长向承租人代理电报递交了准备就绪通知书，称该轮已按合同规定，在各个方面准备就绪，可以装载6 900吨散装玉米。11月23日，发货人已将所有货物备齐待装。由于天气恶劣，直到11月27日（星期五）港口检疫官才得以到锚地检查船舶。检查发现货舱内有害虫，随即下令进行熏蒸。11月30日熏蒸完毕，发货人称12月1日的14：00时接受备妥通知。但由于无空泊位，直到12月7日才靠泊装货，12月13日装货完毕。船舶在港停留达20多天，船东向承租人索赔滞期损失。由于双方不服仲裁裁决，该案交到上诉院。船东称，合同规定不论检疫是否办理，都可起算装卸时间，租船人应当赔偿滞期损失。在上诉院，邓宁法官、CAIRNS 法官及 ROSKILL L.J.法官最后裁定，只有递交了有效的准备就绪通知书，装卸时间才可以起算。本案例中船长递交的准备就绪通知书称，船已按合同规定在各方面备妥，可以装载玉米，但卫生检疫官却发现货舱中有害虫，根据有关法律须进行熏蒸才可装货，这说明该轮事实上并未备妥，递交的准备就绪通知书无效。船舶备妥是指在发出准备就绪通知书当时事实上备妥而非在将来某时备妥。船舶事实上备妥是发出准备就绪通知书的先决条件。卸货前，舱盖还未打开，但很快便可以打开，准备就绪通知书应视为有效；船在锚地，未取得当地警察的装货许可，发出的准备就绪通知书可以视为有效；"THE DELIAN SPIRIT"案中未办理检疫，准备就绪通知书可以初步视为有效。但此案中船舶事实上并未备妥，发出的准备就绪通知书应视为无效。

判例3："THE APOLLO"（1978）LLR203

"APOLLO"轮被一家公司期租。1972年3月交船时，船上两名船员患胃肠炎，怀疑为斑疹伤寒被遣下船（事后确诊为伤寒）。船上其他人员没发现病症。租船人命该轮驶往利比里亚的 LOWER BUCHANAN 港装货。3月27日22：24时该轮抵达装货港锚地，但到3月28日05：00时才有空泊位。3月27日23点，卫生检疫官员对该轮进行检疫，获悉在上一港有两名船员怀疑患有伤寒而被送医院。28日03：00时检疫结束但未通过。除此之外，船舶其他方面均已备妥。28日上午，检疫官员对船员及饮用水进行化验。29日08：30时化验结束，结果显示船员无传染病。09：45时，检疫官员对厨房、卫生设施等地进行消毒，10：30时发放了卫生合格证。船随后被安排靠泊装货。租船人事后向船东索赔从3月28日00：30时至29日10：30时租金及耗油损失11 725美元。

本案争议在于，租船人是否可以提出上述索赔。回答此问题，首先要弄清楚该轮在锚地等待是何方、何时、何原因造成的。显然，办理卫生检疫是造成该轮等待的根本原因。这又回到了船舶完成检疫是否是例行手续的问题上。由于该案的特殊性，仲裁员将其交给法院裁定。

在法院，MOCATTA 法官裁定，根据租船合同，由船东提供船舶和船员，而船员被怀疑患有传染病在上一港被遣下船这一事实阻碍了卫生检疫合格证书的发放。若只是个例行手续，它不会给船舶造成什么延误，但此案中情况不同。因怀疑有传染病，检疫官员依据法律规定，必须进行抽样化验和必要消毒，确认没有问题才能签发合格证书。正是这一过程造成船舶延误，理应由船东负责。检疫前的待泊时间由租船人负责。

判例4："THE PUERTO ROCCA"（1978）LLR253

该案仍涉及海关检查手续与装卸时间起算问题。"PUERTO ROCCA"轮被航次租用运载散装玉米到利物浦港卸货。合同第47条规定，在卸货港船舶须办理海关手续，租船方代理人在工作时间收到船长的准备就绪通知书后，不论靠泊与否，装卸时间从第二天的第一工作期间开始起算；第50条规定，如遇港口拥挤导致船舶抵达港口后不能立即靠泊，按第47条规定递交准备就绪通知书，装卸时间相应起算。1977年11月4日16：45时，该轮抵达卸货港锚地，16：50时向租船人电报递交了准备就绪通知书。但租船人随即拒绝了该通知书，声称该轮尚未根据租船合同第47条规定办理海关手续。鉴于该港在锚地根本不办理海关手续，船东在声明保留第一个准备就绪通知书同时，于11月8日将船驶入一个非卸货泊位，办理并通过了海关检查，随后又于12：00时向租船人发出第二个准备就绪通知书。租船人接受了该通知书并于11月9日08：00时起算装卸时间。

合同双方对起算时间产生争议。鉴于此案情况复杂，仲裁员递交高等法院裁定。在高院，MOCATTA法官审理后裁定，鉴于该港锚地无法办理海关手续，合同规定无法执行，应视为无效条款。因该轮事实上靠泊时便顺利通过了海关检查，本身不存在办理障碍，故第一次递交的通知书有效，装卸时间从11月5日08：00时起算。

判例5：The "New Forest" ［2008］1 Lloyd's Rep.504

这是一个关于SOF的证据效力的判例。该案中，SOF虽未如租约所约定的由各方共同确认，但法官依然认为SOF具有很强的证明力。

案情

"New Forest"轮执行一个从巴西到中国的航次租船合同，租约第11条约定"滞期费和速遣费依据事实记录进行计算，该事实记录应由船东委托的装、卸港的代理出具，并需经船长及装港/卸港港务部门共同确认。"租约约定因坏天气导致的装卸货停止时间不计为装卸时间。

船舶到达卸货港中国烟台并提交了NOR，但由于吃水问题，船舶在靠泊前需要减载，双方对于以下过程并无太大异议：在烟台过驳需要浮动和移动的吊机，两者从载货船中将货物转移至驳船。一个浮吊通过拖轮拖至船边，橡皮浮筒（Fenders）安放在船边以确保安全，驳船在旁边接收货物。因为坏天气，浮吊和驳船返回泊位。

2005年3月11日，船东主张滞期费并随附SOF，承租人拒绝了该主张，虽然事实记录提及了坏天气，船东主张事实记录存在错误，真正使得卸货延误的原因是缺少驳船和过驳时需放置在两船中间的浮筒。

判决

法官认为，尽管租约中"on the basis of"的措辞并不足以使得SOF具有最终证据的效力，然而，SOF仍然具有很强的证明力，即使它没有满足"经船长及装港/卸港港务部门共同确认"的条件。即使在租约未约定SOF的证据效力时，SOF仍具有很强的证明力，这是因为SOF是在当场制作的，与当事人在事后很长时间之后才获取的其他证据材料相比，在没有欺诈、过失的情况下，它是最能反映事实的证据材料。在可以提供SOF或类似文件的情况下，法庭倾向于在此基础上作出结论，因为其他事后很久才取得的证据在证明力上往往不尽如人意。

判例6：The "Front Commander"［2006］2 Lloyd's Rep.251

这是一个关于提早装货条款的解释和装卸时间起算问题的判例。

案情

2003年12月7日，双方签订航次租船合同，以Asbatankvoy格式合同为基础，受载期为2004年1月9日至10日，合同并入Asbatankvoy格式的常见附加NOR和早装条款（early loading clause）如下：

附加条款第31条：...the vessel shall not tender notice of readiness prior to the earliest layday date specified in this charterparty and laytime shall not commence before 0600 local time on the earliest layday unless charterer Consents in writing ...

附加条款第33条：If charterer permits vessel to tender NOR and to berth prior to commencement of laydays，all time from berthing until commencement of laydays to be credited to charterer against laytime and/or time on demurrage.Saved time to be split 50/50 owners/charterers.

2004年1月6日，承租人给船东发了以下内容的邮件：charterers confirm NOR to be tendered on arrival Escravos，and to berth/load as soon as instructed thereafter by terminal.

2004年1月7日，承租人发了以下邮件给船东：Front Commander will

tender NOR on arrival, ie 8 January 00：30 and we want her to berth/commence loading 8 January. 船舶于8日中午12点靠泊。

双方主张

船东主张从靠泊开始到9日00：01时的一半时间计算为装卸时间，承租人主张装卸时间应从9日06：00开始起算，因为承租人始终没有同意装卸时间应提早起算。

判决

英国高等法院的法官支持了承租人的主张，认为承租人没有给出书面的同意确认装卸时间可以提早起算，承租人只是同意可以提早装货，该同意并不代表承租人同意装卸时间提早起算。但是上诉法院的法官推翻了高等法院的判决，支持了船东方的主张。

法官从以下3个角度说明了装卸时间提早起算的问题，具有较大的现实意义：

（1）如无相反约定，在装卸时间之前提早递交NOR，则装卸时间从受载期开始起算；

（2）如无相反约定，在装卸时间之前提早递交NOR，承租人指示船舶开始早装，装卸时间并不提早起算；

（3）依据本合同的早装条款，早装的一半时间应当记为装卸时间，对于该点，承租人的行为/邮件表明：①其同意提早递交NOR、靠泊和早装；②以上同意以书面作出；③船舶确实提早靠泊并早装。

其法律后果是：①承租人已放弃要求船舶不可早于受载期前装货的权利；②即使没有承租人的说明，船东可于9日前提交NOR；③承租人要求靠泊和装货是一个有效的航次指示，该指示在第31条的范围之内；④船东不可拒绝承租人的该指示。

8.案例英文信息

A Dispute in Demurrage for A Trading Company

Abstract： With the subject of a dispute in demurrage faced by A Trading Company, this case describes the whole process of the disputes between A Trading Company and H Shipping Company, between A Trading Company and their Seller and Buyer. The detailed description reveals the relevant stipulations in both sale contract and charterparty with regard to laytime and demurrage, the statement of facts in both loading port and discharging port, the different calculation results. It reflect the dispute nature. The second part of the case is of theoretical analysis and comments from the writer.

Key words: laytime, demurrage clause, WWWW, NOR

案例使用说明

一、教学目的与用途

本案例适用于"国际贸易实务"、"国际货物运输"和"国际物流"课程中关于装卸时间和滞期费知识点的教学。案例的编写目的是通过案例中描述的各争议焦点的讨论，引导学生领会装卸时间和滞期费计算的相关规则和计算方法，培养学生处理滞期费问题的实践能力。通过阅读、分析和讨论本案例资料，帮助学生思考和掌握下列具体问题：一是装卸时间和滞期费问题在买卖合同和运输合同履行中的重要性；二是装卸时间和滞期费计算的相关法律规定；三是装卸时间和滞期费的约定方法和计算方法；四是船舶抵达和船舶准备就绪的判定规则；五是滞期费索赔的实践技能。

本案例的概念难度、分析难度和陈述难度均适中，适用对象包括国际贸易专业、国际物流专业和国际商务专业的本科生、研究生以及国际商务专业学位研究生。对于缺乏专业基础理论知识的本科生，可以根据教学大纲，有选择地引导阅读案例相关材料，熟悉装卸时间和滞期费的概念，重点掌握装卸时间起算的基本原则和计算方法；对于缺乏实践经验的研究生，可以引导其将所掌握的理论知识运用于本案例每一个具体问题的分析，对案例中争论的几个焦点问题，作出自己的是非判断，锻炼其处理实际问题的综合能力。

本案例规划的理论教学知识点包括：

（1）装卸时间和滞期费问题在合同中的重要性；

（2）装卸时间和滞期费约定的基本方法；

（3）装卸时间起算的普通法原则；

（4）滞期费计算的基本方法。

本案例规划的能力训练教学内容包括：

（1）正确约定合同装卸时间的能力；

（2）履行合同中避免滞期费产生的实践能力；

（3）正确判定船舶是否满足抵达条件的能力；

（4）正确判定船舶是否满足准备就绪条件的能力；

（5）阅读和归纳装卸时间事实记录并正确计算装卸时间和滞期费的能力；

（6）解决滞期费纠纷的能力。

二、分析思路

本案例的理论教学知识点是航次租船合同中的滞期费计算问题。根据教学目的和案情，建议案例讨论按照下列思路进行：

首先，引导学生讨论装卸时间和滞期费计算的一般性原则。按照顺序讨论：滞期费和速遣费的含义是什么？装卸时间的概念是什么？WWD的含义是什么？SHIN和SHEX的含义是什么？EIU和UU的含义是什么？装卸时间起算的条件是什么？何谓船舶抵达、备妥和准备就绪通知书递交？WWWW的含义是什么？

其次，引导学生讨论装卸时间计算的技术性问题，包括：计算的依据是什么？计算时应扣除哪些事项？分别计算、平均计算和可调剂使用的概念分别是什么？一旦滞期永远滞期和不连续计算的规定有何区别？责任中止（cesser）条款的含义是什么？

再次，讨论双方装货港滞期费计算是否合理的问题，包括：L轮在长江口待泊的时间应否计入装卸时间？该轮在长江口待泊时在法律上已经准备就绪，并可以递交准备就绪通知书了吗？该轮从长江口到南通港泊位的航行时间可以计入装卸时间吗？联检的时间、验舱的时间以及验舱未通过的时间应当计入装卸时间吗？坏天气时间应当如何处理？五个货舱没有同时工作应当如何理解？

之后讨论双方的卸货港速遣费计算是否合理的问题，包括：两个合同的货物同时卸货，装卸时间应如何计算？收货人因包装污染拒绝卸货导致的时间损失应如何计算？

最后，引导学生讨论买卖合同下非租船方的装卸时间保证义务问题。首先应当让学生明白，这个问题已经超出了运输合同范畴，而是进入了买卖合同的范畴，但由于二者在装卸时间和滞期费问题上紧密联系，必须展开讨论，并且本案例中已经涉及这个问题。讨论应当包括：买卖合同中是否应当对此问题作出约定，其意义是什么？在合同无明文约定情形下，非租船方是否有义务保证装卸时间？

在完成上述问题讨论后，还可以引导学生讨论一个延伸问题，即滞期费/速遣费的索赔时间和诉讼时间问题，前者是一个合同约定的问题，后者是法律规定问题。

三、理论依据及分析

1.掌握滞期费计算原则和方法的重要意义

滞期费的本质是航次租船合同中约定的，当租船人用于实际装货或卸货的时间超过了合同约定的允许时间，就超过的时间按照约定的费率补偿给船舶出租人的时间损失赔偿。一个航次租船合同下能否产生滞期费和产生多少滞期费，除了取决于合同中约定的允许时间多少和滞期费率的高低外，更主要的取决于影响货物装卸不利因素的多少和影响程度有多大。滞期费率的高低主要取决于航运市场的运价水平。在航运市场高涨时，一艘10万载重吨船舶的滞期费率可达每天10万美元，高得令人咋舌；而当航运市场处于低谷时，同样船舶的滞期费率可能不到1万美元。但无论滞期费率高或低，一个航次中如果产生了滞期费，承租人总是需要按照租约约定对船东作出赔偿的。在滞期费率一定的条件下，能否产生滞期费以及滞期费有多少主要取决于相关因素的影响程度。例如，装卸港口拥挤造成的待泊时间越长，滞期费就会越多。在航运市场高涨时期，如果一艘海峡型船舶待泊一个月，滞期费可能高达上百万美元之多，那对承租人来说就是一场灾难。因此，学好用好装卸时间计算的原则和方法的重要性不言而喻。

尽管滞期费的约定来源于租船合同，但买卖合同也涉及这个问题，主要原因是负责租船的贸易方（是买方还是卖方取决于买卖合同约定的贸易术语）常常无法控制对方港口的货物装卸。如果能够在买卖合同中将对方港口的装卸时间保证转嫁给对方，至少对方港口可能产生的滞期费责任就通过买卖合同而转嫁出去了。这一点，对于中间贸易人而言显得尤其重要。像本案例中的A，如果他能够在采购合同中把装货港的滞期费责任约定给中国的卖方C，把卸货港的滞期费责任约定给越南的买方Y，那么，A在租船合同中的装卸两港的滞期费支付义务就全部转嫁出去了。

本案例中，A就只注意了租船合同中的装卸时间和滞期费约定，而忽略了在两个买卖合同中分别与卖方和买方约定装卸时间和滞期费，结果，只有自己承担装货港口发生的滞期费损失了。

2.应妥善地约定装卸时间

能否产生滞期费以及金额多少，首先取决于租船合同中允许的装卸时间多少，因此，妥善约定装卸时间就非常重要。租船合同中的装卸时间条款看上去非常简单，常常只有一句半句，但其中学问却很大。

装卸时间和滞期费条款是航次租船合同的重要条款，也是最容易产生争议的条款。在英文中，装卸时间一词是laytime，lay在英文中有停靠、躺下之意，船舶平日都是在移动（move）的，只有在装卸货物时才会（to）lay，因此用于装卸货物的时间就被称为laytime了。简单地说，laytime就是船东免费给予承租人装卸货物的时间，超过了laytime，船东要向承租人额外收取费用，即滞期费。

影响货物装卸的因素有很多，一些因素是可以预见的，一些因素则由于信息闭塞而无法预料，但在商谈租船合同或买卖合同的装卸时间问题时，一些常见的影响因素总是应当考虑到的。

港口的装卸效率是首先应当考虑的问题。合同约定了装卸货物数量之后，究竟需要多长时间完成货物装卸，首先取决于港口的装卸效率。装卸效率高，需要的装卸时间就短，否则就会长。

另一个需要考虑的因素是天气和节假日的影响。对于租船人而言，尽管可以在租约中将这种影响在装卸时间中扣除，但如果遇到等泊，前述因素会导致泊位上船舶的装卸时间延长。如果不能规定待泊时间中不良天气和节假日也扣除的话，租船人就要承担这种影响带来的时间损失了。

港口拥挤往往是导致滞期费的一个重要原因，在绝大多数情况下，港口拥挤带来的时间损失都要由租船人来承担。因此，在洽谈租船合同的装卸时间条款时，承租人需要十分谨慎，在了解装卸港口的拥挤情况后，尽量多争取些装卸时间，甚至应当考虑变更装卸港口。

装卸时间和滞期费背后的原理是，当承租人未能在租船合同中约定的装货和卸货时间内（如租约约定的是固定的装卸时间）将货物全部装完和/或卸完，一般认为，承租人就违反了租船合同的约定，属于违约行为，此时承租人可能需要向船东支付违约损害赔偿。

在英国法下，当一方违反合同时，非违约方有权向违约方主张损害赔偿（damages）。如果双方在合同中约定了违约损害赔偿的金额或损害赔偿的计算方式，则该损害赔偿为议定赔偿（liquidated damages），即损害赔偿的金额是事先已经约定的，那么，在该项损害发生时，违约方就应当按照约定向受损害方作出赔偿，这是滞期费赔偿的法律基础。

对于装卸两港的装卸时间如何处理，有装卸时间分别计算、平均计算与共用三种常用的处理原则。

装卸时间分别计算是指分别规定装货港口和卸货港口的装卸时间，分别计算各个港口的滞期费，索赔时只作金额上的相加或扣减，不允许作时间上的加减。

装卸时间平均计算则不同，它允许用一个港口的速遣时间去抵扣另一港口的滞期时间。因为速遣时间和滞期时间的含金量是不同的，所以这种规定对承租人是有利的。

装卸时间共用的含义是，把合同允许的装货时间与允许的卸货时间加总看作一个总的允许时间，两个港口的允许时间可以调剂使用。此时，如果合同规定"一旦滞期永远滞期"，结果就不好说了。

在本案例中，A没有在租船合同中就装卸两港的装卸时间如何使用作出约定，结果只能被认定按照装卸时间分别计算的方法处理。如果能够约定装卸时间平均计算或共用，那么，A就可以用在胡志明市节省的时间去冲抵在南通港滞期的时间，从而减少滞期费支付金额。

3. 如何界定船舶的抵达

装卸时间确定之后，接下来的问题是如何规定装卸时间的起算。装卸时间的起算点是个重要的分水岭，起算之前的船舶时间消耗由出租人承担，起算之后的时间消耗就要由承租人承担了。如何起算装卸时间涉及双方的经济利益，特别是在船舶到达港口后需要在锚地或港外等候区域等候很长时间的情况下，能否起算装卸时间，争论更加激烈。

国际上的通行做法是，规定装卸时间在船长有效地递交了货物装卸准备就绪通知书后的某一时间开始起算。这样，如何构成准备就绪通知书的有效递交就非常关键。根据普通法和国际通行惯例，准备就绪通知书的有效递交（或者说装卸时间起算）必须满足以下3个条件：第一，船舶必须抵达合同规定的装卸港口或泊位；第二，船舶必须实际上准备就绪，可以装卸货物；第三，准备就绪通知书必须按规定的方式和时间递交给被通知人。

（1）泊位合同下的船舶抵达

把装卸货物的地点规定为某港口的具体泊位的合同，或承租人有合同明示的权利选择一个泊位的合同，被称为"泊位租船合同"；把这个地点规定为某个港口的合同，被称为"港口租船合同"。判断一个合同究竟是泊位租船合同还是港口租船合同，主要依据的是合同的相关措辞。

在泊位租船合同下，船舶只有抵达指定泊位才被视为抵达。船舶虽已进入港口，但未靠泊之前仍不能视为抵达船舶，没有具备递交准备就绪通知书的条件，装卸时间不能起算，等泊时间只能由出租人承担。

根据普通法的"契约自由"原则和《海商法》第98条"航次租船合同的装货、卸货期限及其计算办法，超过装货、卸货期限后的滞期费和提前完成装货、卸货的速遣费，由双方约定"的规定，上述不利于出租人的普通法原则可以通过合同的相反约定予以改变。通常方法有：

一是规定"不论靠泊与否"（whether in berth or not，WIBON）。"不论靠泊与否"的含义是当船舶抵达装卸港口的锚地后，不论船舶是否能够靠上约定的泊位，都视为船舶已经抵达，就可以递交准备就绪通知书，装卸时间就可从那时起按规定计算。

二是规定"待泊时间计入装卸时间"。"待泊时间计入装卸时间"的含义是船舶等待泊位的时间损失应当计入装卸时间。

三是规定"船舶抵港即可靠泊"（berth reachable on her arrival）。这种规定的含义是：承租人保证船舶到达港口时，可马上安排靠泊，否则将赔偿出租人待泊时间损失。

在泊位租约下，有时船舶无法抵达泊位是承租人原因造成的，即所谓承租人的阻碍，使得装卸时间无法起算。例如，货物没有完全备妥，港务局不准船舶靠泊；在车船直取条件下，收货人没有备妥接运车辆，港务局不准船舶靠泊；或者收货人没有履行货物进口手续，船舶不许靠泊卸货等。这时，应视为船舶已经抵达，装卸时间应按规定起算。

（2）港口租船合同下的船舶抵达界定

在港口租约下，船舶必须抵达合同约定的港口，才能满足"到达"的要求。该要求包括两个方面：第一，船舶必须到达港内；第二，船舶可任由承租人立即、有效地调遣。

对于港口的定义，BIMCO的《解释定义》规定：港口（port）是指船舶装货或卸货的区域，而不论是在泊位、锚地、浮筒或类似装货或卸货地点。港口也包括船舶等待依次进港的惯常地点，以及船舶按指示依次进港或必须等待依次进港的惯常地点，而不管该地点与上述区域距离的远近。"不论进港与否"（whether in port or not，WIPON）条款可以解决上述问题。WIPON条款的含义是：船舶抵达了港口惯常的待泊地点，不论该地点是否属于港口范围内，出租人都可以递交NOR，并按规定计算装卸时间。

关于"承租人可马上有效处置"问题，它的核心意思是承租人一旦有了泊位，可以马上通知船长，船长可马上去执行靠泊指令。

本案例中，出租人和承租人对于南通港装卸时间的计算发生了争议。由于南通港当时没有空闲泊位，L轮抵达长江口后，只能在那里抛锚待泊，而长江口明显在南通港的范围之外，L轮没有抵达南通港，按照前述原则，装卸时间是不能起算的。然而，该航次的租船合同中规定有WWWW，其中的一个W就是"不论抵港与否"，按照BIMCO的《解释定义》，船舶抵达长江口就应视为抵达约定的港口，装卸时间就可以起算。出租人正是按照这个解释和合同约定计算的。但是，承租人却认为，船舶没有抵达南通港，因此不能起算装卸时间，只有L轮抵达南通港后才能起算，承租人正是按照这个思路计算的。显然，承租人没有正确理解合同的相关规定，或是故意所为。

4.船舶的准备就绪

装卸准备就绪是指适航的船舶在货物装卸的各有关方面已做好了准备。装卸准备就绪包括法律上准备就绪和实体上准备就绪两个方面。

（1）法律上的准备就绪

法律上的准备就绪是指船舶完成了港口当局、海关、卫生检疫以及移民局等政府部门要求的各类进港文件申报并获得相应的进港准许证书。几乎所有的国家都制定相关法律，对国际航行船舶进出本国港口规定海关、卫生检疫和移民局方面的申报及检查程序。如果进港船舶不能通过检查，将无法获准进港装卸货物。因此，传统上船舶通过这类检查就成为装卸准备就绪的重要方面。

在卫生检疫方面，各国的港口都设有船舶检疫锚地，来自国外的船舶需首先进入检疫锚地等待港口国卫生检疫官员登轮检验检疫。检验检疫的主要内容是检查船舶是否来自疫情国家、船员是否持有传染病疫苗接种证书

（vaccination certificate）、是否患有传染病，以及船舶是否带有病虫或鼠害等。如果船舶无法获得检疫合格证书，便不能获准靠泊装卸货物，这将直接影响承租人调遣使用船舶。因此，船舶没有通过检疫，便不能起算装卸时间。

在海关检查方面，任何国际航行船舶在进入一国港口之前都必须履行海关申报手续。通过检查的船舶会获得一份通关单并可以进港装卸货物，否则船舶将被滞留并听候处理，此间船舶不允许进行装卸作业。因此，船舶没有通过海关检查，便不能起算装卸时间。

移民局对船舶的检查主要是对进出境人员进行检查登记，检查是否有偷渡者。如果船舶被查出有违反移民局规定的行为，很有可能被禁止装卸货物。因此，没有经过移民局检查的船舶也不能进港装卸货物，也不能起算装卸时间。

就船舶在法律意义备妥一项来说，以大法官邓宁勋爵为代表的英国法律界认为，如果船舶在海关、移民局检查、卫生检疫以及港口当局要求方面不存在妨碍货物装卸诸种问题，就可以递交装卸准备就绪通知书，装卸时间就可以起算。相反，如果在上述方面存在问题，致使船舶无法立即装卸货物，则船长就不应递交准备就绪通知书，即使递交了通知书，也应视为递交无效，不能起算装卸时间，何时船舶真正事实上准备就绪，可以进行装卸作业，何时再起算装卸时间。

应当注意的是，上面介绍的是英国普通法下确立的原则，根据契约自由原则，如果租约中作出相反约定，应以租约约定为准。再者，大陆法中尚无这种规定，租约双方要改变普通法的原则，需在租约中明文约定。例如，常见租约中规定的"不论通过检疫与否"（whether in free pratique or not，WIFPON）、"不论海关清关与否"（whether customs cleared or not，WCCON），就与当前的普通法原则相同。

（2）实体上的准备就绪

实体上的准备就绪是指船舶、与货物装卸有关的设备和货舱都已准备妥当，靠泊后即可立即进行装卸作业。船舶实体上的准备就绪主要涉及以下几个方面：

① 船舶的吃水应能保证顺利进港靠泊。如果需要减载，合同中应当规定由谁负责减载及减载时间由谁承担。如果规定由承租人负责并承担减载的时间，则减载时间应当记入装卸时间；如果未经承租人同意，出租人自己加载使吃水超过限制，这时就不能认为船舶已经备妥。

② 相关设备准备就绪。与装卸有关的起货机、吊杆、滑车、供电和舱盖的开启等许多方面，应处于正常有效的工作状态，吊货索具（如吊货钢丝、吊货勾头等）还必须持有合格检验证书。有的合同甚至约定，船舶靠泊时，吊杆应当处于立起状态，货舱舱盖应当处于打开状态，以便靠泊时可立即开始货物装卸。

③ 货舱在装货前必须保持干净适货。货舱干净是针对所有装货的舱室而言的，所以，部分舱室不合格应视为全船未准备就绪。标准的租船合同中一般都规定货舱干净、干燥要求。运输特殊货物时还会在租约中附加一条"船舶通过检验"条款，规定如果靠泊后不能通过货舱的干净、干燥、无味、无锈、货舱内衬、护货板等方面的检验，就视为船舶未准备就绪，不能起算装卸时间。这样船舶抵达后的所有时间损失都由出租人承担，或中庸一些，规定重新整理货舱直至重新检验合格的时间应从装卸时间中扣除。

④ 压在上面的货物（overstowed cargo）应当移开。在卸货港，对于积载在下面的货物来说，如果压在上面的货物尚未卸下或移开，就无法开始卸货。这时船舶对于下面货物的货主来说就没有准备就绪，已发出的准备就绪通知书对该货主来说也是无效的。只有压在上面的货物卸完或移开后船舶对该货主才实际上准备就绪，在该货主收到出租人重新发出的准备就绪通知时才可以起算装卸时间。如果出租人疏忽没有重新发出准备就绪通知书，则承租人无须承担该货物起卸前的时间损失。

本案例中，船舶抵达南通港后顺利地通过了联检，意味着L轮在法律方面已经准备就绪，在长江口递交的准备就绪通知书应当视为有效，可以起算装卸时间。然而，在随后的货舱检验中，由于货舱不干净，没能通过检验，应当视为该轮在实体上没有准备就绪，因此在长江口递交的准备就绪通知书应当视为无效，装卸时间不能起算。遗憾的是，双方的租船合同对此没有作出明确的约定，只约定船舶抵港时货舱应当能够通过适货检验，而没有约定如果不能通过，装卸时间应当如何起算。因此，出租人只扣除了货舱没通过检验到再次检验通过的那段时间，而承租人则认为船舶实体上没有准备就绪，在长江口递交的准备就绪通知书是无效的，装卸时间只能从L轮靠泊后起算。双方的争议就是这样发生的。

5.准备就绪通知书的正确递交

船舶装卸准备就绪通知书是由船长直接或通过船舶代理向承租人、发货人、收货人或他们的代理人以一定形式发出的关于本船已经抵达港口并在各方面做好了装卸货物准备的通知。它的作用有两方面：一是通知货方船舶已经准备就绪并可以进行装卸作业，请其做好相应安排；二是启动装卸时间计算时钟，开始按规定计算装卸时间。

准备就绪通知书的递交（tendering of NOR）必须符合要求，否则等于没有递交，装卸时间不能起算。一般情况下，准备就绪通知书的递交应当符合以下要求，如果租船合同有特别约定，还应当满足合同特别要求：

（1）递交的形式符合合同规定。准备就绪通知书的递交可以通过口头形式，也可以通过书面形式，应按照合同的约定递交。

（2）被通知人必须正确，即船长应当按照合同约定向相关人递交。

（3）应当在工作时间递交。几乎所有的租约都规定准备就绪通知书需在工作时间内递交。这样，在非工作时间内递交的准备就绪通知书就被视为在下一个工作时间递交的。

本案例中，L轮船长根据船东的明确航次指令，正确地递交了装卸两港的准备就绪通知书，所以，合同双方在这个方面没有产生任何争议。

6.正确计算装卸时间和滞期费

装卸时间的计算是按照租约装卸时间条款的规定，按照起算原则，扣除应该中断或除外的时间，计算承租人为完成货物装卸实际使用的时间。实际使用的时间（time actually used）超过合同规定时间（time allowed）的部分，称为滞期时间（time on demurrage），根据租约规定的滞期费率（demurrage rate）便可计算出滞期费数额。如果实际使用时间少于规定的时间，称为速遣时间（time saved），应根据合同规定的费率，由出租人向承租人支付一定的奖金，即所谓的速遣费（despatch money）。

速遣费的规定方法通常有两种：一种是按照节省的工作时间计算（working time saved，WTS），即计算时，从实际完成装卸时间到允许的装卸时间届满这段时间中扣除合同约定的除外时间；另一种是按照节省的全部时间计算（all time saved，ATS），即以从实际完成装卸时间到允许的装卸时间届满这段时间为计算基础，不扣除合同约定的除外时间。以哪种方法为准，应在合同中约定。

滞期费/速遣费的计算依据以下文件进行：

（1）租约。严谨的租约都有一条专门条款对装卸时间、起算原则、中断和除外时间，以及装卸准备就绪通知书的递交等作详细规定。这些规定是计算装卸时间的合同依据。此外，如果租约广泛的免责条款中涉及滞期费计算，也应一并遵照执行。

（2）船舶装卸准备就绪通知书。船舶代理人都会按照船长递交的通知书内容，再重新制作一份正式的准备就绪通知书，转交给货方。装卸准备就绪通知书是计算装卸时间的重要依据。一般情况下，没有递交准备就绪通知书是不可起算装卸时间的。但如果船舶已靠泊作业，尽管没有准备就绪通知书，装卸时间仍可以在开始作业时起算，但船舶在此前的待泊时间不应计入装卸时间。

（3）装卸时间事实记录或装卸时间表。装卸时间事实记录（laytime statement of fact），有的船舶使用装卸时间表（laytime sheet），是以记载船舶从到达港口锚地或惯常等泊地点时起，到货物装卸完毕时止的全部期间内，船舶的动态、装卸作业的起止时间、待时的起止时间及原因等事项的详细记录。

装卸时间事实记录的内容主要包括：船舶抵达时间、NOR的递交及接受时间、引航员登船引领时间、靠泊时间、海关检疫完成时间、每天装卸作业起止时间、星期日、节假日、不良天气、装卸设备故障、等待货物和等待接运工具等中断或除外事项的起止时间，以及装卸完毕时间和装卸货物数量等。

装卸时间事实记录是计算装卸时间的事实依据。它通常由船舶代理人根据船长或港口的作业记录编制而成。装卸作业完毕时，船长、货主或其代理人须对记录的事实逐一核对，没有异议后，船长、发货人、收货人或其代理人在该文件上签字。签字后的装卸时间事实记录船长保留一份，船舶代理人转交出租人、货方各一份。

（4）合同约定的其他必备文件。

有了上述文件，出租人便可以制作滞期费/速遣费计算单，然后将此表连同合同规定的文件交给承租人索要滞期费。在发生速遣费时，这些文件通常由承租人作出，向出租人索要速遣费。

滞期费是一种合同约定赔偿，按照英国普通法原则，一旦产生后，就与合同约定的除外条款无关，即允许的装卸时间用满之后，合同约定的除外时间就再也不应从滞期时间中扣除。这就是滞期费的"滞期连续计算"（demurrage runs continuously）原则，也称作"一旦滞期，永远滞期"（once on demurrage, always on demurrage）。其含义是在开始进入滞期后，所有的除外时间都算作滞期时间，如遇星期天、节假日、坏天气等都不再作扣除。通常，这一原则被写在租约中。如果承租人欲改变这一状况，须在租约中规定"滞期费不连续计算"（demurrage per like days as laytime），即进入滞期后，也应像计算装卸时间那样，对该中断或该除外的时间都予以扣除。

本案例中，租船人和船东的滞期费计算依据和程序都是正确的，但计算结果却不同。问题发生的根本原因是运输合同对装卸时间的扣除约定不明和计算时对约定的相关条款理解有误，或是故意所为。在南通港的装货时间计算中，船东根据租船合同中规定的 WWWW 条款，装卸时间从船舶抵达长江口递交了 NOR 后的第二天上午 06：00 时开始起算，这是符合合同约定的，而租船人却将这部分时间扣除了，从船舶靠泊后才开始起算，这是违反合同约定的。而在 24 日的装卸时间计算中，货舱检验没有通过的那部分时间在船东的计算中被扣除了，这是合理的，但租船人的计算却奇怪地没有扣除。事实上，如果合同没有特别约定，货舱检验没有通过应当视为船舶没有事实上准备就绪，那么，从船舶抵达长江口到货舱再次检验通过这段时间都不应当计入装卸时间。

四、关键要点

阅读本案例并正确回答讨论思考题，需要学生把握以下要点：

（1）不仅运输合同需要约定装卸时间和滞期费问题，买卖合同也同样需要。

（2）妥善约定装卸时间和滞期费需要专业知识。

（3）必须在合同中明确约定船舶的抵达问题。

（4）必须在合同中明确约定何谓船舶的准备就绪。

（5）必须在合同中明确约定船舶准备就绪通知书的递交方式。

（6）滞期费的计算必须依据相关的文件进行，做到有理有据。

五、课堂教学计划建议

本案例可以作为专门的案例讨论课来进行。如下是按照时间进度提供的课堂计划建议，仅供参考。

对于本案例教学，建议在给出本案例前，教师用 50 分钟的课堂时间预先讲授相关知识，并在相关知识讲授完毕后，立即给出本案例素材和讨论思考题，然后根据思考题的数量将全班学生分成若干组，每一组分配一个问题，要求各组在课后阅读案例材料，根据所学知识对分配的问题作出分析性答案，并将主要分析依据和结论做成PPT。然后准备100分钟时间全班同学听取汇报和教师评论。课中计划：

简要的课堂前言，明确主题：2～5分钟

小组发言：每组10～15分钟，控制在80分钟内

引导全班进一步讨论并进行归纳总结：15～20分钟